MANHATTAN ATMOSPHERES

MANHATTAN ATMOSPHERES

Architecture, the Interior Environment, and Urban Crisis

DAVID GISSEN

University of Minnesota Press
MINNEAPOLIS | LONDON

This book is supported by a grant from the Graham Foundation for Advanced Studies in the Fine Arts.

A version of chapter 1 was published as "Exhaust and Territorialisation at the Washington Bridge Apartments, New York City, 1963–1973," *Journal of Architecture* 12, no. 4 (2007): 449–61; copyright 2007 Taylor and Francis, http://www.tandfonline.com/. A version of chapter 3 was published as "The Architectural Production of Nature: Dendur/New York," *Grey Room*, no. 34 (Winter 2009): 58–79; copyright 2009 by Grey Room, Inc., and the Massachusetts Institute of Technology.

Published by the University of Minnesota Press
111 Third Avenue South, Suite 290
Minneapolis, MN 55401-2520
http://www.upress.umn.edu

Library of Congress Cataloging-in-Publication Data
Gissen, David.
Manhattan atmospheres : architecture, the interior environment, and urban crisis / David Gissen.
Includes bibliographical references and index.
ISBN 978-0-8166-8070-2 (hc)—ISBN 978-0-8166-8071-9 (pb)
1. Interior architecture—Social aspects—New York (State)—New York—History—20th century. 2. Architecture and society—New York (State)—New York—History—20th century. 3. Manhattan (New York, N.Y.)—Buildings, structures, etc. 4. Manhattan (New York, N.Y.)—Social conditions—20th century. I. Title.
NA2850.G57 2014
720.9747'109041—dc23

2013040912

Printed in the United States of America on acid-free paper

20 19 18 17 16 15 14 10 9 8 7 6 5 4 3 2 1

CONTENTS

ACKNOWLEDGMENTS

I HAVE BEEN DEVELOPING *Manhattan Atmospheres* for almost the entirety of my academic career. It is the product of my research and academic studies, but it also came about through the support of friends, colleagues, archivists, and numerous others.

I first discussed, debated, and wrote the ideas within this book in 2004 with my PhD supervisors at the University College London, Matthew Gandy and Adrian Forty. Many of the most exciting insights in these chapters came about through their questions, proddings, and critiques. At my various defenses, Adrian, Matthew, Erik Swyngedouw, Murray Fraser, and T. J. Demos provided intellectual fuel for arguments and debates surrounding this period and its architecture.

Funds for research, travel, and illustrations for this book were generously provided by the Graham Foundation for Advanced Studies in the Fine Arts, the California College of the Arts, the Pennsylvania State University, and the Seed Fund, San Francisco, California.

From the project's beginnings to its last moments in production, I relied on archivists and librarians at a number of institutions and organizations. These include Mike Chrimes, London's Institute of Civil Engineering (ICE); Barbara File, the Metropolitan Museum of Art, New York; Mary Daniels and Ines Zalduendo, the Loeb Library, Harvard Graduate School of Design; Stephen Sinon, New York Botanical Garden Library and Archives; Sidney Druckman, the Battery Park City Authority; Janet Yoder and Nicole Soriano, Pelli Clarke Pelli Architects; Linda Scinto, Cathy Chase, and Kevin Roche, of Kevin Roche John Dinkeloo and Associates; and librarians at the Library of the New York Branch of the Environmental Protection Agency, the Peabody Library at The Johns Hopkins University, the Avery Library at Columbia University, and the Real Estate Board of New York. Several chapters include interviews; I am particularly grateful to Hazel Henderson, who spoke to me in 2005, and to Carolyn Iu, who clarified several aspects regarding trading rooms (many of which have been decommissioned) at the World Financial Center.

Portions of *Manhattan Atmospheres* were published in journals and presented at academic events. I thank Reinhold Martin, Felicity Scott, and Thai Smith, of the journal *Grey Room;* their criticisms gave this project a more sophisticated tone at a significant point in its development. Ben Campkin, director of UCL's Urban Lab, invited me to contribute my work on the Washington Bridge Apartments to an issue of the *Journal of Architecture* he coedited with Paul Dobraszcyk. Pier Vittorio Aureli, Eeva-Lisa Pelkonen, Robert Stern, Marikka Trotter, Esther Choi, Greig Crysler, Jordan Geiger, Lisa Tilder, Javier Arbona, Tirza Latimer, K. Michael Hays, Timothy Hyde, Antoine Picon, and William Saunders invited me to their various institutions to lecture and discuss aspects of *Manhattan Atmospheres.* D. Graham Burnett, Tom McDonough, and Sylvia Lavin publicly debated the ideas within this book with me at various events. The inimitable Geoff Manaugh invited me to transform my research into contemporary design ideas in his exhibition *Landscape Futures.*

My editor at the University of Minnesota Press, Pieter Martin, and the anonymous reviewers of this manuscript provided key criticisms that vastly improved the book. Kristian Tvedten and Ana Bichanich helped locate and develop illustrations for the book. Jeremy Rountree was instrumental as a research assistant at key stages of the project's development. Colleagues critical to this work's success include Stephen Beal, Mark Breitenberg, and Melanie Corn of the California College of the Arts, and Dan Willis of the Pennsylvania State University.

Finally, I thank my many friends and family for their support. I dedicate this book to my wife, Rachel Schreiber. I happily dedicate so much of my life to Rachel, so this book is simply a much smaller but nevertheless necessary gesture.

INTRODUCTION

From Urban Nature to the Maintenance Environment

POSTWAR NEW YORK CITY has long been a source of study for historians, urbanists, geographers, and sociologists to better understand the disintegration of the socionatural systems that bound this city together. This city's great park networks, sanitarian and reformist projects of light and air and water networks of the nineteenth century, the public works and landscaped road networks of the mid-twentieth century—all became degraded physically and financially between the 1960s and the 1980s. Images of flooded streets from burst water mains, blackened air, collapsed highways, blighted public spaces, landscapes of burning buildings, and sickened trees typify our understanding of the built and natural landscapes of Manhattan during these years. The site of this time period, which extends from the end of an industrial era to a postindustrial one, has been termed the "crisis" or "disaster" city.[1] It has become a renewed source of interest for historians, geographers, and artists as the harsh economic policies of this time and place appear to have been repeated within the cities of contemporary United States and Europe and as the last vestiges of the important marginal and gritty sites that emerged during this time in New York become developed.[2] During this period in New York's history, the grandeur of the City's socionatural project appears to have sputtered or become an atomized version of its former self, a shadow, though it nonetheless continued in pocket parks, sites of urban activism, occupations of desolate landscapes, and an eventual preservationist attitude toward existing nineteenth-century landscapes.

As visceral as this image of the City is, and as critical as the responses to it were, this book identifies another socionatural project fostered during these years. In addition to the more localized, activist, and preservationist projects, the socionatural project of New York City also continued during this time, but within the interior environments of the City's monumental late-modern architecture. There, behind sheets of tinted and mirrored glass, the vaporous cooled and warmed atmosphere of postwar architecture became a site within which visions of urban socionature within this city were hatched. If the earlier and more public structures, networks, and systems that integrated social and natural processes supported the City's industrial-era economies and subjects, the environments generated within the City's architecture during this time evoked a far different political and economic future for the City that produced a far more complex urban and somatic effect. The postwar and late-modern architectural environment became laced with the social and political tensions and dramas that define the experience of the City at this particular historical moment.

In this book, I trace the rise of architecture as a key site of environmental production and support within a restructuring New York City, an interior realm of physical and material urban maintenance. During the urban tumult of the 1960s and through the recoveries of the 1980s, corporations, institutions, governmental officials, architects, engineers, and landscape architects seized upon the architectural environment's myriad physical characteristics—its sealed interior atmosphere, stable temperature, and calibrated humidity—refashioning these constituent features into a project for the City's emerging late-capitalist urban economy. The sealed environment of buildings entangled with efforts to gentrify neighborhoods and rebuild verdure; became sites of conservation for cultural artifacts in museums; and promoted postindustrial labor within the offices of the downtown financial center. Architects elaborated on this emerging environmental form, developing buildings with a pronounced emphasis on surfaces and abstract forms that suggested both the context for monumental interior environments in the City and its emerging and complex urban milieu. The buildings and environments that emerged in New York City were caught within the histories and geographies of emerging economic industries, demographic goals, and development plans that would reimagine the City's historical sites and nature in a postindustrial form. Situated within the spaces of neighborhood redevelopments, corporate-office complexes, and city parks, the environments within buildings were created within urban sites that intersected with, if not outright fostered, other, better-known aspects of New York's economic transformations. The demographic displacements staged in the City's neighborhoods, corporate reinvention of its public spaces, and the rise of its powerful cultural institutions and financial centers are integrated into the development of these environments. These environments within buildings are both a poorly understood aspect of a critical period within New York City's history and aspects of a phenomenon that helped usher in features of contemporary urban experience.

As the following chapters argue, the architectural environment became reimagined as an integral and growing aspect of New York City's postindustrial development; but the types of environments formed in New York also intersected and resonated with architecture found in other cities and with larger disciplinary concerns.[3] The environments explored throughout this book were embedded within Western transnational architectural debates and concepts such as the megastructure and late-modern and postmodern architecture. They can be identified within debates on fostering nature in cities, cultural heritage, and international finance. Throughout this book, we connect phenomena in New York City with other historical, disciplinarian, and global developments, and the environments within New York City were certainly caught within transurban historical, disciplinary, institutional, and governmental webworks. But by examining how a seemingly globalized phenomenon—the conditioned interior space of late-modern buildings—became fashioned specifically to address the concerns of the transformations within this city, we unravel a new type of history of these spaces and of cities more generally. We bring to this environment an urban understanding that joins its technological, climatological, and architectural-historical interests while continuing to tie the formation of late-modern architectural languages to the formation of particular spaces and times.[4] Taking the approach of various histories that identify powerful phenomena by investigating specific architecture and art within the historical transformation of specific cities, I chose to examine a series of architectural environments with a pronounced geographical and historical specificity.[5] The environments that I examine in New York—sealed megastructural apartments built over highways, interiorized verdant corporate atria, late-modernist museum expansions, enormous late-modern trading-room interiors, and others, such as *Bürolandschaft* office interiors, enormous convention centers, and the atria-hotel concept of John Portman and Associates—are all key late-modern formations, several of which originated here. But they are all here, and all are entangled in critical ways with New York's important historical landscapes, its world centers of real-estate development and global finance, and its growing power as the cultural center of the West. The environments I examine did not happen to be here; rather, they were reworked into the very tissues of the City's transformation. Today, sociologists and geographers argue that this period of New York's history is critical to understanding various contemporary spatialized phenomena, particularly as many socioeconomic practices of contemporary cities were first staged in New York City at this time.[6] I also believe that the environments within New York City's late-modern buildings are critical components for further understanding the constituent material features of the late twentieth-century postindustrial metropolis and this era of urban development more generally.

The environments developed within the buildings of restructuring New York City were some of the most politicized forms of nature found in the City; but we lack an urban history of these spaces, one that explains how these environments entangled with and reinforced the discursive and material structures that stitch together this city, its objects, and its subjects. The environments that emerged here must be understood as a transmogrification of both urban nature and architecture in the City that furthered the goals of late-modern global urbanity. This book provides us with some necessary historical perspective to reconsider this environment's ascendant role, its relation to the history of late-modern urban architecture, and its intersection with our contemporary postindustrializing economic order. Equally important, this book provides a framework for considering other possibilities of architecture and environment within this and other cities. Architecture might take on some new, as yet unimaginable role within cities, rooted in a critical understanding of their environment as a historical and geographical urban artifact.

AN URBAN HISTORY OF THE ARCHITECTURAL ENVIRONMENT

By writing the architectural environment into the environmental history of New York City, we brush up against many historical narratives regarding the relationship of architecture to this postwar city, disciplinary notions of architectural autonomy, and postwar histories of urban nature. According to the dominant narratives of New York's urban history, its socionatural project unraveled between the mid-1960s and mid-1970s.[7] Physically and municipally, the City appears to have ceased addressing the health of its subjects in the manner of the earlier reformist urban projects of the nineteenth and early twentieth centuries. These earlier urban projects were rooted in nineteenth-century theories of urban sanitation and beautification, capitalistic investments and spatial reforms, and medical and bacteriological sciences; they reached monumental expression with the construction of large-scale socionatural networks, such as parks and water systems, highway systems, and massive housing and urban-redevelopment schemes that reworked nature into historical real-estate structures.[8] Specific examples of these projects at the beginning and end of these processes include the completion of New York City's Croton water systems in the nineteenth century and the development of public-housing tracts in the City in the immediate post–World War II era. This critical latter project emerged from a European intellectual context that imagined potential links between architectural form and the socionatural transformation of the City. The "tower in the park" that defined public and subsidized housing not only advanced a particular architectural form as a key urban type but also evoked the transformation of the urban fabric into a site that acted as a counterenvironment to urban density, expedient forms of commercial land exchange, and uncontained industrial pollution. Several contemporary historians excavated the problematic ways these structures were wielded by developers and municipalities as sites of urban segregation and problematic forms of urban investments, but we should recall that, as troubling as the social history of these projects may be, they contain an architectural grammar that ultimately emphasized a biophysical integration of domestic urban sites into a stable and integrated urban-architectural superstructure.[9]

Between the 1930s and early 1950s, as New York City rose to become the largest industrial-era city with the largest labor force in the world, the City's infrastructural and planning projects extended throughout the City's boroughs. Under the public-works leadership of Robert Moses, the intellectual traditions of U.S. and European planning were implemented through coordinated federal, state, and municipal investments. Enormous highways, greenways, park systems, and housing tracts complemented the City's already-monumental public parks and water networks.[10] The capital of capitalism was also the capital of a reworked form of urban nature. Despite the intensity and integration of scales of New York City's socionatural project, by the late-1960s, this coordinated system suddenly transformed into more modest urban proposals, disentangled from notions of urban and natural transformation and the multigovernmental system of financing. This was the result of declines in manufacturing within the City and a corresponding loss of tax bases, as well as a recession that hit the City especially hard in the late 1960s. The reformist, sanitarian, and bacteriological project unraveled, and architecture and planning appeared to cease addressing the City on a socionatural, somatic level. Such infrastructural disentanglements were further exaggerated during the City's critical financial crisis of 1975. In that year, the City's major banks coordinated a strike in which they refused to continue loans to the municipal government; to avoid bankruptcy, a multidisciplinary board of the City's high-ranking business executives devised ways to cut the City's budget, which would fall 33 percent over the next three years. The cuts impacted virtually all the City's infrastructural services—from parks to subways—but the City's agencies with health responsibilities were particularly affected by the reductions in funding. The notion of the municipality as a spatialized center of physical support, which was already questionable in the ten years before the fiscal crisis, was further eviscerated. In place of the funding of public works, business interests let loose a program of fiscal austerity and proto-neoliberalism that shifted urban spatial production to business and cultural tourism.[11]

These shifts were not solely economic or governmental; they can also be detected within localized critiques of New York's planning, architectural, and urban-disciplinary shifts developing within the United States and Europe between the early 1960s and late 1970s. Postwar architectural and urban critiques began as a series of reassessments of earlier and modern reworkings of the City that appeared as brutal forms of architectural and bureaucratic rationality, instrumentality, and positivism.[12] Jane Jacobs, to cite an early and particularly famous example, convincingly shifted the terms of urbanism away from a Moses-era focus on regional architectural and urban integration and its architectural grammar. In the place of aggregated blocks and expanses of urban verdure, she provided an analysis of the individual nineteenth-century New York City "block" structure and its "community" as the basis of architectural–urban connectivity. Her analysis was powerful and influential, but, more critically, it illustrated the loss of authority—moral, scientific, or otherwise—of earlier forms of large-scale planning. Such critiques were pervasive; they appeared within neighborhoods where massive projects were staged, and the desire for community and the turn against biophysical economic urban integration formed core aspects of other early-1960s transdisciplinary urban critiques within European situationism or the work of Team 10.[13]

In coming to terms with the legacy of modernism, architects theorized new parameters for relationships between architecture, subjects, and the City outside earlier and integrated biophysical conceptions. In addition to the critiques already mentioned, in London, the writing of Reyner Banham and the work of the Archigram group reoriented the scale and language of technologically oriented modernist architecture toward the inflections of urban mass consumption. Here, the somatic transformation embedded in the distribution of plumbing or heating in the City became reworked as an expression of individualist consumerism: insulated spaces dotted with a connective tissue of individuated environmental machinery. The architects Robert Venturi and Denise Scott Brown attempted to salvage architecture's public contract by tying architecture to the urban logic of the commercial strip, advancing a new form of urban contextualism also situated within postwar consumerism.[14] This communicative project was also taken up with the notion of a corporatized and reworked public sphere in the writings of Charles Moore. In New York City and Italy, Peter Eisenman and Aldo Rossi theorized a new, postscientific engagement with the postwar City, a formalized and politicized form of architectural "autonomy" that demanded the isolation of architecture relative to the capitalist City and its technologies.[15] By the mid-1970s, Eisenman would be aligned with a group of neomodernists known as the "whites," Moore and others with the historicist "grays." These latter consumerist, contextualist, and autonomist approaches of Venturi, Brown, Moore, Eisenman, and Rossi formed much of the intellectual foundation of what architect and critic Charles Jencks would theorize as architectural "postmodernism." Although postmodernism was pervasive in architecture and other arts, spreading to many global and cultural urban centers, according to David Harvey, "New York became the epicentre of postmodern cultural and intellectual experimentation" because of the transformation in the City of urban labor and governance.[16]

In tandem with these governmental transformations and urban and institutional critiques, throughout 1960s and 1970s New York City we see buildings and infrastructural projects, both proposed and realized, becoming disentangled from any self-evident and explicit engagement with the City as a socionatural form, and the language of architecture and urbanism appearing to lose a transformative somatic position within the grand ambitions of urbanism and planning. Although some infrastructural works continued as the City's economy recovered in the mid-1980s, such as the expansion of New York City's water systems in the 1980s and 1990s and the development of green spaces along its waterfronts from the 1980s through the 1990s, these efforts were unhinged from explicit notions of urban and human physical health. These infrastructural projects lacked a modernist pretense according to which otherwise unhealthy urban environments transform into more healthy ones via the transformation of urban nature.[17] As the City shifted toward containing the largest postindustrial economy in the West, its earlier socionatural architectural and urban forms, water systems and parks, transformed into more explicit supports for the City's burgeoning real-estate economy.[18] Such shifts were systemic and related back to the disciplinary formation of new architectural ideas; a new urban sensibility can be detected within various postwar, experimental, and postmodern architectural approaches that stretch from 1960 to the late 1970s. In several cases, images of iconic, industrial-era socionatural spaces in Manhattan become the backdrop for a proposed and radical postindustrial architectural relationship. The proposal of Buckminster Fuller to dome Manhattan (1960); Archigram's Walking City collage (1964), situated in New York's West Side port; and Rem Koolhaas's notions of buildings operating within intensely isolated Manhattan blocks or fantastical visions of waterfront redevelopments (1978) are among a larger group of images that used the crumbling industrial-era landscapes of New York City as a foil for a spatial sensibility that projected the erosions of modern urban relationships that were already under way.[19] These projects contrast the prewar spaces of Manhattan against a deinfrastructuralized relationship between architecture and urban nature. Postindustrialization was a latent aspect of a more explicit visionary moment within architecture.

The urban restructuring of New York City became a model of urban restructuring both in the United States and Europe, with important and systemic ramifications for the conceptions of architecture, space, and cities in an era of deindustrialization and municipal-governmental withdrawal.[20] By the early 1980s, important studies within the fields of architectural history, cultural theory, anthropology, and urban geography explored, charted, and critiqued the seeming disconnections between architecture and the urban spaces in which it was situated. Manfredo Tafuri suggested that the unraveling of the Western city as a synthetic architectural and urbanistic project rests on the failures of regional planning to connect buildings to urban processes, something he traced to the postwar era both in New York City and in other American cities. For Tafuri, the failures of planning illustrated the subsequent autonomy of architecture. Tafuri focused on the formal aloofness of postwar modern architecture relative to its surrounding urban environment—its inability to control the shape or socionatural contours of the city. Fredric Jameson similarly argued that lurking within a postmodernist architectural program was a desire to disconnect the interior of architecture from the city. Using the mirrored-glass Bonaventure Hotel in Los Angeles as his example, he argued that postmodernism was less a turn toward the urban context, in the manner advanced by Venturi and Scott Brown, and more a process that reoriented architectural interiors into themselves with often disorienting visual effects of mirrors, escalators, plants, and water. Within Jameson's writing, the postmodern interior becomes a dizzying antiurban analogue to the disorientations and violence of global capital, a site of nature disconnected from any urban aim. From the late 1970s throughout the 1990s, architectural environmentalists and urban geographers similarly examined the rise of the postmodern and global corporate architectural interior as a new, climate-controlled, and isolated form in the city, held behind a taut wall of shimmering glass. Mirroring the assessments of Tafuri and Jameson, they argued that architecture takes on another, more autonomous project within the global city. Within these studies, nature, as a transformative urban force, drops out of the urban and architectural project, and architecture rises as a more individualized historical practice, the environment within its spaces providing "comfort" and a more ornamental conception of natural artifacts.[21]

As significant as the urban transformations staged in New York City were, as important as their lingering effects remain on this and other cities, and as critical as the aforementioned disciplinary insights remain, we might reconsider the ultimate status of architecture relative to this city's long and particular project of socionatural reconstruction. Many of the architectural environments built in New York City between the 1960s and 1980s reveal that the nature–architecture relationship did not simply disintegrate, and demonstrate how these environments related to the old sites of urban nature. Many of these buildings suggest numerous strategies that extended the socionatural project of this city and reworked its historical spaces, but in a vastly different form than that envisioned years earlier. Between the early 1960s and mid-1980s, the biophysical tenor of this city's socionatural project did not completely disappear; rather, as New York City entered an era of financial crisis and then rose to contain its powerful postindustrial economy, this project continued, but it became reified in a new and more intensely architectural form. Such architecturally situated environments suggested new sites and scales of urban biophysical support, engaged with the City's earlier socionatural landscapes and networks but now oriented toward the people and things imagined to be critical to an initially nascent and then burgeoning postindustrial economy. The postwar building boom resulted in corporations building large concentrations of verdant, indoor atria for the maintenance of urban flora; museums experimenting with large spaces where conditioning systems preserved objects in often environmentally performative ways; and finance-oriented corporations generating vast and influential air-conditioned trading rooms servicing the City's financial markets.[22] As these environments rose, the highways, parks, and working waterfronts that defined New York's socionatural project were not simply abandoned, nor did "public" nature simply and solely come inside. Rather, the new architecture and its environment mediated a transformation of the City's critical earlier sites of socionatural production, orienting them toward an emerging conception of the City. Such spaces were built atop landscaped highways, in Central Park, or on the City's historic working waterfront. As these architectural projects suggested sites of support within the City's architecture and transformations in its historical structure, it also suggested powerful and troubling relationships between architecture, socionature, and the social and political structure of the City.

If theorists and critics considered the postwar architectural environment to be a form of individualized technoconsumerism or a potential bubble of urban isolation, collectively the architectural environments constructed in New York City suggest other possibilities: they illustrate various efforts by architects, developers, landscape architects, and institutions to urbanize the material conditions produced by the architectural environment—the ability of the late-modern architectural environment to support plants, art, machinery, and people—into spatial and economic projects specific to the goals of New York's late-capitalist urbanization. If the earlier and more public urban and socionatural structures and systems of reformist eras supported New York City's industrial economies and subjects, the environments generated within the City's postwar architecture evoked an entirely different political-economic character that produced a far more complex urban and somatic effect. Developers and architects imagined the potential environmental resistance of late-modern space—its sealed curtain walls and the atmosphere within it—entangling with efforts to restructure the demographics of the City's neighborhoods. For architects and landscape architects, the comfort zone of office buildings became a new site within which to imagine a new corporate nature that could respond to the City's collapsing forms of public nature; engineers developed new atmospheric parameters within buildings that facilitated new ideas about environment and trade in Wall Street's trading rooms, a new environmental milieu for the finance workers within an emerging and critical economy. Museums and their architects imagined new types of environments that would enable them to consolidate culture in the City's largest museum, the Metropolitan Museum of Art, all in the name of physical and atmospheric stability and conservation. The atmospheric environments within buildings figured in discussions spanning from the transformation of New York City into a center of international culture, to the future position of the City as the financial center of the world.

The urbanized environments in New York contained specificity, but they also entangled with disciplinary efforts within architecture to reimagine buildings for the postwar American city. Architects developing buildings throughout this period in New York, from Kevin Roche John Dinkeloo and Associates in the late 1960s to Cesar Pelli and Associates in the mid-1980s, were part of a larger group of practitioners who imagined the interior environment becoming a form of urban content and architectural representation. Their often abstract, monumental, mirrored-glass and aluminum-sheathed work sought ways to transform the language of an earlier generation of modern architects, but their work was not easily located within postwar architectural theory (because their work lacked ironic allusions to historical architecture or explicit forms of ornamentation). In coming to grips with this work, Charles Jencks called their work "late-modern," a label I embrace. For Jencks, late-modern architecture was both pragmatic and exaggerated modernist forms but lacked the referentiality, representational irony, and humor of postmodernist architecture. Jencks further described this type of late-modern architecture as "silver." Jencks's coinage of this term was used by architectural students at the University of California Los Angeles in the early 1970s to relate to the pronounced use of mirrored curtain-wall glass and aluminum among architects such as Cesar Pelli (then based with Victor Gruen in Los Angeles), Anthony Lumsden, and others. Writing in 1976, the architectural historian Kenneth Frampton described the architecture of Roche and Dinkeloo and of Pelli as "silvery"; in his use, it was a simultaneously descriptive and derisive term that evoked the enormous institutional wealth that often funded these architects' projects. The idea of a "silver" architecture contrasted bodies of work being theorized in New York: "white" and "gray" architecture.[23] The descriptor "silver" also evoked this architecture's changeable environmental quality, which differed from contemporary postmodern architecture that expressed more semantic architectural effects. But silver also evokes notions of temperature (such as quicksilver or mercury), light, and other environmental effects. Throughout this book, I examine the formation of this particular aesthetic of aluminum, mirrored glass, and abstraction, arriving at an interpretation in which I see this work as a material representation of architecture as an emerging system of urban environmental production.[24] Today, the few who write about "silver" architects chiefly associate the label with the architecture of mid- and late-1970s Los Angeles, but this book recovers a "silver" project within Manhattan.[25]

The new architectural environments rising in New York emerged from late-modern architectural concepts, but they also found themselves implicated in furthering modern and even early-modern socionatural, economic, and geographical relationships. Postwar discussions of space, indoor air, and maintenance reconfigured much earlier, predominately nineteenth-century discourses developed within this city on the interior as an urban refuge. The embedded fears of urban air and pollution, literally engineered out of buildings and aestheticized in their impervious skins, evoke ideas of a "miasmatic" city overtaken with fouled air.[26] In addition to these concerns, the connections between architectural environments and the subjects and objects within them continued concepts that linked metropole and its antipode, more typically associated with the late nineteenth and early twentieth centuries. For example, the old economic networks between the City and the global South reappeared in the spectacle of exotic indoor vegetation moved into the City's atria and in the distant cultural artifacts brought into conditioned rooms in the City's museums. In both cases, sophisticated architectural interiors became sites that situated and ultimately naturalized unmoored objects within a new global architectural and urban context. In both cases, a presumably late-modern architecture became entangled in an older politics of power in the City. Although architecture made certain historical relationships reappear in the City, these relationships were not at all obvious or transparent. One of the key functions of this study is to demonstrate these historical and geographical interconnections and to recognize the few who identified them at the time.

THEORIES OF AN URBAN ARCHITECTURAL ENVIRONMENT

As is becoming clear, this book identifies links between the architectural environment and the socionatural and socioeconomic transformations embedded within a specific moment within New York City. To better investigate the interrelationships between architecture's history and the City's forms of socionature, I often turn to geographical interpretive techniques. In particular, I utilize recent geographical theories of cities, nature, and environment found in literature on urban-political ecology, urban-environmental studies, and, most significantly, "the urban production of nature." This latter body of literature offers an antinaturalistic theory of environment and cities that provides insights into how urbanization produces forms of and ideas about the nature we encounter in the city.[27] Its authors—chiefly Matthew Gandy, Maria Kaika, and Erik Swyngedouw—combine key insights from Henri Lefebvre on the production of space, urban-environmental ideas of networks from William Cronon, Neil Smith's notions of the "production of nature," and ontological and epistemological theories of nature and society drawn from Donna Haraway, Bruno Latour, and Gilles Deleuze and Félix Guattari.[28] Literature on the urban production of nature represents a deft synthesis of "postnatural" thought and examines relationships between urban processes, such as the capitalization of land, the industrialization of labor, and the forms, meanings, and power of nature that are produced within cities. Authors of this literature interpret how something as seemingly simple as the realization of a glass of water in the city is not only a technological feat of production but also a vast assemblage of concepts and material, from historical concepts of cleanliness and health to enormous investments of capital in municipal bonds. A glass of water, in such an analysis, is a hybrid "metropolitan" object, a "cyborg" made in and through networks of cash and social, economic, and political concepts that course through the city.[29]

Most literature on the urban production of nature primarily investigates a particular city's historical and contemporary parks, water, and waste systems. This literature examines how such systems entangle with the urban political and economic orders of their time. Within this work, the water infrastructure of twentieth-century Guayaquil is integrated into the colonialization of the City's economy; the park systems of nineteenth- and twentieth-century Manhattan become entangled in processes of modern, high-capitalist investment; and the Los Angeles river is recovered as a site of political-ecological contest in twenty-first-century Los Angeles.[30] Ultimately, this literature leads me to understand that the air breathed within buildings, like the glass of water drunk in the city, is a site of urban tensions and representations. Through these methods of analysis, we can develop a novel geographical and architectural-historical technique to analyze the architectural environment, but, more significantly, we can begin to link the architectural environment to specific urban formations.

The great water infrastructure of nineteenth-century New York City was tied to the City's industrialization, capitalization of land, urban-reform movements, and City Beautiful aesthetics. In a similar vein, I believe that the powerful rise of the technologically sophisticated architectural environment within this city operated as both a physical representation and a tool of contemporaneous urban phenomena. Consider the following terms, often studied as key processes and formations evident in the restructuring of Manhattan: "gentrification," "culture industry," "postindustrialization," "finance industries," and "global city." These processes and economic realities describe urban transformations as cities restructured from an earlier industrial-economic base. Various historians have identified how these processes can be linked to developments in urban planning, art, and architectural form both within this city and in others.[31] I believe that concepts from geographical literature on the urban production of nature enable us to understand how these urbanized processes and phenomena informed the development and experience of this city's vaporous, fleeting interior environments. Within this study, an economic urban phenomenon such as gentrification, among other possible examples, entailed not only transformations to the social and visual experience of the City but also a little-understood reimagining of the environmental experience within buildings and the relationship (the visual sense) of a building's interior environment to the City. Gentrification (like the other terms mentioned) becomes formed and reformed through architecture, but within the hands of various agents it also becomes a set of relationships integrated into a new interaction between subjects, architectural spaces, and environments that rework these preexisting relationships within the City. As we shall see, the environments examined within this book become aligned with late-modern urban processes and economic structures. They become powerful milieus integrated into the goals and aims of New York City's late-modern urbanity.

Equipped with these epistemological techniques, I seek to better identify and ontologically theorize this pervasive environment that courses through the City. Architectural historians have argued that the technologically sophisticated environment within late-modern buildings represented a new form of "well-tempered" or "conditioned" environment. Such terms emphasize these spaces as counterenvironments—spaces in relation to, but set apart from, the City. In the late 1960s, Reyner Banham offered one of the first histories and theories of the atmospheric, lighting, and acoustical aspects of modern space. He described this epiphenomenon as the "well-tempered environment." This concept emphasizes the modernity of the architectural environment, its pronounced use of heating, ventilation, cooling, lighting, and acoustical improvements. His theorization articulates the way the features of temperature, humidity, light, and sound are brought under mechanical control. The "well-tempered" environment existed in contrast to the unpredictable and uncontrollable weather and pollution outside in the City. It was simply nature improved, mechanical art over raw nature and urban industrial pollution. As we understand how architectural environments become tools of urban power, their spatial character expands beyond Banham's particular focus. They not only exist in contrast to the given environments of the City, they become entangled in a wider web of urban relationships and concerns. In the manner of literature on the urban production of nature, we might excavate the urban economic order and power that lie hidden within the architectural environments of the last forty years. But, in addition to expressions and tools of an economic order, the architectural environments also become extensions of institutional authority, power, and care—what Michel Foucault called "bio-power." This latter term, initially developed by Foucault in a philosophical and historical context in the mid-1970s, has been elaborated more recently in a political and theoretical context by Giorgio Agamben, Michael Hardt, and Antonio Negri. "Bio-power" names a new form of dispersed authority that appeared in the eighteenth and nineteenth centuries and replaced older, monarchial forms of power. Bio-power is that form of power which supports a human subject's life and the subject's instrumental relationship to a state economy. Social institutions such as the family and workplace, spaces such as the house and hospital, and discursive formations including health and medicine exhibit and form bio-power. These are power structures that maintain us physically as reproductions of the authority and power of state governance. Foucault conceptualized his idea of bio-power as an aspect of his critique of Marxist theories of state governance and Marxism's more situated notions of a class-based power. In contrast to the forms of power examined by Marx and within Marxist writings, a Foucauldian conception of power is more dispersed and pervasive.[32]

In my analysis, I draw on the concept of bio-power to formulate a more complex understanding of the urban status of the architectural environment, but I also am interested in a neo-Marxist interpretation that attempts to excavate those activities that are both reified and fetishized within the architectural environment. In aligning the aforementioned theories, I ultimately turn to a specific concept of "maintenance" formulated in New York in the late 1960s that describes the urban role of the architectural environment. In some ways, this is a literal physical description of what the architectural environments explored in this book do: they maintain the subjects, objects, and spaces critical to this moment in the historical transformation of the City. But my use of the term draws on concepts and theories of maintenance that are far more complex and that enable us to integrate many of the ideas I have mentioned. In 1969, five years before Foucault first wrote on bio-power, a New York City artist, Mierle Laderman Ukeles, wrote an extended theoretical text on the concept of maintenance in the City. Her "manifesto" on maintenance both documented and focused on acts of physical maintenance as a critical practice that configured the experience of the City and its institutions. Ukeles's writing appeared at a critical time in the history of maintenance within New York. In addition to problems with air and water pollution, New York experienced several garbage strikes, and the City witnessed the beginning of a growing postindustrial service-oriented workforce. She explored the reality of maintenance as a more critical aspect of the future of the City and, equally significant, the way practices of maintenance could become a new intellectual and material territory. Within her thought, activities such as garbage collection, cleaning objects, and preserving threatened cultural artifacts become categories of thought, ontological reflections on the status of objects within the City's systems of power. Ukeles's writings and activities were part of conceptualist art practices that simultaneously deemphasized the production of objects and oriented art practices toward a Kantian concern for the contingency of aesthetic experience. Within her own forty-five-year art practice, she made work that uncovered the hidden networks of maintenance—janitorial work, conservation work, and garbage collection, among many others—that move throughout the spaces and economies of everyday and institutional life in New York City.[33]

Ukeles's ideas informed the concepts in this book in their historical and geographical specificity: she was one of the first to identify spatialized forms of power embedded within the spaces and institutions of postwar New York City. One of Ukeles's observations is that a precondition of late-modern institutional authority—that is, the particular power of museums, archives, or financial institutions to act—was maintenance. This could entail the public upkeep of space itself, but it also entailed other systems of maintenance as a form of authority. In a passage of her manifesto often overlooked by her contemporary commentators, Ukeles further positioned maintenance as a socionatural practice, a form of urban nature production that extended the socionatural project of the modern city—but inside. Mirroring the late-1960s discussions of buildings examined in this book, such as Kevin Roche and John Dinkeloo Associates' Ford Foundation Building or the expansion of the Metropolitan Museum of Art, she proposed bringing all manner of degraded urban material into museums, creating "a container of polluted air . . . polluted Hudson River water . . . ravaged land," where it would be publicly "de-polluted, . . . rehabilitated, . . . and conserved" by a series of technical and what she called "quasi-technical" processes. Maintenance ultimately rebuilds and protects nature, objects, and the subjects that encounter these things, but inside.[34]

Ukeles's concept of maintenance forged critical developments in both contemporary conceptual and feminist art practices and histories, as it concentrated on maintenance as an invisible, underexamined, and highly gendered and classed activity.[35] Her ideas have appeared in recent architectural-theoretical discourse, in the writing of Hilary Sample (who coined the term "maintenance architecture") and Jorge Otero-Pailos. In this latter context, 1960s concepts of maintenance become lenses onto the ontological status of care within architecture. That is, within these authors' writings, they employ the term "maintenance" to examine how the cleaning and upkeep of architecture enable us to develop a more nuanced philosophy of modernism. Both Otero-Pailos and Sample concentrate on the washing of architectural surfaces and the visual obscuring of the cleaning labor in buildings, especially in the context of modern architecture. Such activities are among the myriad activities that make modern architecture modern.[36] Ultimately, my concept of "maintenance" and use of the term are different than the work Sample and Otero-Pailos describe; my goal is not to align contemporary architectural thought with conceptual art. Rather, maintenance enabled me to identify the specific powers spatialized within the architectural environments under analysis in this book. It enabled me to understand and link several strands of theoretical reflections on subjects and objects together: Foucauldian theories of power and its productive role, Marxist analyses of reification and fetishization, Deleuzian reflections on territoriality, and even a Kantian concern for the contingency of objects and their experience. Through an expanded concept of maintenance as a socionatural activity, we might begin to adequately identify and theorize the tenor of environmental production within the architectural environment. Maintenance emerges as the new precondition for the appearance of objects and subjects as critical components in a nascent late-modern urbanism. That is, the presence of art, nature, and subjects in the late-modern city is based on isolated systems of support that make these things appear in particular spaces and sites. Within this particular study, the City's late-modern architecture rises as the production site for a maintenance environment; here, maintenance and its particular urban power are given a more explicit and monumental form.[37]

PRECEDENTS OF THE MAINTENANCE ENVIRONMENT

As this book employs interpretive techniques and language to better communicate and objectify the architectural environment within a specific urban scenario, it enters into a dialogue with existing studies, histories, and theories of both architecture and cities. This includes Reyner Banham's aforementioned book, *The Architecture of the Well-Tempered Environment*; architectural-theoretical books on the architectural environment such as Luis Fernandez Galiano's *Fire and Memory: On Architecture and Energy*; the technological history *Air-Conditioning America*, by Gail Cooper; and works of science studies that examine architectural environments, such as Michelle Murphy's *Sick Building Syndrome*. Among the historical studies on the architectural environment, this book's most obvious precedent is Banham's *The Architecture of the Well-Tempered Environment*. Banham's book is often regarded as the first book on the history of heating, ventilation, and air-conditioning, but in reality it is the first book to examine the technology of the architectural interior as an environmental totality. The modern architectural environment interested Banham because he believed its history fulfilled the thesis advanced in his earlier book *Theory and Design in the First Machine Age*. That is, modern architecture became modern when it literally absorbed, and was ultimately transformed by, technological systems. Banham's story essentially narrates the transformation of architecture by technological systems. *Manhattan Atmospheres* does not update Banham's book; it's not a critique of technologically driven histories of architecture (that battle was waged long ago); rather, it brings the history of the architectural environment into a different intellectual and urban context. This book interprets the architectural environment in ways that Banham could never have historicized in the late 1960s, because both the urban implementation of the technologies he examined and their architectural grammar were only beginning to be staged.

In addition to reconsidering existing works on the architectural environment, *Manhattan Atmospheres* potentially demonstrates new possibilities for bridging discursive and materialist explorations of environment and nature within the field of architectural history and theory. Many contemporary critical architectural historians—chiefly Reinhold Martin, Felicity Scott, and Mark Wigley—critique the concept of environment within architecture as a fetishization and naturalization of largely sociopolitical power relationships.[38] Without denying that environment can become naturalized within past and present architectural writing, I attempt to understand ideas of environment within architecture anew, via the aforementioned geographical literature. I aim to demonstrate that environments are certainly representations, but I also consider more closely the histories of the specific things—plants, art, the very constituent material of the air—that often constitute spaces that architects have described as "environments." Such things are often overlooked in the contemporary critical literature. These things and ideas point toward biophysical dreams and realities that should not be dismissed outright because they can be or have been described as "environments."

My geo-architectural mix also simultaneously builds upon, but ultimately differs from, other contemporary geographical turns in architectural writing. Recently, many contemporary architectural theorists have turned to geographical literature and concepts to elucidate an understanding of space as sublimated within economic, political, and natural flux. The recent work of Keller Easterling turns to geographical conceptions and empirical data to consider how contemporary space is immersed in unseen economic and governmental forces. This "logistical" interpretive framework advances built space as a dependent and ultimately malleable conduit of data and information. Such logistically oriented writing often insightfully aligns late-modern space with late-modern economies, but I often find this architectural writing to have the effect of rendering the world of objects and representations (whether aesthetic or instrumental) in a sweeping, data-ridden milieu from which we have no escape. Such an approach is mirrored in the more depoliticized Deleuzian and more geologically inspired architectural writing of Sanford Kwinter. Like Easterling, Kwinter imagines a world with no outside, where the city becomes analogous to physical geographical flows within which individual subjectivity and social representation evaporate or become sublimated.[39] In contrast to both Easterling and Kwinter, throughout this book I objectify the architectural environment as something intelligible, representational, and architectural, something from which we can stand apart to understand and observe. Of course, the architectural environment seethes with data (the concept of a "comfort zone," for example, is based on parameters of climatic data), and I find contemporary logistical architectural theory useful in thinking about space, but the intellectual thrust of this book is to transform something that may appear to be purely the product of logistical flux into something we might see with a more objectlike character. Finally, my approach differs from a recent approach to geo-architectural analysis that equates geography with architectural scale. In this interpretation, architecture becomes geographical when it takes on the dimensions of a city, region, or landscape.[40] But what I understand from geographical literature such as that on the urban production of nature is that a glass of water or an interior is as geographical as a megastructural building.

Manhattan Atmospheres also expands the ideas of several books on urban environmental history. These include important works on New York City by Matthew Gandy and Julie Sze, and critical works on urban nature by Maria Kaika and Mike Davis.[41] The relationship between Gandy's and Kaika's books is theoretical and methodological, as these two books utilize the ideas of the urban production of nature to foster an understanding of how cities produce and generate environments that reflect their particular political economies. My book differs from these, as I not only explore architecture and aesthetics—a critical dimension missing in these works—but also bring the history of nature production inside. As this book *urbanizes* the discussion of the architectural interior environment, it also *architecturalizes* urban political ecology and writings on the urban production of nature. In addition to suggesting new possibilities for interpreting architecture and architectural technology, this work also contributes to literature on the cultural, social, and spatial transformations of New York City between the 1960s and the late 1980s. The important studies of Neil Smith on the economic reality and cultural imagery of gentrification in New York City; Rosalyn Deutsche on the operationalization of art and "public culture" for the purposes of demographic restructuring; and Christine Boyer on the architectural imagery of South Street Seaport and the World Financial Center are all model studies of contemporary New York City.[42] Although they differ in theory, ranging from the Marxism of Smith to the Foucault-inspired concepts of Boyer, each study registers many of the transformations in New York via the public spaces of the nineteenth century. Spaces such as Tompkins Square Park, Madison Square, and the Lower Manhattan Waterfront become barometers of urban restructuring processes. In the most direct sense, this project adds to literature on the restructuring of New York City by taking the discussion *inside*; the key studies of urban change in New York City that I have mentioned contain a decidedly "outdoorist" take on the socionatural and spatial transformations rendered in the City, registering virtually all of these transformations in the most palpable public places.

Finally, this book offers a different visual and aesthetic register with which to evaluate what New York City appeared to be immediately preceding, during, and after its "crisis" years. Artists, filmmakers, authors, journalists, and other urban chroniclers often represented New York City from the late 1960s through the mid-1980s as a city on the verge of crumbling into utter, desolate ruin.[43] During this period, the city became, and still is, the visual language for the American image of urban crisis. Wasted landscapes of graffiti, sickened trees, urban wildlife, flooded streets, and violent urban neighborhoods have become a dominant language through which to interpret the City's various economic and social pressures. But this book suggests another reality lurking within the City's crumbling cityscapes: the architectural environments in this book suggest that architecturally sophisticated, technologically inflected spaces might also bear the imprints of urban crisis. Rather than simply reinforcing the language of a desolate, crisis-era "urban pastoral," they enable us to visualize the crisis city via the counterenvironments built to mediate crisis. By additionally positioning the spaces that I examine in this manner, I am not arguing that they were in any way just or appropriate responses to urban crisis. In fact, many of the chapters in the book ultimately question the pursuit of these spaces and the ideas behind these spaces. Rather, these architectural environments simply illustrate the ways that some concept of "city" was potentially realized in and through the architectural environment, in and against the city as it was imagined. Although this book certainly contributes to the history of New York, I ultimately hope that the ideas I explore inform analyses of late-modern socionatural spaces in other cities as well, particularly as these spaces and the ideas behind them intersect with architectural conditions.

THE MAINTENANCE ENVIRONMENTS OF NEW YORK CITY

In the chapters that follow, not only do we begin to uncover the matter and ideas embedded within the maintenance-oriented environments that participated in the restructuring of New York City, we also uncover the significance of this architecture to the constitution of the contemporary city. The following chapters are organized both historically and geographically. We begin in the early 1960s, examining a complex of towers in the upper reaches of Manhattan Island spiraling through the City's "central business district"—the heart of postwar planning activity and the epicenter of the reworking of the City—and we conclude in the 1980s, with another complex of towers at the opposite end of Manhattan.[44] Although there is a chronological stream sequencing the chapters, each chapter traces the interdevelopment of specific architectural-environmental concepts within specific and important neighborhoods, precincts, and structures. In each chapter, we see how environmental ideas and the specific historical characteristics of a neighborhood—its demographics, economy, and transformation—intersect to produce distinct interrelations between environment, subjects, objects, and the political-economic pressures acting on the City. Although each chapter contains enormous specificity in excavating particular aspects of urban history, each relates the specific cases to more general theoretical concerns within architecture, urbanism, and environment.

The book begins with a history of a project that was once critical to New York's transitional urban development: the Washington Bridge Apartments and Extension. From an architectural and urban-historical perspective, this "megastructural" development sits at the dividing line between modern and late-modern architecture, the industrial and postindustrial city, and architectural planning and interiors. This is a massive, aluminum-skinned, megastructural "air-rights" project designed by Brown and Guenther and once fostered the postindustrial redevelopment of Washington Heights. The Bridge Apartments were built within one of the most environmentally inhospitable sites in Manhattan, and they were conceptualized as simultaneously offering an environmental refuge from the polluted atmospheres of the City—a general concern within this city—and promoting postindustrial forms of domesticity. The apartment buildings also claim a significant distinction in the history of architecture and environmental concerns: they were prominently featured as one of the first megastructural projects in Reyner Banham's study of building types, and they were the first building interiors analyzed by the Environmental Protection Agency. Chapter 1 begins to excavate the historical relationships between these buildings' role in the transformation of Washington Heights, the brief rise of megastructural developments as environmentally transformative planning tools, and the desires of architects and atmospheric scientists to construct counterenvironments within the interiors of buildings in New York City. Through this chapter, we begin to understand how the seemingly ubiquitous spaces of late modernity were fashioned to represent certain spatially specific environmental agendas. This chapter offers an environmental and architectural interpretation of Manhattan's demographic neighborhood restructuring as the construction and experience of an "environment" within the environment.

As the City's new postindustrial architectural environments offered an environment apart from the crumbling atmospheres of the City, they also became experimental sites for repositioning more traditional forms of urban nature that appeared under stress in the City's parks and streets. Chapter 2 examines the development of indoor atrium gardens and their ascendant role as a site of nature production within a city famous for the grandeur of its public parks. Corporate atrium gardens emerged first in New York City with Roche and Dinkeloo's Ford Foundation Building garden; by the 1980s, New York City's Midtown East neighborhood had the largest concentration of atrium gardens than any other neighborhood in the City or in any other city in the United States. But more than the scale of these gardens, this chapter examines experiments conducted by a range of architects, landscape architects, and scientists to implement these atrium spaces in New York from the late 1960s to the mid-1980s. In addition to these architectural efforts, the New York Botanical Society sought ways to connect the possible forms of nature in New York to office architecture and environments. Responding to the onset of the City's financial crisis, it examined how vegetation could be grown in the stable atmosphere of the "comfort zone" of office buildings—70 degrees Fahrenheit and 50 percent humidity—and how that transformed what we understand both the interior environment of buildings and urban nature to be. In doing this, the society not only transformed its institutional role but also began to transform the meaning of plants and the implications of corporate space. I argue that the atmosphere within the City's office buildings emerged as a distinct geographical climate to support nature in New York City, something that began to be shaped through architecture and intra-architectural relationships.

Chapter 3 explores how cultural institutions developed interior environments to further transform New York City into an international and postindustrial cultural center. The Metropolitan Museum, in particular, emerged as a site where architecture's late-modern environment facilitated the securing and display of important international cultural artifacts. I explore this via a history of the Metropolitan Museum of Art's entry in the competition to house the Egyptian Temple of Dendur, a sought-after artifact in the late 1960s. What made the Metropolitan's proposal unique is that whereas most museums sought to place the temple outside, in a setting closely mimicking its original Nile landscape, the administrators of the museum argued that the sealed and protected environment of late-modern architecture was most suitable for the temple. The Metropolitan successfully hinged the discussion regarding the future home for the temple on the particular atmospheric environment that would surround it, something that would mitigate urban pollution and seemingly conserve the object from the fluctuations caused by weather. I argue that the Metropolitan Museum and its architects positioned the late-modern architectural environment to develop a type of power over cultural objects. But, in developing a space to house the temple, the museum became involved in controversies over the transformation of the original Dendur site in Egypt and the impact of its expansions into Central Park. The result was an enormous level of debate regarding the relationship of architecture, environment, and natural sites transformed through processes of cultural consolidation and preservation.

Chapter 4 takes us to the trading halls of Lower Manhattan. Here, we see how engineers and architects reconfigured the architectural environment to support the laboring bodies of the City's postindustrial economic industries and networks. In this chapter, I examine how the intensely cooled and conditioned environment of trading halls in Lower Manhattan entangled architectural-biotechnical machinery, data systems, and the ephemeral center of "the market" with the people within it. I explore how these rooms offered an experience and form that associated "environment," "labor," and "data" in ways that continue into the present. I also examine how this particular environment became urbanized within the architecture and interiors of Cesar Pelli and Associates, architects who symbolized New York as the center of world finance through a largely environmental image of architecture. I argue that features of the late-modern architecture of finance ultimately monumentalized the maintenance environments of the City as a form of ascendant socionature of the City's postindustrial economy.

These chapters argue that our understanding of New York's socionatural project must expand to include the matter and spaces that lie outside traditional sites of socionatural contest. They argue that our understanding of "environment" within buildings must be unhinged from both a purely technohistorical interpretive framework and a completely amaterial, discursive investigation. *Manhattan Atmospheres* argues that the environments within buildings should be understood as having the potential to become material-representational artifacts—an expression of power—just like other aspects of a city's urbanized socionature. The environments examined here related to a specific time and place, but aspects of them appear in a still-emerging postindustrial urban consciousness. The legacies of maintenance environments can certainly be found in urban-architectural environmentalist discussions both in this city and in others: contemporary debates surrounding urban developments that promote healthy interiors, filtered air, and green and sustainable atmospheric engineering within the complex milieu of cities; and discussions of art, plants, and nonhuman life and the appropriate metrics we employ to maintain these objects and living things within architecture.[45] But, more critically, the legacies of architectural and environmental maintenance can also be found in architectural and art practices that interrogate the way architectural environments prefigure the experience of space and objects. Most significantly, the discourses surrounding these environments permeate our perception of the environmental support structure of a late-modern global city.

If the legacy of nineteenth-century cities was the vast networks that tied subjects into expansive socionatural urban systems, the legacy of crisis-era New York was the atomization of urban-environmental support into more discrete, architecturally situated sites. Today, the vestiges of the City as a physical system that somatically supports the populace are found behind the silvery curtain walls of the global city. We will see how environments explored in this book entangled with a diverse range of subjects, from the use of buildings as protective environments in the City and discussions of indoor air that fosters the health of workers, to the appropriate atmospheric and museological context for the world's cultural heritage. Many of these debates continue to be carried on at an urban level within municipal and disciplinarian arenas in New York and other global cities. Finally, in considering these interiors and their architecture, we might remove any lingering myths or sentiments about where socionatural production is in the postwar city. When we do this, I think we will have a better sense of how the City enters into a late-modern and nascent global stage of the urban productions of nature. The City, its environments, natures, and atmospheres are always there to be reshaped, but reshaped in the most politicized ways.

1 PROTECTION

Megastructures and Environmental Gentrification

FROM THE MID-1950S THROUGH THE LATE 1960S, the class structure of New York City transformed from its working-class industrial base to a corporate and service-based economy. In the early 1950s, the City held the majority of manufacturing jobs in the larger metropolitan region, but by the late 1960s it held the least, losing jobs to deindustrialization, the migration of manufacturing centers to the U.S. South, and automation.[1] As manufacturing fell, service-industry employment rose by almost 50 percent, and Manhattan's industrial-labor force was quickly supplanted by the workers of a new, "postindustrial" economy, which made a corresponding impact on all strata of the City's population and precincts.[2] Such transformations in labor fed into spatial transformations within the City: sites of former industrial areas and working-class residential areas often became degraded as a result of closures and a loss of population. From the 1960s to the 1980s, as the populations of these neighborhoods fluctuated, many eventually became arenas for potential new middle- and upper-class forms of economic and neighborhood development. These transformations of New York impacted the social, demographic, and physical features of the City in many different and recognizable patterns and forms. For those studying the eventual displacement of working-class residents by wealthier ones, aspects of the City's spatial mechanics typically become characterized with the term "gentrification." This term, coined in the early 1960s, coalesces around the idea that the "gentry"—literally, the ownership class—problematically seizes the devalued historical spaces of the industrial city as tools for its own spatial reproduction.[3] The processes of gentrification in New York City, which often transformed neighborhoods with alarming speed, became a target of scholars who positioned cosmopolitan urbanism as a liberatory force and ultimately demanded a "right to the city" for all.[4]

Most studies of New York City's gentrification focused on the *spatial* attributes of urban change within this city, particularly the cultural, physical, and demographic transformations of historically representative neighborhoods and the spatial alienation of those about to be dispersed.[5] Gentrification in New York had a particular visual and spatial language: gentrification entailed not only forms of historical connoisseurship but also alignments between art and performance in the transformation of the historical fabric of the City.[6] But gentrification in New York also contained a more generalized political-economic structure that fed into its spatial languages. In attempting to understand why the degraded sites of American and European cities became gentrified so quickly, the geographer Neil Smith argued that gentrification was actually a dialectical process of spatial impoverishment and reinvestment: as capital is withdrawn from historical sectors of cities and they turn into crumbling, degraded areas, it makes these areas potentially desirable targets of financial and spatial revitalization. This "rent-gap" theory, as it became known, suggests that the type of urban degradation that rippled through various neighborhoods of New York from the 1960s through the 1980s had financial value within an urban capital economy, as it promised a potential and significant return on future investments within these areas. Thus, the types of economic and demographic changes and pressures affecting a city's neighborhoods have a direct relationship to the simultaneous "discovery" and transformation of these neighborhoods throughout the 1960s, 1970s, and 1980s. In his later studies of gentrification, Smith expanded on this spatial-economic interpretive lens, articulating what he called New York's particularly "frontierist" attitudes and revanchist gentrification techniques. This latter work examined how neighborhoods in Manhattan were presented as strange landscapes to be forcefully wrested from working-class and poor communities to enable wealthier forms of development.[7]

Studies of New York's gentrification, that is, studies that emphasize the economic, spatial, and representational dimensions of the urban displacements staged here, are forceful. But missing from most of these studies and theories of the displacements of this postindustrializing city are the ever more troubling and continuous socionatural and *environmental* mechanics of urban dispersion that ran alongside its spatial and economic history. Because most studies of urban displacement focus on the city as a spatial and economic system, we miss this powerful component of how cities change. And although a few commentators offer a novel understanding of the environmental inequities and imbalances between various neighborhoods of late-modern New York City, we lack an understanding of how the degradation, representation, and rebuilding of "environments" in the 1960s and 1970s became systems of alienation as well.[8] Postwar neighborhood redevelopment and change not only engaged with the representations and redistributions of historical imagery within cities but engaged with representations and redistributions of spatialized environments as well. In more general terms, we lack a history and theory that describe how the rendering of these new environments became a system that intersected with the displacements and situatedness of the inhabitants of cities. For forty years, "gentrification" described the seizure of space from one class by another, generally with a preservationist and conservationist aesthetic; we now need a language that describes the contemporaneous reconstruction of urban environments and the corresponding evictions. This demands a new interpretive framework and language.

Certainly, the reconstruction of New York City into a postindustrial form was both a spatial and an environmental project. The very descriptor of a city after ("post-") industry articulates the obvious environmental transformation embedded in this shift in labor. But, like gentrification itself, the environmental transformation of cities via the rebuilding of actual socionatural conditions was far more complex than just the removal of existing industrial forms of production. As we will see throughout this book, the production of new architectural environments in Manhattan often involved the production of a whole new set of socionatural relations that reworked this city's historical socionatural relations. In other words, the proposing and building of new environments that appeared with urban displacements should not simply be understood as an illustration of those displacements. At the very least, they should be understood as a precondition of displacement, and in some instances they could be more forcefully understood as an agent of it.[9]

In tracing a parallel and *environmental* form of urban demographic transformation, we might go back to the period stretching from the early and mid-1960s to the early 1970s, a period when the processes ultimately described as "gentrification" were beginning to be staged within the City.

If gentrification was a process that entailed the withdrawal and investment of capital into the City's degraded historical spaces as well as the visualization of the City's neighborhoods as urban outlands, some environmental form of displacement would most likely entail a similar dialectical process. That is, we might look to projects that not only have "environment" as their topic of analysis but also begin to suggest the withdrawal and intensification of the architectural, environmental support system, as well as the colonization of environment itself. What I am calling an intensification of environment entails the pronounced use of an architecture (in this case, potentially sealed and air-conditioned) to maintain the subjects and objects of a city in the face of real and imagined environmental pressures. What I am calling a withdrawal may simply be the absence of such a use, or the purposeful neglect of biophysical forms of maintenance. This process relates to much of the work examined within this book, all of which protects things and people or otherwise divides parts of a city into maintenance environments and their externalized opposite, often in environmentally degraded "frontiers."

In locating these processes within this particular historical moment, we can turn to several of the most visionary postwar projects for New York; many call a new city into being on top of its old industrial form. These projects include Buckminster Fuller's proposal to mechanically condition a portion of Manhattan under an enormous dome (1959–70), Paul Rudolph's proposal to develop housing over the City's Lower East Side in his Lower Manhattan Expressway ("LOMEX") project (1972), and the Washington Bridge Apartment Complex (1963), made famous by Reyner Banham in 1976.[10] These fantastical works offered some of the first enticing, but ultimately troubling, visions of architects fashioning environments within environments in this city—both protective insides and their opposite.

Fuller's proposal was really several projects drawn over several years. In its first iteration, Fuller imagined a dome covering midtown Manhattan and portions of the East River and Brooklyn, effectively eliminating the "industry" of the East River harbor in and through the interior architectural environment. In another iteration, developed in 1970, he proposed claiming Central Park with the dome, a park that had been considerably downgraded in the public imagination. In its most enduring iteration, a perspective showed the dome covering most of Midtown and a sliver of Central Park in an intense interiorization of the City. In emphasizing the quality of this new urban interior atmosphere, Fuller showed the smoke from the industrial waterfront's Con Edison power plant wafting outside of the protected interior of his proposed new vision of the City. His proposal offered a healthy atmosphere within an otherwise intolerably polluted city.

Rudolph's project assembled housing blocks around transport and ventilation cores, further articulated to prohibit the fumes and noise of the highway below. In one important iteration of the Lower Manhattan Expressway, the architect showed the project well situated within the historical Lower East Side, Soho, and Greenwich Village neighborhoods. His project not only reordered the space above the proposed urban highway but also brought boulevards to the previously industrial spaces within Soho and Tribeca. None of these projects figure in contemporary discus-

Paul Rudolph, Lower Manhattan Expressway proposal, ca. 1970. Library of Congress Prints and Photographs Division, Paul Rudolph Archive (LC-DIG-ppmsca-26450).

sions of the history of gentrification, again because of a spatial and historical focus of its study, versus an environmental one.

Among these early proposed and built late-modern projects that restructured the degraded environments of the City, we might more closely examine the lesser-known but once infamous project the Washington Bridge Extension Complex. This assemblage of five buildings, built over the Trans-Manhattan Expressway and completed in 1963, was a sensation within architectural and planning literature in the 1960s and early 1970s; and it was an inspiration for similar proposals, including Paul Rudolph's LOMEX project. The Washington Bridge Extension project was significant as a controversial and intended manipulation of both the environment and the demographics of the City. The complex utilized late-modern architecture and planning strategies to initiate a physical and experiential juncture between architecture and the environmental degradation of the postindustrial City. Figuring prominently in his 1976 study of "megastructures," the Extension Complex, according to historian Reyner Banham, was the largest realization of the megastructure idea. When it was proposed, the Extension Complex offered an aggressive solution to redevelop crumbling neighborhoods, to negotiate the urban highways that cut through many of these areas, and to situate an emerging professional class within blighted areas of the City.

The centerpiece of the Washington Bridge Extension Complex was a residential complex, the Washington Bridge Apartments, developed for middle-class residents in a significant contrast to the working-class housing of the immediate surrounding area. Setting it above the highway, the developers of the project promised to offer the inhabitants an exhilarating relationship to the City and the highway while providing an environmental refuge from its negative aspects. The apartments figured prominently within national urban demographic and environmental debates, particularly literature on absorbing modern networks into postwar construction and building within potentially polluted urban sites. This portion of the project also included the first building examined as an "environment" by the Environmental Protection Agency, which explored its potential ability to insulate residents from urban pollution. The resulting destructive impact of the highway on this neighborhood, its intersection with the demographics of the apartment complex above it, and the environmental reconfigurations of the new buildings produced an environmental image of neighborhood transformation, a troubling form of literal socionatural deconstruction and reconstruction.

In current forms of architectural scholarship, this project has an uneasy relationship to both studies of "urban renewal" and histories of "gentrification." It cannot be easily classified within the language of renewal because of the architects' and planners' attempts to arrive at an architectural language outside a strictly orthodox modernism (inspired by the Congrès international d'architecture moderne). The project also lacks certain conservation aesthetics—the marked revitalization of architectural-historical districts—that are hallmarks of early forms of gentrification. But these facts just further illustrate the inadequacy of using "renewal" or "gentrification" to describe some of the most forceful techniques of postwar urban displacement. After all, the project's colonization of a degraded urban site was a harbinger for current late-modern architecture built next to de- or postindustrialized sites and other risky environments within which architecture provides some modicum of protection. The Washington Bridge Apartments certainly represented a return of the middle class to the central City, and it articulated novel methods to remake the City's spatial, demographic, and environmental attributes. Virtually all large-scale projects recondition the socionatural relations between inhabitants and their surroundings, but we might argue that these relations become the very substance of this planning project. This project emerged as gentrification became an engine of urban change; nevertheless, the term "gentrification" has never been, and cannot be, easily ascribed to it. Gentrification cannot easily describe the environmental reordering of urban space nor the complex concepts of class restructuring embedded in late-modernist ambitions and aesthetics. It is a harbinger of displacement in the City, but one rendered through a forceful rebuilding of environment.

AIR RIGHTS, POLLUTION, AND ATMOSPHERIC ENCLAVES

Throughout the late 1950s and late 1960s, the municipal government of New York City explored how to integrate the empty spaces created by the City's modern-era transportation networks into new housing and development schemes. The sites of train yards and highways were generally open spaces within the City's boroughs that abutted historically working-class or industrial neighborhoods. Here, modern networks and the historical structure of the City were in an uneasy but historically dialectical relationship. The block structure of the City's spaces of real-estate development existed in contrast to those networked spaces that were held in common—by the city, state, or federal government—and outside of the reach of markets. But if such sites were empty and outside the dynamics of trade, they were also often barren and, in the case of highways, blighted and polluted. Many of them existed in neighborhoods simultaneously impacted by the City's transforming economy, and the presence of these large infrastructural works appeared to destroy neighborhood cohesion. Within the context of a New York City experiencing a disentanglement of the support structure that created such networks and desperately in need of revenues, such sites became intense objects of speculation. The process that began in the 1950s and 1960s with projects such as Concourse Village, Litho Village, Linear City, and the original Hudson Yards Plan continues well into the present, in the development of housing over the City's contemporary Hudson Rail Yards and High Line. These former sites of modern-era networks have become some of the most innovative sites of postindustrial development.[11]

To realize these "air-rights" developments, as they became known, architects and engineers developed new forms of architectural representation that remade networks into legible and believable sites of the urban fabric; the municipal government developed new legal instruments to transform these indeterminate zones into property; and engineers created new forms of engineering expertise to manage the risks of environmental pollution often endemic to these sites. The federal government, which funded most major postwar roadway projects, viewed urban and rural highways as part of an infrastructural city-to-city network underpinning state economies and national defense. From a federal perspective, highways were fundamentally automotive conduits, sites of flow and circulation. Recognizing highways as potential untapped sites of urban development, in 1960 the highway agencies of New York, New Jersey, and California lobbied the federal government to allow urban development within highways. Building over highways would fold these spaces back into the spatial structure of cities. From a municipal perspective, highways displaced the very idea and literal boundaries of urban property, as their forms negated the structure of urban lots and left residual lot forms and pollution in their wake. Such sites often remained, and remain to this day, contested arenas of ownership rights and health within many American cities. Air rights promised to return the dynamics of a real-estate market to these sites and to make an otherwise problematic environmental zone in the City inhabitable.

The literal possibility of air-rights development over roadways in New York City came with a 1961 amendment to the U.S. Federal Aid Highway Act, which overturned the 1956 act that prohibited the development of the space above highways. As the federal government shifted from discouraging nonautomotive development within highways to allowing it, a significant amount of construction over U.S. highways was proposed. Significant amounts of state-sponsored literature also emerged between 1962 and the early 1970s that theorized these projects and the parameters for developing the spaces above highways. Among the proposed development projects, which included convention centers, hotels, and office buildings, the Washington Bridge Apartments figured as a prominent aspect of this activity. The air-rights literature, frequently referring to sophisticated architectural historical precedents, the promise of air-rights projects, and the Washington Heights development, provides a cogent lens through which to view the spatial and environmental connections made within this unique development form.

In addition to addressing the enormous expense and obvious engineering challenges of building above highways, the authors of air-rights literature continuously addressed the physical risks associated with this form of development. A piece of air-rights literature commissioned by the State of New Jersey Department of Transportation contained an entire section on roadway pollution ("Air Pollution Considerations"). The authors considered the ways in which architecture in this context carried intense sensorial pressures and dangers. They warned that developments built near and over freeways presented some potentially hostile, threatening conditions for their inhabitants, particularly the potential problems associated with carbon-monoxide (CO) exposure and noise.[12] The authors of this and other forms of air-rights literature clearly understood highway space as a compromised setting within the City.[13] Nevertheless, these engineers turned to an emerging conception of architecture as a "conditioned" space as a means within which the problems of such intense sites could be rectified. For the authors of air-rights literature, the development of architecture above and adjacent to highways involved a combination of engineering and demographic ideas. Construction over highways was both slow and extremely expensive. Within the context of air rights, the authors believed that certain capital-intensive buildings (primarily offices and massive apartment buildings) could offset the high costs of air rights by building over highways and "CO-proofing" the interiors of buildings. In a section in the October 7, 1961, report *An Information Guide on Air Rights above and below Interstate Highways,* by the American Association of State Highway Officials, the authors considered the intersection of highways and architectural space and technologies. In their examples of compatible uses, the authors suggested structures in which occupants "are usually enclosed in an air-conditioned environment."[14]

Within other postwar contexts, the conditioned interior environment was emerging as a site of "manufactured weather," a response to natural geographical climates.[15] But here, the conditioning of interior spaces took on specific urbanized relationships that revived earlier ideas of the architectural environment. It could suggest the mitigation of disease or health, and within the context of polluted sites or systemic urban pollution more generally, the interior conditioned environment of buildings took on another dimension, as a site within which urban pollution would be mitigated. Such an interpretation of the conditioned environment took hold in New York City particularly in the 1960s and early 1970s.[16] Within this context, indoor air, and the space within which it might be produced, took on a representational quality that partially evoked earlier concepts of the interior, particularly during the height of the City's industrialization in the nineteenth century, when one of the chief functions of ventilation was to mediate the pressures of industrial pollution. Within the context of air-rights development, the interior environment emerged as a representation of health as much as comfort, one that could negotiate urban subjects' relationships to the dangers of a compromised, polluted city.

Nevertheless, within air-rights literature, some doubts were raised about the ability of buildings to mitigate highway pollution and the intelligence of creating residential spaces in these areas: "[T]he occupants of apartment buildings—even buildings with the same quality of insulation and air-conditioning—often may be disturbed by freeway noise, especially during sleeping hours." However, the same authors suggested that such construction might be possible: using the example of the Sutton Place Apartments, a luxury tower partially built over New York's East Side Highway, they concluded that "high-rise apartments can be compatible with freeways under proper circumstances."[17] Ultimately, the development of capital-intensive and environmentally resilient buildings, whether they were office buildings or architecturally sophisticated apartment buildings, was encouraged. These concepts were reiterated in a study funded by the U.S. Department of Transportation and conducted by highway planners who examined the economic returns possible in air-rights development. The planners concluded, "With few exceptions, only high-density projects that are able to sustain high site costs will be able to make economic use of airspace."[18]

The aforementioned literature on air-rights development enables us to understand the often-surprising correlations established by planners between development, highway pollution, and the amelioration of these problems through further, select forms of development. They suggest emerging links between risk analysis, cost-benefit analysis, and other forms of technocratic engagements with urban planning. But, most significant, the air-rights planning schemes of the late 1960s and early 1970s intensified forms of planning that considered the environmental problems of cities as opportunities for development and, furthermore, developed spaces sheltered from those problems. Highway-air-rights housing announced itself as a financially rewarding response to the problems introduced by highway development into a city. In other words, air-rights schemes directly negotiated this new type of polluted landscape that resulted from highway development to enact the inhabitation and potential transformation of these degraded areas of cities.

This discursive trajectory of air rights is mirrored within the urban-environmental history of the Bridge Apartments. The Trans-Manhattan Expressway, which sat under the apartments, cut through the center of the Washington Heights neighborhood on the upper peninsula of Manhattan, a neighborhood that, in the late 1950s, began losing its population of working-class German Jews, Irish, and Cubans. The municipality considered the neighborhood "downhill" in 1954, and in need of redevelopment, a process that began in the early 1950s.[19] By the early 1960s, a city-sponsored audit of the "dilapidated" and "deteriorating" housing of southern Washington Heights concluded that only 25 percent was considered adequate.[20] Such studies chronicled the impact of suburbanization and deindustrialization within Washington Heights; by the 1960s, the overall population of this area of Washington Heights had declined

Demolition of the Trans-Manhattan Expressway, 1960. The Port Authority of New York and New Jersey.

by 27 percent.[21] The Trans-Manhattan Expressway demolition that began in the late 1950s had already destroyed several of what City administrators termed the "softest" areas of the neighborhood. (This term describes areas of the neighborhood that were vulnerable to urban development, through their high level of tenancy versus owner occupancy and/or their dilapidated condition.) It required the demolition of seventy-six buildings housing eight thousand individuals within 1,818 families from a predominately working-class and poor background. The acquisition of the property cost the Port Authority approximately $10 million, with a loss of significant tax revenues for the City. Provisions costing the Authority approximately $400,000 were implemented in the earliest stages of construction for the future development of an air-rights scheme.[22] The City, which, after the Federal Highway Act of 1961, owned the air rights over the state- and federally subsidized highway project, sold the air rights to the Kratter Corporation. The state and municipality advanced the project by offering the developers a state-supported mortgage loan and tax abatements, bolstering the potential financial success of the project.

In 1961, with the ownership of the air rights and the federal approval of air-rights structures secured, Kratter and its architects, Brown and Guenther, unveiled their vision of the Washington Bridge Apartments. The four exceedingly slender, aluminium-clad towers promised a new type of living experience within this neighborhood and the City more generally, cast astride a highway and providing refuge for the 960 apartment units from the fumes and dirt of the highway below. In a study of Washington Heights by the *New York Times*, the transformative role of the proposed Washington Bridge Apartments and the larger Extension Complex becomes increasingly clear. In a 1962 piece titled "Washington Heights Reverses Tide of Urban Decay," the author, Carl Gerwitz, wrote of the environmental beneficence of Washington Heights as an aspect of its enduring appeal: "Thirty years ago, physicians advised their patients to move to Washington Heights for its 'mountain' air and its pure drinking water. The air and the water are still good, but the area—once a prime residential neighborhood—has been stagnating. Today, with a modest building boom underway, civic leaders and public officials are laying the foundation for what they hope will be the rejuvenation of the Heights." Gerwitz also observed that the "conditions" in Washington Heights' deteriorating

Model of the Washington Bridge Apartments. The proposed parks can be seen between the towers. *Architectural Forum* (October 1961): 63.

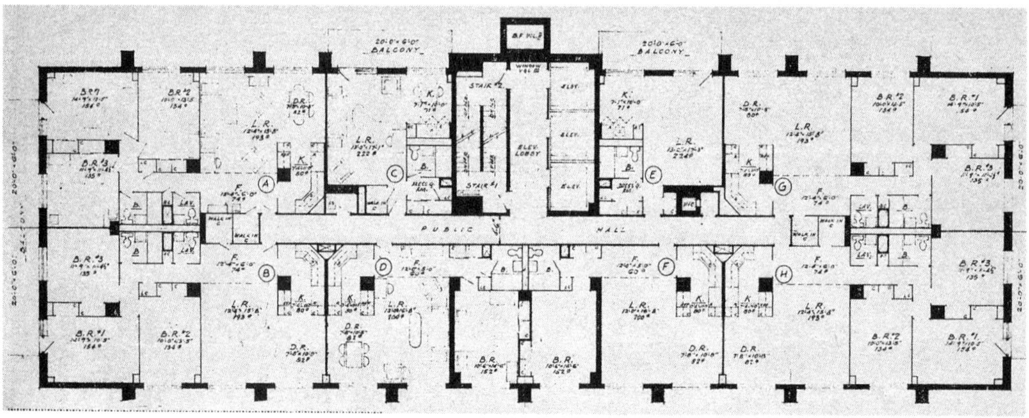

Plan of the Washington Bridge Apartments in *Empire State Architect* (September–October 1963): 31. Copyright Brown and Guenther. Avery Architectural and Fine Arts Library, Columbia University.

Washington Bridge Apartments and Extension Complex under construction. The Port Authority of New York and New Jersey.

neighborhoods were "not bad enough to warrant bulldozing entire blocks. But pocket slums—primarily brownstones and wooden frame houses where families share one room—and many rundown tenements signal the beginning of urban decay."[23] Gerwitz noted that the Washington Bridge Apartments were one of several developments in the area that planners would use "to reverse this trend" and that the apartments were "expected to spur new private initiative—either through new buildings or rehabilitation of existing housing." Paralleling Gerwitz's assessments, Frederick Elias, the vice president of construction for the Kratter Corporation, proclaimed tersely, "One nice building in a bad spot can act just the reverse of one bad apple in a barrel."[24]

The towers' potential transformation of both the highway environment and the demographics in the neighborhood also registers within the complex's architectural representations. The modern aesthetics of the towers clearly contrasted with the soot-stained brick tenement buildings of the immediate neighborhood. In the planning, the towers suggest the continued rejection of the nineteenth-century urban fabric that is a hallmark of modern architecture through the towers' dramatic siting and slim profiles. This is reiterated in the towers' implied—although not actual—link to the bus station and the highway.[25] But the towers' urban relationships were not entirely "high modern"; one of the most novel aspects that the architectural firm of Brown and Guenther developed within the buildings was the use of an aluminium skin on their exterior. This particular feature articulated some of the late-modern urban ideas and relationships embedded within the project. We might understand the use of aluminum on such slender slabs as visualizing the way the architects and planners necessarily viewed the surroundings of the buildings as a complex and compromised "environment."[26] This related to the earlier examinations of Bernard Guenther, who explored the combination of impervious white brick and metal panels in an earlier apartment building, along Sixth Avenue in Greenwich Village. It also related to contemporaneous examinations of an urban tower's resistance to the environmental imprints and impacts of the city in various atmospheric studies of towers. The use of aluminum on the exterior of the buildings, rather than vitreous brick, transposed a material primarily used on environmentally situated objects—ships, airplanes, and automobiles—into architecture. Compared with the red and yellow

RIGHT: View of the Washington Bridge Apartments and Extension Complex. The Port Authority of New York and New Jersey.

BELOW: View of the George Washington Bridge Bus Station and the Washington Bridge Apartments, ca. 1965. Library of Congress Prints and Photographs Division, Historic American Engineering Record (HAER NY,31-NEYO,161—20).

bricks used for the surrounding Washington Heights apartment buildings and tenements, aluminum was a material ascribed with "resistance" to both physical and biophysical characteristics. It could be easily cleaned of environmental imprints—dust, smoke, and soot—even as it appeared to allow environmental forces to pass over it. As the Bridge Apartments were some of the first apartment buildings in the United States to be covered in this material, not to mention the first with such an unusual site, this choice merely articulated the stakes and imagery within the overall planning concept.

The thin aluminium-clad slabs suggested the buildings' environmental resistance and restructuring, but, like a ship plowing through water, it also suggested "environment" as the ultimate context of the development. An advertisement in the *New York Times* illustrates the developers' and architects' intentions, the potential luxury of the buildings, and the way these factors entangle with the buildings' aesthetics:

> Opening Tuesday, September 4th New York's spectacular middle-income housing achievement!
>
> Here are the first completely aluminum-clad tower apartment buildings in Manhattan, located on one of the highest points on Manhattan Island. These four 32-story aluminum towers are built directly over the bridge approach . . . offering you true "in-the-sky" living with unsurpassed views! Truly breathtaking!
>
> Bridge Apartments has spacious layouts, 20-foot balconies . . . modern conveniences and luxury touches everywhere.
>
> Bridge Apartments tenants will have available for their convenience, a block-long park, playground facilities, and restful sitting areas, all safely protected from street traffic.
>
> Transportation: the new Port Authority Bus Terminal is a block away; subways and buses to everywhere are readily accessible; unexcelled auto connexions to all highways and expressways.[27]

Together with the Nervi-designed bus station (which began construction in 1961), the entire complex appeared to be an innovative exercise in the physical and environmental aspects of urban planning and highway development. *Empire State Architect* noted the technical innovations of the apartments, the aluminium skin, the massive platforms with ten-foot-deep girders that supported the apartments, parking, and a public park—all above the highway.[28]

CRUMBLING ATMOSPHERES

The Washington Bridge Apartments and the Washington Bridge Bus Station were sensational new elements in New York City's postwar planning efforts. Although the bus station, designed by Pier Luigi Nervi, was far more innovative architecturally, both buildings were lauded in the architectural press. *Architectural Forum* critic Donald Canty reflected the general critical approval in his admiration of the construction system in the Nervi bus station. Canty particularly noted the techniques Nervi used to ventilate highway fumes from the bus station with formally robust concrete work;[29] the extensive use of aluminium curtain walls in the Brown and Guenther building appeared to be an equally innovative response to the conditions of the highway below. Photographic representations of the interior spaces of the Bridge Apartments in the architectural press emphasized the unusual and fantastical views. From the apartments in the western tower, one viewed the George Washington Bridge and vistas of the Hudson River and surrounding cliffs; from the eastern tower, one saw the Cross Bronx Expressway and the various bridges connecting Manhattan into the Bronx. Within the middle towers, the balconies extending out of the Bridge Apartments offered vertiginous views of the highway below.

In 1963, the Bridge Apartments began to fill with tenants. The towers imbued the formerly tenement-laden residential neighborhood with a sense of technological futurism. The architectural critic Fred Bernstein recalled "being dazzled by the sleek, aluminium-faced buildings, which resembled the Girder and Panel building sets I loved to play with. To my mother, who had grown up in a Bronx tenement, and my father, the child of the Williamsburg 'projects,' the shiny new buildings by Brown and Guenther were luxury housing."[30] The Bridge Apartments quickly filled with tenants, but the project also emerged as a symbol of the risks involved in then-contemporary urban design. According to Bernstein's own account of the earliest years of the towers, visitors to the buildings had

Manhattan and Cross Bronx Expressways: view from the tower of the Washington Bridge Apartments. Copyright Charles E. Rotkin/CORBIS.

View from the Washington Bridge Apartments of traffic and the aluminum skin of the neighboring tower. *Architectural Forum* (March 1967): 69.

doubts as to the trade-off of the relatively affordable rents within a project that potentially exposed its residents to the pollution and noise of the highway. Although developers promoted proximity to the highway as a visual and functional amenity, these visitors saw the potential pitfalls of pollution and noise. And, although the Bridge Apartments' developers advertised that their architectural efforts would bring residents into a spectacular relation with the City in a protected context, several of the initial architectural and planning features were dropped because of cost overruns. Features eliminated in the final project included a cap over the highway, an integrated ventilation system for the buildings' interiors and park spaces, and an air-conditioning system for the buildings. All would have provided additional protection for residents in the removal of fumes.

The inherent risks of the project were apparent to some in its earliest stages. According to Hazel Henderson, an environmental activist, many within New York City voiced opposition to a project that not only naturalized the driving of highways through urban areas but also seemed to performatively trade environmental risks for questionable demographic goals. Henderson, who helped form the group Citizens for Clean Air between 1963 and 1964, recalled, "We protested the construction of the apartments. These protests began before the buildings were even constructed. We just thought, how could you make anyone live there above the highway?" She continued, "We used scientists, architects, and planners at Columbia University to back up our own problems with development in New York City."[31] In 1964, Henderson fostered the first study of the air surrounding the Bridge Apartments, conducted by the City's Department of Air Pollution Control, which concluded that the pollution level in the area was undesirable but "not dangerous."[32]

Without adequate protection from the highway's fumes, the new residents of these buildings began to protest almost immediately, and the protests became publicly visible in 1967. Ridiculing the early advertisements for the Bridge Apartments, one reporter on the buildings wrote, "'New York's Most Fabulous Big-Family Opportunity' . . . Many of the development's 960 tenants . . . would not go along with the description of life above a 12-lane highway." One tenant who lived on the fifth floor of the building discussed the interior of the apartments and the highway below: "If I were to open the windows you would soon find yourself shouting . . . the noise becomes very irritable. It's constant. It can drive you to distraction." Another tenant discussed the infiltration of fumes into the interior of the apartments: "We just moved from the 14th to the 28th floor to try to get away from the fumes. . . . We have to rent air-conditioners from the management to keep our windows closed to keep from being asphyxiated.'"[33] Residents of the building illustrated the problems of the buildings by conveying to reporters that apartments were being vacated almost daily. Curiously, if it were not for the apartments' brazen siting, architectural concept, and particular demographics, these accounts would never have materialized in such a public form. Numerous areas of the City suffered from terrible pollution, but this building in particular was publicly positioned as a possible solution within which architecture and planning could transform the intolerable environments of the late-modern city. Its failures merely illustrated the deep-seated desires contained within the overall enterprise.

In response to the complaints of these tenants and the residents who surrounded the development, Henderson's group sought ways to restructure the ground beneath the buildings to remediate the highway fumes. Their ultimate proposal involved bridging the open spaces between the apartments, thereby sealing off the apartments from the fumes below, and venting the fumes up and over the apartment units. The costs of protecting the apartments totaled approximately $500,000, based on estimates from the Port Authority, which were about the same as the improvements that had been cancelled before the construction of the Bridge Apartments.[34] However, the state expected the owners of the buildings to pay the expense; and the executive for the owners claimed that because the ultimate environmental situation of the building was deemed not dangerous, the managers and owner of the building would not take any steps to address complaints about noise or automobile exhaust.[35] In recounting his work on the apartments, Bernard Guenther, the architect, stated that he was "very concerned about the noise and pollution factors . . . but the highway was being finished at about the same time as the buildings, and we couldn't fully assess what impact the traffic would have." The blame for the exposure was placed with the Port Authority: "As a condition of its agreement for the use of its air rights, the Port Authority required that the spaces between the buildings be left open to facilitate the ventilation of the bridge approach." Guenther continued, "Leaving the spaces open helped their pollution problem . . . and it helped create ours." Like Henderson, Guenther argued that platforms would "seal off the highway, which would be ventilated through exhaust ducts leading to the building's roofs."[36]

In 1967, Henderson's group arranged for Senator Robert F. Kennedy to come to New York City to address the relationships between planning, pollution, and state-level monitoring of urban-environmental deterioration. In a heavily publicized tour, Kennedy flew across Manhattan in a helicopter, observing some of the City's most polluted sites. At the conclusion of his tour, he visited with residents of the Washington Bridge Apartments. Kennedy was struck that voices had to strain to hold a conversation on the building's terraces because of noise, and by the residents' consistent complaints of "dirt, dust and fumes" that "made it impossible to use the terrace or open the windows."[37] At the conclusion of his visit, Kennedy addressed Henderson's Citizens for Clean Air, where he delivered a speech that attacked the invidious nature of carbon monoxide in New York City and the planning of the Bridge Apartments, and demanded the immediate amelioration of these problems:

> The second major source of pollution is carbon monoxide. Carbon monoxide from cars and trucks comprises roughly one-third of the pollution in New York City's air. Although it currently is less of a threat to our health than sulfur oxides, the Public Health Service found that carbon monoxide reaches dangerous concentrations in a number of areas in the city, such as tunnels or heavily traveled streets and highways. One area is in the vicinity of the George Washington Bridge Apartments which I visited this morning. These apartments are located directly over the Manhattan approaches to the George Washington Bridge where clouds of carbon monoxide and other car exhausts constantly billow up to poison the surrounding air. Residents of these buildings are continuously exposed to excessive levels of carbon monoxide, an exposure that can lead to decrease in mental acuity, creates cardiac symptoms in patients with heart disease, promotes fatigue, headaches, dizziness, nausea, vomiting, and can cause death.
>
> . . . The choice of this location for these apartments, astride one of the most heavily traveled highways in New York City, shows a total disregard for environmental factors on the part of our city planners. Immediate relief is needed for the residents of these apartments. I urge that Federal, State and City funds be used on a crash basis to build a vapor-proof barrier over the sections of this interstate highway that pass underneath these apartments.[38]

We can question the presumed disregard for environment that surrounded the planning of this development, yet such a vocal call to alleviate the pollution problems of a single housing project was unprecedented in New York City. The actions of Citizens for Clean Air and Kennedy's attention to the risks involved in the creation of the Bridge Apartments were significant for their time. Importantly, Kennedy called for an infrastructural solution to the pollution besetting the Bridge Apartments. This differed from the more architectural and technical proposals for the site. In other words, missing from Kennedy's attack was a reiteration that these buildings were environmental enclaves.

CYBERNETIC ATMOSPHERES

The important "vapor-proof" barrier was never built at the Washington Bridge Apartments, yet continued efforts of local, municipal, state, and federal groups to rethink the project and the desire for the City to realize additional air-rights developments resulted in the first federally funded study of the indoor air of a building. Funded by the newly formed Environmental Protection Agency (EPA), the study specifically focused on the relation of automobile pollution, architecture, and urban planning in the mitigation of pollution within buildings. Beginning in 1970, the agency conducted a two-part study of the efficacy of New York City building and planning practices in the protection of interiors from the perils of the automotive city. Titled "Indoor-Outdoor Carbon Monoxide Pollution Study," the study is, in retrospect, a central element in the rethinking of cities, planning, and buildings along intensive parameters and a document that imparts the potential health significance of the "sealed environment" in which we now predominantly experience the architecture of cities. Focused on the Washington Bridge Apartments, the introduction to this study's final report is worth quoting at some length in order to convey the goals of the research:

> The considerable interest which exists today on the part of architects, urban planners and others in air rights buildings for dwellings, schools and offices is a natural consequence of the fact that 60–70% of the downtown areas of major American cities consist of paved roadways. The high value of land in such areas makes the concept of buildings, which span these roads, economically attractive. It is clear however, that the impact of traffic generated air pollutants on the air quality within such buildings requires assessment to be sure that the health of the occupants is not endangered. In order to make such an assessment, the Air Pollution Office of the US Environmental Protection Agency contracted with the General Electric Company in May of 1970 to make an intensive study of air quality and traffic relationships inside and outside of two buildings in New York City. One of these buildings was an air rights, high rise, apartment dwelling known as the Washington Bridge Apartments, which straddles the Trans Manhattan Expressway near the approach to the George Washington Bridge. The second building was chosen to provide a comparison between an air rights building and a more conventional high-rise structure located on a canyon-like street in midtown Manhattan. This

> second structure was a twenty story office building located at 264 West 40th Street, just east of Eighth Avenue.[39]

The latter structure was located near a similarly heavy-trafficked area within a block's length of the Port Authority Bus Terminal, and the street received traffic coming into and out of the Lincoln Tunnel. As part of the project, groups of scientists established carbon monoxide laboratories within both groups of structures. Each was linked via computer-processing machines to technically advanced sampling equipment and laboratories in Cincinnati, Ohio. For five months, scientists measured carbon monoxide levels in these buildings, as well as "the wind, temperature and traffic conditions which occurred at each site." Using computer-modeling equipment, the scientists concluded that carbon monoxide levels in the buildings were related to the volume of automobile traffic, the level of nonautomotive emissions such as cooking equipment and building incinerators, humidity and heat levels, and, most significant, the configuration of the site and buildings.[40]

In engaging in these analyses, the scientists were not only measuring indoor air but also expanding the strategies of environmental-monitoring efforts to meet the emergence of new urban threats and risks. The environmental threats of late-modern cities suggest new urban webworks that move beyond the direct and visual measurements of pollution within the industrial city. The research process at the Bridge Apartments reflects a "cybernetic" turn in urban management in the late 1960s. In general terms, this conception of urban management integrates constant analyses of urban space—often using computers, airplanes, or even satellites—with a more flexible engineering and planning apparatus that can respond quickly to various urban dangers, from blight to pollution. The rigging of the Bridge Apartments into this type of cybernetic pollution-monitoring system foregrounded the most contemporary building systems that monitor indoor air quality from centralized locations thousands of miles away.[41] It also implemented the types of data collection necessary when developers and state agents position buildings in sites that subject inhabitants to high environmental risks.

Within the technical assessments of their report, the authors of the EPA study concluded that the configuration of the Washington Bridge

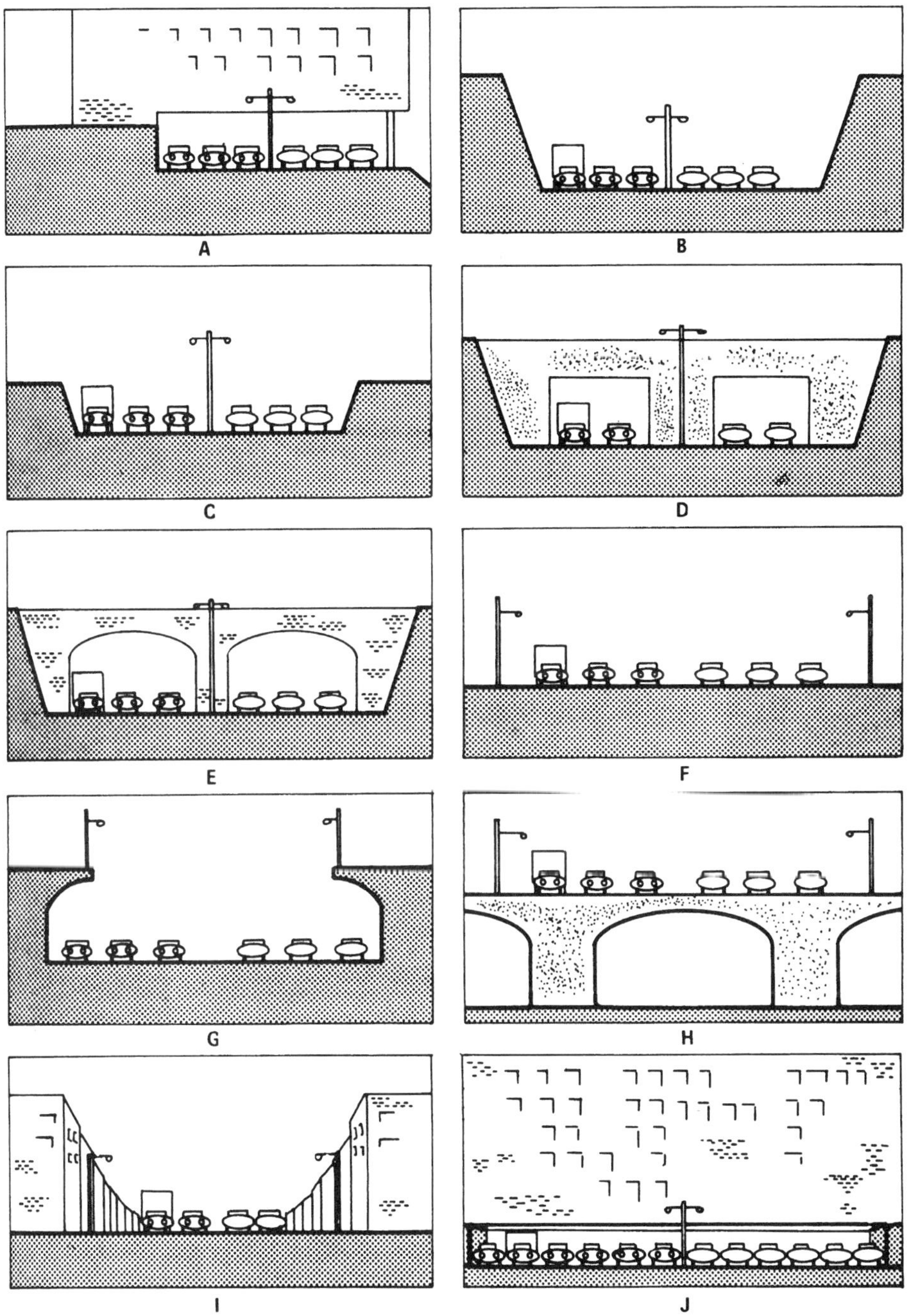

Illustrations from a study on urban air pollution. Jerry Kurtzweg, "Urban Planning and Air Pollution Control: A Review of Selected Recent Research," *Journal of the American Institute of Planners* 39 (March 1973).

Apartments actually encouraged the drawing of fumes from the roadway into the space surrounding the buildings. Because of building physics, the structures' surrounding air actually had higher levels of carbon monoxide than the roadway below. However, the study's most interesting conclusion was that the prewar office building, with its casement frame windows and brick skin, contained even higher levels of indoor air pollution. Although the prewar building was traversed by 7,000 cars per day and the air-rights buildings by 150,000, the concentrations of carbon monoxide in the former building were much higher. The study thus acknowledged the problems of air-rights architecture but concluded that, as a planning form, it was no worse, and was in fact better, than buildings that constituted a much larger aspect of the built landscape of the City.

Remarkably salvaging the Bridge Apartments, the authors of the study argued for the continuation of these types of structures as strategies to combat the environmental risks of the late-modern city. In their guidelines for future planning, the authors wrote what might be the first postwar guide to armoring buildings against the environmental problems of cities, an idea that will reappear within this book's Epilogue:

> The data obtained in this study indicates that the pollutant level internal to buildings is greatly influenced by traffic and the height above the traffic and by "stack effects" internal to the buildings. Accordingly, the following guidelines are suggested: 1. Special attention be observed to seal the lower floors of new buildings to exclude traffic generated CO [carbon monoxide]. The specific number of floors to be sealed should be determined from forecast data on traffic volume on predominant adjacent highways. 2. Where possible, major entrances into buildings should be located such that prevailing road winds blow parallel to them. Building sides which face major urban roadways should be as tight as possible. 3. Air rights structures should be designed to provide ample spacing between buildings to permit dilution. This spacing should be based upon forecast data on traffic volume and speed and the length of covering over the highway. 4. Consideration should be given, when long sections of a highway are covered, to force ventilation systems which exhaust pollutants from the "tunnels" between air rights structures at heights above their roof levels. 5. Convection paths internal to buildings should be minimized. Elevator shafts could be under a slight positive pressure from an air source drawn from the outside of the building approximately ½ the height of the building. 6. Elevator control rooms at roof level should be force

> ventilated to the roof to reduce the entrapment of pollutants in tall buildings. 7. Internal pollutant sources, such as parking garages within the building, etc., should be force ventilated outside the building parallel to and over the center of the highway over which the building is constructed. The pressure at the exhaust point should be inversely proportioned to the horizontal distance from the nearest receptor.[42]

Not only is this a vision of urban architecture in purely scientific terms, it also presents architectural planning (and air rights in particular) as imperiled by risks within and surrounding the structure. Onc might argue that the conclusions of the study present a latent desire to enact a new, detached role for architecture relative to cities. The Bridge Apartments may suggest (and the EPA document certainly furthers this idea) that the "outdoors" offers little environmental benefit for the development of a healthy enclave within a city. The EPA document suggests that the future viability of the Bridge Apartments rests on its ability to unhinge itself from its surroundings. The study by the EPA, though done in the name of protecting the health of the inhabitants of these buildings, offers little evaluation of the planning goals of the Bridge Apartments, particularly as they relate to the highway beneath or the surrounding neighborhood. The EPA concludes that the Bridge Apartments are simply a less technically sophisticated approach to a reasonable form of urban and environmental planning. In other words, architecture's relationship to the problematic socionatures of cities is simply one of disentanglement.

These conclusions suggest a somatic and urban vision for architecture quite different from the one developed within the programs of high modernity. If that latter and earlier system sought to stitch the modern subject's physical needs into an overall formal and infrastructural urban ideal, the concepts explored at the Bridge Apartments suggested a biophysical program of detachment that is nevertheless tied to a larger, urban-demographic vision. We might see the Bridge Apartments as a representation of some emerging and larger urban and environmental mentality: the colonization of the industrial city with individualized environments protected from the threats of late-modern urban infrastructure. We might see those air-rights concepts that immediately followed the Bridge Apartments, such as Rudolph's LOMEX proposal, as an attempt to bridge the desire for environmental autonomy with a similar, though larger, urban program. Nevertheless, the same problems evident in the Washington Bridge Apartments are evident in these other representations as well—the embrace of automotive space and the development of a physically integrated but environmentally protected space above. This high-profile urban air-rights project of the early 1970s and the related proposal by architect Ulrich Franzen suggested a more sophisticated assemblage of planning strategies to achieve new environments adjacent to and above roadways.[43] Also mirroring the development attitudes of the Bridge Apartments, the first iterations of the Confucius Plaza development in the Chinatown area promised a new, more technically sophisticated form of restructuring than that staged in Washington Heights. Like the Bridge Apartments, Confucius Plaza incorporated middle-income apartments and public programs: a school and park. But the project's architects, Horowitz and Chun, proposed the more aggressive, if not altogether absurd, strategy of siting the building on the proposed refurbished exit ramp of the Manhattan Bridge's upper platform. Again, the goal was to appropriate an otherwise "completely wasted space . . . where motorists, backed up across the Manhattan Bridge, would have thrown their crushed cigarette packs," stated a spokesman for the project. Like the Bridge Apartments, Confucius Plaza was advertised as "a structure that will combine shelter, education and transportation" and that would address the problems of building above a roadway. Enhancing the ideas present in the Washington Bridge Apartment's architecture, Horowitz and Chun proposed the first use of an extensively sealed curtain wall on a large-scale middle-class apartment tower in New York City. The developers of the project, Daniel Z. Nelson and Leon DeMatteis Construction, acknowledged "that there were 'obvious problems' in wrapping a highway around a school and an apartment house—noise, vibration and pollution from exhaust fumes." However, they claimed that "[s]tudies are being made and we are confident that these problems can be solved."[44] The building, which was literally wound with traffic, would yet again offer an image of a protected space in an otherwise intolerable zone of the City.

As developments such as Confucius Plaza circulated in the City's popular and architectural presses, the problems of the Washington Bridge Apartments were being forgotten. Following a rent strike in the early 1970s that protested the deteriorating conditions in the building and the rising rents, many of the initial residents of the building departed.[45] The

Preliminary design, Confucius Plaza, Horowitz and Chun. Photograph by W. F. Chun, from Robert A. M. Stern, Thomas Mellins, and David Fishman, *New York 1960: Architecture and Urbanism between the Second World War and the Bicentennial* (New York: Monacelli Press, 1995), 152.

striking tenants claimed that the management did not adequately maintain the building's services, and the buildings quickly became known for their crumbling water and electrical systems. The apartments often flooded, and their ambiguous relationship to the highway led to numerous lawsuits between the City and the buildings' owners, primarily regarding responsibility for problems of the highway caused by leaks and structural problems and vice versa. In the ensuing years, the Bridge Apartments became a locus for the primarily working-class Dominican residents who immigrated into Washington Heights in the 1980s. As the work of contemporary historian Sarah Sze notes, this particular ethnic and national group continues to bear many of the environmental inequities of Upper Manhattan. The Washington Bridge Apartments are often mistakenly viewed as "projects" for poor New Yorkers. Although they are inhabited by many residents who receive housing assistance from the city and state, the rents in the apartments remain expensive for this particular neighborhood. The apartments, however compromised, are well-lit with natural light and have spectacular views. The apartments' actual history remains obscured by their present state; and their continued role as some of the better housing in a neighborhood that remains exposed to problems from the pollution of automobile exhaust is obscured by the impression of the buildings' stained facades.

LEGACIES OF ENVIRONMENTAL RESTRUCTURING

By the mid- and late 1970s, the Bridge Apartments were considered an embarrassment within the urban-planning literature of American cities, but in 1976, architectural historian Reyner Banham recuperated the entire Extension Complex as a significant precursor to the "megastructural" projects of the late 1960s and 1970s that he explored in his work *Megastructure: Urban Futures of the Recent Past*. This book traced the history and "demise" of the megastructural idea from the early 1960s to the mid-1970s. In *Megastructure*, Banham wrote that the Bridge Apartments were the largest realized megastructure, a claim he articulated in a comparative analysis that showed profiles of the Bridge Apartments relative to other built megastructures, such as the Centre Pompidou in Paris and Habitat in Montreal, among other projects.[46] Banham's book was not the first work on megastructures; earlier, primarily Japanese discussions of architectural megastructures concentrated on the relationship between the infrastructural fixity and architectural flexibility typical of the form. Megastructures aspire to be architectural analogies of a completely modernized city. But in his book, Banham also introduced the notion that megastructures take on the envirotechnical functions of the city.[47] This absorbed the megastructure into one of Banham's ongoing interests: architecture reduced to a system of environmental modification. As Banham noted, the architects of megastructures often suggested that their structures offered an entire urbanism that remediated the "extreme" nature of their natural and urban environments—whether this was the hazards of an urban highway, a postwar ruinous landscape, or the heat of a desert in Algiers. We might contrast Banham's environmental reading of city space and highway space to the contemporaneous "semiological" readings of these spaces advanced by Venturi Scott Izenour, which became hallmarks of a postmodern urbanism. In this latter work, the environmental intensities of the city are transformed into communicative signs versus biophysical effects. For Banham, the sun retains its sense of an external "nature" to the city, albeit taking on an ambiguous quality; whereas for Robert Venturi and Denise Scott Brown, the sun is just another aspect of a mediated consumer strip.[48]

Banham extended his environmental reading of the megastructure into a larger historical narrative in which the megastructure's historical precedents included exploratory architectures, such as ships, spacecraft, and oil rigs. In his typically technophilic (and vaguely sarcastic) fashion, he included as an illustration of the power of megastructure the following observation on a late-colonialist project for Algiers, the Cité-paquebot project by Wladimir Gordeef (1954): "Intended to make life comfortable for white colonials in the Sahara Desert—it is not necessary to go into outer space or the ocean deeps to find an environment that is hostile to somebody!—sealed and self-contained like an ocean liner . . . , Gordeef's luxury living machine had its apartments opening off a vast air-conditioned communal space."[49] Within this project and its peculiar context, we find an early yet potent internalization of the City that will be mirrored in further projects explored in this book. In folding the Washington Bridge Apartments into this narrative that included submersibles, oil rigs, and postwar colonialist architecture, Banham uncovered an important architecture–nature role latent within the megastructural concept: its promise (whether actualized or not) to restructure the existing subject–environment relations of cities into concentrated zones, something that the history of the Washington Bridge Apartments illustrates as an ultimately failed yet important initial goal. This sentiment is further elaborated within Banham's comparative analysis of megastructures: showing the Bridge Apartments, Centre Pompidou, and Habitat projects together, among lesser-known schemes, one senses the larger concept of urban and environmental restructuring that moves through megastructures. Many of the projects Banham illustrates comparatively were controversial efforts to re-create the given environment of industrial cities into a more postindustrial form. The Washington Bridge Complex, Habitat, and the Centre Pompidou literally sat on top of important sites in the industrial history of their respective cities: a historic immigrant neighborhood, a former industrial harbor in Montreal, and an important market district in Paris. Through Banham's examples, we sense the megastructure as an emerging yet short-lived global and postindustrial architectural sensibility, a form that simultaneously acknowledges the dissolution of historical urban relationships between architecture and infrastructure and understands architecture as the new site for urban biophysical support.

In the conclusion to *Megastructure*, Banham wrote that the megastructure was a failure because of its paradoxically totalizing environment, contradicting its promise of flexibility found within its form. The megastructure's technophilic forms appeared to sublimate all architectural meaning into instrumental use and relations. But we might argue that one of the megastructure's ideological failures—albeit one celebrated by Banham—was its aggressively uneven distribution of "environment,"

Wladimir Gordeef, Cité-paquebot, Algiers, 1954. From Reyner Banham, *Megastructure: Urban Futures of the Recent Past* (New York: Harper & Row, 1976), 44.

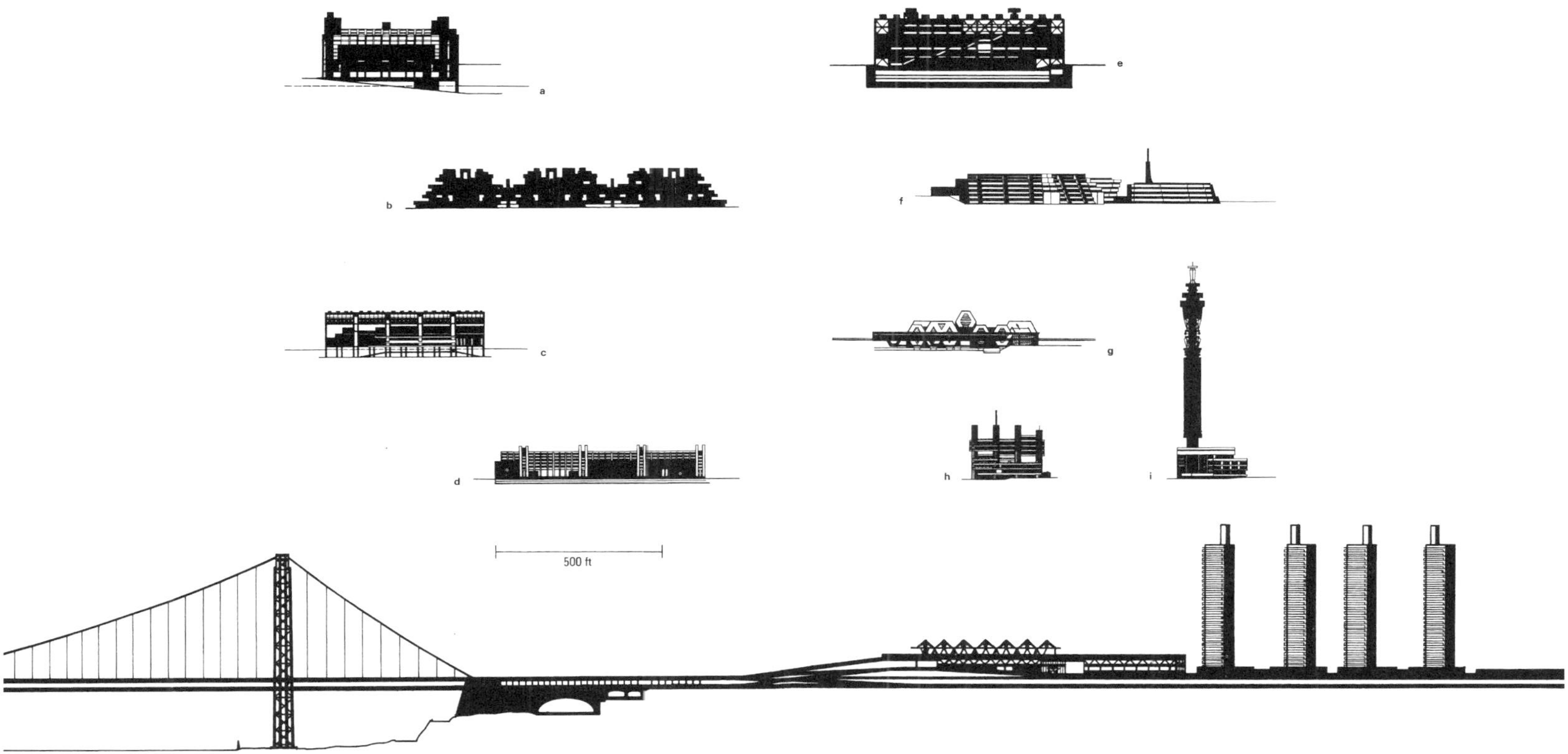

Illustrations of megastructures shown at same scale. The Washington Bridge Apartment complex is in the lower-right portion of the double-page illustration. Drawing by Mary Banham, from Banham, *Megastructure*, 128–29. Reproduced by kind permission of Mrs. Mary Banham and Shelley Power Literary Agency. Copyright 1976 Mary Banham.

understood as the sum conditions necessary to support an urban populace. The formal aesthetics of the megastructure were rejected as totalizing by Banham and later architects, particularly those advocating various alternative late- and postmodern architectural approaches. Yet, as we shall see in the next chapters, the concepts of environmental intensification and differentiation staged within megastructures became features of those latter architectural grammars. If the Algiers project illustrates his beliefs, then this intensification and unevenness become justified for Banham, precisely through its ability to mediate difference. In the case of the Bridge Apartments, environmental intensification and differentiation were tools of urban development.

In considering how to further theorize this form of architectural and urban-environmental manipulation—one fostered by the state and municipality, given form by architects and developers, charted by Banham, and continued to this day—we might turn to a philosophical concept of environment articulated more recently. In his writings on environment, power, and contemporary architecture, the philosopher Peter Sloterdijk argues that beginning in the twentieth century, the breathable environment became the material of power and governance. In its most extreme form, this system of power was manipulated as a tool of violence that denies the conditions for life. He calls this form of power "atmoterrorism." Sloterdijk suggests that by the postwar period, the violence within manipulations of "atmosphere" found within modern warfare began to extend into the most mundane transformations of spatial environments. He claims that "the principle of air-conditioning" imparts the notion of "disconnecting a defined volume of space from the surrounding air" but suggests that the resulting different environments develop separately and problematically from each other. For Sloterdijk, simply demarcating two unequal environments within the larger "environment" contains the potential of violence.[50] We might see the Bridge Apartments and other related megastructural projects as analogous to the conditions analyzed within Sloterdijk's theories. Formally, technically, and spatially, megastructures emphasized an emerging yet incomplete internalization of the urban environment, often in the name of somatically supporting a city's emerging urban subjects.

Ultimately, the Washington Bridge Apartments represent a significant and monumental attempt to position architecture and its internal environment relative to the collapsing environmental tissues of a deindustrializing New York City. In this specific case, we see architecture utilized to potentially negotiate the "intensities" of degraded urban environments—exhaust, particulates, noise—in parallel with the demographic transformation of a neighborhood. The planners of the project turned the literal environment (the air circulating around this site) into a form that might be captured and isolated within a city. This environment acquired value as both an objectified thing that could be traded (the air rights above the highway that were bought and sold by the city and the state) and a substance that could be transfigured into something more inhabitable. Although the Bridge Apartments failed and still appear extreme, the specific constellation of ideas embodied at the apartments continued into additional projects within this city, but at a more nuanced scale. In addition to the examples I have briefly reviewed in this chapter, we can also add another. In the mid-1980s, developers Thomas Lee and the Henry Street Partnership proposed more tempered versions of air-rights planning in the neighborhood directly abutting the Manhattan Bridge in Chinatown. In what the Koch administration dubbed the "Special Manhattan Bridge Planning District," both developers proposed creating an enclave from the fumes of the Manhattan Bridge for three luxury-apartment buildings.[51] While not appearing to be megastructural planning efforts, these buildings exhibited an environmental strategy that extended the concepts of the planners of the Bridge Apartments. Here, degraded sites became potential large-return investments if architecture guaranteed some level of protection.

Ultimately linking pollution, architecture, and demographic goals, the forces behind the Washington Bridge Apartments entangled with material and discursive urbanization strategies that continue to motivate forms of urban redevelopment. This complex and others represent the reinterpretation of the architectural environment as a site of protection that nonetheless suggests a potential transformation of the City. This strategy differs from both the modernist integration of architecture and planning and contemporaneous strategies of gentrification. We tend to consider gentrification as a process of historical revitalization, but these projects suggest how other types of architectural grammars move with neighborhood change. Similarly, if the curtain wall of late-modern architecture could represent emerging ideas of corporate space, subjectivity, and commodities, within the context of these neighborhoods in Manhattan it could take on other associations, such as the capture of the environment itself.[52] Today, this type of architecture continues to rise above and against the historical spaces of the City's industrial-era neighborhoods. Desires for "sealed," "protected," or "filtered" interior environments that are safe from the invidious pollution (both real and imagined) of their surroundings are discursive features of interiors and of contemporary urban experience in New York, particularly since the attacks of September 11, 2001 (see the Epilogue). Rather than representing the end of an era of naive architecture with New York City, the Washington Bridge Apartments contain within their construction an emerging form of architecture that negotiates the potentially threatening matter of the City as a force of urban change.

2 GROWTH

Corporate Atria and the Cultivation of Urban Nature

IF THE INTERIORS OF NEW YORK CITY'S architectural developments suggested a more protected environment in response to fears of the City's endemic pollution, they were also becoming more verdant. In the 1960s, architects, landscape architects, and scientists reconceptualized the environment of the City's office buildings as a type of climate that might grow plants and trees in large indoor gardens. The first of these rooms was the Ford Foundation Garden of 1967, built in Midtown East, and developers, architects, and institutional researchers positioned these rooms as a site where the City's flailing socionatural project would be stewarded and maintained. The City's famously wan outdoor street trees were one of many vivid examples of the challenges of growing vegetation in the polluted environment of an industrial city.[1] By the mid-1970s, in a mostly postindustrialized Manhattan and a bankrupt city wanting of funds to maintain parks and green areas, the City's anemic trees remained as illustrations of the continued contradictions between urbanization and the ornamental nature that appeared to be its counterpoint. Through the efforts of architects, landscape architects, institutions, and developers, the new office buildings rising in the Midtown area of the City were imagined as sites for extensive plantings of indoor nature that were both protected from urban pollution and climatically stable. The nature grown in them provided a staging ground for relationships between the urban subjects and environments of the City's postindustrial economy. The first of these indoor gardens presented curious new challenges and questions regarding the vestiges of "nature" found within late-modern architecture. Plant specialists and landscape architects attempted to interpret what the environment of late-modern architecture was, in both urban and geographical terms. They imagined the modern office building's plentiful light and atmospheric features as a representation of divergent geographic zones, and landscape architects and horticulturalists sought to identify those species of plants that would thrive in the unusually consistent indoor climate. As architects, developers, and horticulturalists realized successful plantings within this context, Midtown East became an epicenter of indoor plants for offices. Questions arose as to the role of these plants and their function within corporate space. By the late 1980s, the sheer volume of plants being grown throughout office buildings in New York City and other cities made the indoor atmosphere of late-modern architecture a new lens through which to reevaluate the natural and productive capacities of architecture more generally.

Significantly, the "greening" of Midtown's interiors also intersected both with the transformation of office work in Manhattan and with the particular transformations of this portion of the City. By the 1970s, office employment was the largest form of labor in the City. As the City hobbled through its financial recovery between 1977 and 1986, it gained 300,000 jobs, with 184,000 of these jobs in the financial-services sectors that were concentrating in Midtown. By 1986, the total number of workers in the financial sector was more than 600,000.[2] In addition to the expansion of the corporate workforce in the 1970s and 1980s, the number of women generally, and married women specifically, increased in the American office workplace. By the 1990s, 50 percent of married women were employed full-time, and 50 percent of all women were employed full time—a 17 percent rise from the late 1970s. Both the employers and employed in this large white-collar workforce were far more mobile than earlier pools of workers that primarily concentrated in urban centers; the rise of a more heterogeneous workforce also corresponded with the increasing suburbanization of office work. Companies relocated to the suburbs for several reasons: to be nearer to the places where executives lived, to attract women with families to the workforce, and to avoid the combined real-estate expenses and congestion of Manhattan.[3]

The designed landscapes of suburban office campuses visualized an alternative milieu of the office significantly different from that of the urban office tower. These suburban campuses disentangled the visual grammar of "workplace" from "city" within and through the design of landscapes. In many ways, the office-tower gardens of midtown Manhattan were a response to the transformations in nonurban work settings, but they also extended long-standing planning goals to integrate gardens into Midtown. Images of park systems, landscaped roadways, and verdant plazas appeared in the earliest postwar planning schemes for the area, including the Capitol Street Plan (1948), developed by the New York Institute of Architects, and the Urban Design Manhattan Plan (1966–69), developed by the Regional Plan Association. Both proposals imagined a new network of parks and gardens that extended the area's existing small-scale green spaces, oriented primarily toward office workers. The planners of both systems proposed parks devoid of recreational programs, a contrast to the postwar efforts of Robert Moses and other employees of the New York City Parks Department to orient City parks to populist sports.[4] Despite the forcefulness of these efforts, by the late 1960s, the ability to realize any new park spaces in New York City was hampered by a planning strategy that viewed the production of urban landscapes as a coordination of federal, state, and local capital investments. With the collapse of the tissues that held together this political-economic apparatus, the corresponding productions of nature that emerged from it also disappeared. As Midtown East increasingly transformed into a space of corporate work, the planning of green spaces shifted from those forms of nature production situated within the state's sphere—the "outside"—to one situated within the corporation's sphere—the interior of the office building and its immediate environs.

The indoor gardens of Midtown East emerged from standing planning goals in the neighborhood, but they also built upon an established role of *indoor* greenery as a counter to urban industrialization in Western metropolises. Beginning in the nineteenth century, the planners of urban indoor gardens incorporated vast spectacles of indoor foliage that provided verdant oases that contrasted with the landscapes of labor. The Palm House at Kew, in London, to cite one of the earliest and most famous examples, offered a parallel indoor world, with warmth, humidity, and tropical vegetation that contrasted with the environmental depravity of the industrializing city. This space channeled technological innovations and imperial explorations toward the fabrication of an urban counterpoint. Nevertheless, the space at Kew must be understood as one of myriad spaces illustrative of, not separate from, the processes of modern industrialization. Inspired by the practices at Kew, the early planners of the

New York Botanical Garden built its gardens' indoor conservatory (1902) on the British model and filled this glass-and-iron structure with species of plants from territories falling within the reach of U.S. colonial expeditions. Like the British model, the New York Botanical Garden provided a space that contrasted with the industrial character of the City through its invocation of an exotic and environmentally hospitable world maintained through the technological advances of industrialization. The extension of these practices into a postindustrial context built upon these earlier precedents in both the notion of urban counterpoint and the bringing of foreign environments into the City. But, as we shall see, the office building provided a form of indoor climate completely different from these earlier prototypes.

By the mid-1980s, a large conglomeration of publicly accessible, indoor, climate-controlled corporate landscapes were concentrated in the Midtown East development zone, the area bounded by Thirty-Fourth Street to the south, Sixtieth Street to the north, and Fifth Avenue to the west. These spaces were enacted via influential designs and landscapes, financially lucrative codes developed by the city government, institutional affiliations, and the robust horticultural industry. Plants and building systems intertwined in the concepts of architects Kevin Roche John Dinkeloo and Associates and Edward Larrabee Barnes Associates; innovative mechanical engineers Cosentini Associates and Loring Associates; landscape architects Dan Kiley and Zion and Breen Associates; and Mark Morris and the scientists and horticulturalists of the New York Botanical Garden. Together these people, firms, and institutions demonstrated that nature could be convincingly reterritorialized within the environment of a postwar office building. In doing this, they realigned New York City's historical urban institutions responsible for maintaining nature, recast an understanding of what the interior environment supports and represents, and participated in a larger process that recalibrated the historical relationships between global cities and their antipodes.

THE GARDEN'S ENVIRONMENT

In the mid-1960s, the planners of the Ford Foundation Building, located on Forty-Second Street and Lexington Avenue, explored how the systems and organization of an office building might produce an indoor garden of rich flora. Like earlier planners, the managers and architects of the building wished to expand the neighborhood's existing network of parks and gardens. However, at the Ford Foundation they wished to accomplish this via their understanding of the unique thermal environment of an office building. The Ford Foundation Building's managers; architects Kevin Roche John Dinkeloo and Associates; and landscape architect Dan Kiley produced a 200,000-cubic-foot volume of skylighted, curtain-walled, air-conditioned space that effectively grew more than twenty thousand plants.[5] This group of managers and experts conceptualized the garden as a place to redirect urban office work in a more "humane environment" that differed from the surrounding Midtown East landscape.

The Ford Foundation was one of a series of early works of Roche Dinkeloo, a practice that emerged from the recently reorganized office of Eero Saarinen, who employed Roche and Dinkeloo but who tragically and suddenly died at an early point in his career, in 1961. In the projects inherited from Saarinen, such as the John Deere Headquarters, the IBM Pavilion, the Oakland Museum of California, and the Ford Foundation, Roche and Dinkeloo extended Saarinen's interest in urban monumentality but added additional and often antithetical ideas regarding "environment" and what they termed "antiarchitecture."[6] They used these latter concepts to describe fleeting experiences of spatial effects that acted against the perception of the architectural-figural object so important to the character of monumental architecture. In a recent interview, Kevin Roche mentioned his interests in both concepts of monumental visibility and specific effects such as the shifting reflections produced in spaces with multiple mirrors, the experience of interior vegetation that transforms over time, and material effects that emphasize picturesque experiences of industrial materials, such as the firm's continued use of Corten steel, which rusts to an orange finish.[7] In contrast to the monument's fixity against a changing landscape, Roche Dinkeloo's concepts of environment emphasized changeability. In several cases, Kevin Roche understood these

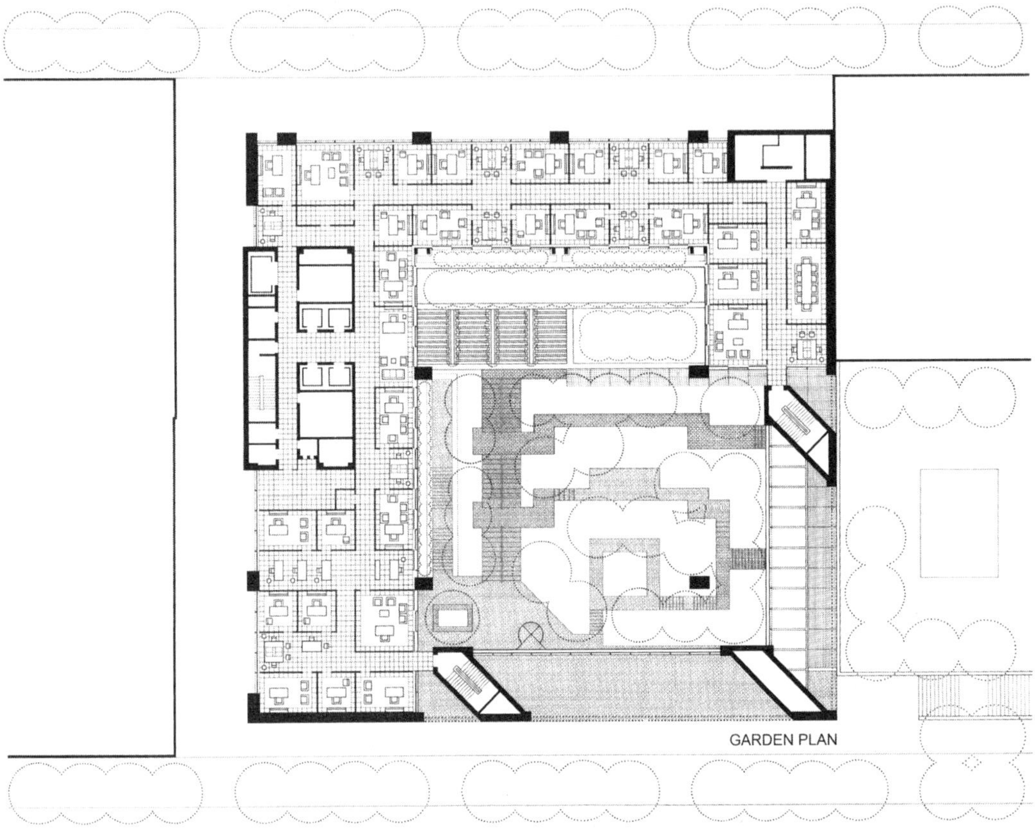
GARDEN PLAN

environmental effects to be reproductions of an earlier and often premodern form of spatial experience and one that softened the effects of massive modern buildings.

The Ford Foundation was one of the firm's earlier buildings within which monumental visibility and scale were integrated into a more changeable and natural conception of the architectural environment. This related to the firm's emerging interests as well as to the particular mandates given the architects by the foundation's managers. In reflecting on the intentions of the project, Ralph G. Schwartz, the Ford Foundation's director of building planning and construction, claimed, "We want to bring

ABOVE: Ford Foundation, view of indoor garden, Roche Dinkeloo Associates and Dan Kiley Landscape Architect, 1967. Courtesy of Kevin Roche John Dinkeloo and Associates, LLC.

OPPOSITE, TOP: Plan of Ford Foundation Headquarters. Courtesy of Kevin Roche John Dinkeloo and Associates, LLC.

OPPOSITE, BOTTOM: Ford Foundation, view of indoor garden, Roche Dinkeloo Associates and Dan Kiley Landscape Architect, 1967. Courtesy of Kevin Roche John Dinkeloo and Associates, LLC.

nature closer, we want to give the man who spends most of his time in an office a more habitable environment."[8] Jonathan Barnett, one of the chief planners of Midtown, wrote that the foundation's garden "stands between the sealed environment of a modern office building and the increasingly harsh and uncontrolled urban landscape outside."[9] Here, environment negotiates both a concrete environment—that of office architecture—and a city's degraded external atmospheric environment. In a similar statement, the installer of the landscape, Everett Conklin, wrote that he wanted "the subtle aromas of plants and flowers and of the newly turned furrow" to contrast with "the smells of partially burned hydrocarbons, dioxides and other pollutants."[10]

Not only was the garden for the Ford Foundation grown in an office building, on an unprecedented scale for the time, but also the garden was grown in one of the most polluted sectors of Manhattan. The air-pollution problem emerged from the Queensborough Bridge, which shuttled traffic into and out of Midtown East, and the Con Edison electrical generating station four blocks away, on East River Drive. In 1965, the municipality released a report on urban air pollution that vividly illustrated the daily effects of poor air quality on the urban populace as the equivalent of "smoking two packs of cigarettes per day."[11] The situation was exacerbated in 1966 when a deadly smog hovered over the City, driving sufferers of asthma and emphysema and other residents with bronchial vulnerabilities to City hospitals. In addition to forming commissions to monitor emissions from electrical plants and building incinerators and heaters, Mayor John Lindsay took the extreme measure of proposing a traffic ban in the heart of Midtown East, along Fifth Avenue between Forty-Second and Fifty-Seventh Streets. The traffic ban was to be in effect on consecutive Saturdays as an experiment to reduce automotive emissions. The notorious pollution of the area prompted, among other schemes, the aforementioned proposal by Buckminster Fuller to dome midtown Manhattan. Although described as a cold-war vision of a city, in actuality Fuller's proposal centered as much on protecting the Midtown populace from its neighboring pollution.

To realize the garden in this admittedly complex and unforgiving environmental context, the architects, landscape architects, and mechanical engineers examined how the office building might cross-pollinate with structures and systems already used to grow plants in highly controlled and polluted contexts. Discussing the technological development of the landscape at Ford, Dan Kiley wrote that he was influenced by horticulturalist Frits Went's (Kiley called him "Fritz Wendt") work on the production of indoor commercial crops in urban contexts.[12] Went developed methods to grow plants for export within the Dutch colonies and, after immigrating to the United States in the 1930s, he worked at the California Institute of Technology. There, he developed the idea for the "phytotron," a fully air-conditioned environment for the growing of commercial crops that maintained constant temperature and humidity levels and that was effectively developed in response to pollution in the urban environment. In the phytotron, Went "was able to establish climatic conditions for maximizing productivity of many important plant crops; to find that optimal day and night temperatures were vastly different for each plant and among plants; to study circadian rhythms under specified conditions; and to make significant discoveries about air pollution."[13]

Went demonstrated that plants placed in the protected and uniform environment of the phytotron grew better than plants grown in the polluted and environmentally variable atmosphere of a city.[14] In the 1930s, Went revolutionized conceptualizations of organism–environment relations by arguing that if the parameters of pollution content, wind, temperature, light, and moisture were all maintained at a consistent level, one could continuously predict the growth of plants and trees.[15] His ideas eventually migrated into more public settings when he was asked to conceive and ultimately curate what he called the "Climatron." This similarly engineered environment housed a plant exhibition in the Missouri Botanical Garden in St. Louis, realized and developed inside a geodesic dome. Went's vision of life as a mechanical versus a biological and specific system remains one of the most contested and controversial legacies of high-modern biology. For the historian of science Georges Canguilhem, it is precisely such a mechanical vision of life that gives life a specifically modern character. This in turn enables the specificity of life to be downplayed in favor of more broad institutional and state systems that ultimately manipulate life to a particular human and rationalized form. For Canguilhem, it is the vision of the environment (in Went's case, its specificity) that ultimately conditions the forms of life that may be achieved within it.[16]

The Climatron, developed by Frits Went, 1960. Library of Congress Prints and Photographs Division, Historic American Buildings Survey (HABS MO,96-SALU,105L—12).

Embracing this particular and modern vision of plant life, Kiley and the engineers Cosentini Associates used both the material and theoretical concepts from Went's phytotron. They envisioned the office building as an environmental totality that might be repurposed to cultivate greenery. For example, to water the garden, they used a concept directly from Went's phytotron for drawing condensation from the climate system into the plants' soil, thus enabling constant watering, even in times of water rationing. They implemented this type of system into their original proposal. Atmospherically, Kiley used but effectively reversed Went's concepts. The Ford Foundation's climate system would presumably limit pollution, but it would be required to maintain the parameters of human comfort, as per the discourse on climate control inherited from the 1940s. If the parameters of the indoor climate were known and unchanging, as is the case with the office's "comfort zone," then using Went's ideas, Kiley and his team imagined that they could predict with some precision the best plant and tree species for a garden grown in this milieu. In developing the indoor garden, the architects and landscape architects explored those species of verdant life that could survive in the aggressively neutral climate of an American office interior. In this effort, Kiley's key innovation was to reconceptualize the comfort zone of the Ford Foundation's climate systems as a geographically specific ecosystem, a representation as much as a set of parameters. Kiley interpreted the combination of stable temperature, humidity, and available moisture levels as closely mirroring the outdoor "summer climate of Virginia or North Carolina." Kiley explained his rationale: "We chose many woodland plants for this court primarily because they can tolerate low humidity. The plants had to be fitted to the tolerance limits of the space. Ideally for humans, humidity should be about 40 to 50 per cent. In winter with the air-conditioning system operating, the humidity in here is only about 10 to 15 per cent. Any more moisture would have been more than the mechanical system could take. So these factors ruled out any tropical plants which would have required much more humidity."[17] The landscape architects, together with the architect, chose species from Virginia and North Carolina to form the imagery of the garden, most prominently magnolias from Virginia, but also azaleas, jacaranda, evergreen pear, cryptomeria, camellia, fuchsia, andromeda, star jasmine, mondo grasses, roundleaf and tassel ferns, spleenwort, red bougainvillea, creeping fig, and blood trumpet vine.[18] The garden species chosen by Kiley reflected both his interpretation of the office's comfort zone and more general notions that certain temperatures were the borderline (or "isotherm") of urban civilization.[19] Heat and humidity were geographical representations in both the larger cultural and the more specifically architectural discourse surrounding the Ford Foundation's garden.

The managers of the Ford Foundation, Roche Dinkeloo, and Kiley had enormous ambitions for the garden, when completed, hoping to "fill the vertical void" with the magnolias "rising up to 150-foot heights."[20] The space was to be a model for future office development. Although it was a promising vision of a future form of nature production in the City, the planners of the garden could not develop a system that could overcome either the road pollution in Midtown East or the biological cycles of the

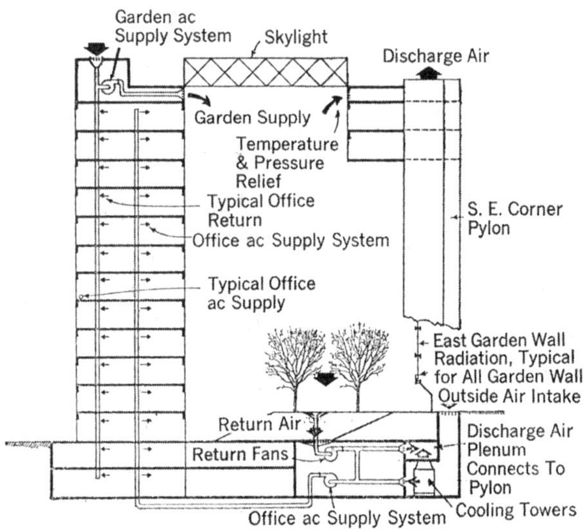

Atmosphere and garden diagram of the Ford Foundation "office building or greenhouse." From *Ashrae Journal* (June 1968): 48. Cosentini Associates.

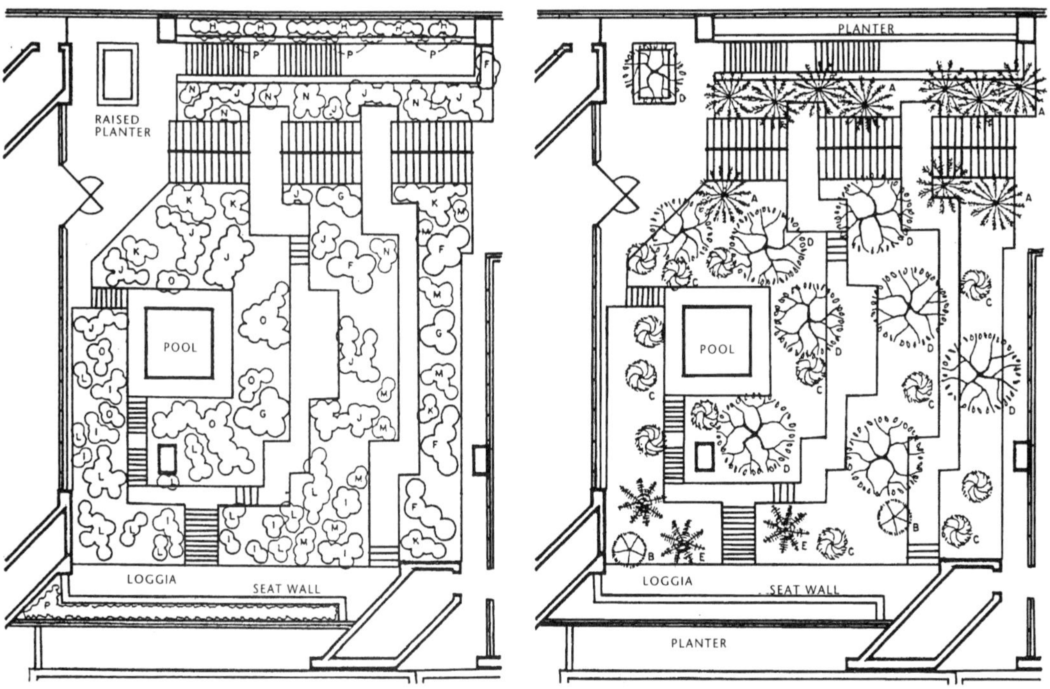

Planting diagram of the Ford Foundation garden, Dan Kiley Landscape Architect. From Dan Kiley and Jane Amidon, *Dan Kiley: The Complete Works of America's Master Landscape Architect* (Boston: Little, Brown, 1999), 67. Copyright 1999 by The Office of Dan Kiley.

plants laced throughout the garden. Soon after completion, air pollution from the busy roadways of the precinct—the very thing the garden was to be a refuge from—infiltrated the air systems that were designed to support the garden. By 1970, many of the plants and trees showed the same problems as those grown outdoors in New York City. Moreover, the landscape technicians had failed to account for the diurnal swings that effectively turn plants "off" in hibernation cycles. The winter temperatures in the mid-Southeast, which typically hover at 40 degrees Fahrenheit, are crucial to the health of plants and trees. The lowest recorded temperature in the Ford Foundation was 63 degrees. Due to this and the unanticipated low light levels, many of the plants suffered stress from the constant stimulation by the office building's climate systems. The combined climate and pollution stresses killed much of the foliage in the garden and limited the ability of the magnolias to grow properly.

The irony of the Ford Foundation's inability to produce a garden in Midtown East was not lost on one of the garden editors of the *New York Times*. As Kathleen Teltsch wrote, "The foundation which has helped revolutionized agricultural methods in Asia, seems to have its troubles growing laurel in Manhattan."[21] This only illuminated the high stakes for Ford in maintaining this space. In addition to generating a new office culture and management scheme, the garden also reflected the primary "product" of the Ford Foundation, the development of innovative landscapes. In postwar American corporate architecture, architects frequently incorporated their clients' innovations into their buildings. Lever House, the headquarters of the soap company, employed sophisticated window-washing equipment; the curtain wall of Saarinen's GM Headquarters contained the same gasket that revolutionized windshield design; and here at the Ford Foundation, we see the production of an innovative garden in the headquarters of the foundation that developed innovative methods for producing agricultural landscapes in some of the world's most hostile political and natural climates. Now Ford's management team hoped to produce a landscape that argued for the office building as a new agent that entangled both corporate and agricultural management in the architectural production of urban nature. This corporate production of nature held high stakes for the company: it would retain Ford's image as the producer of innovative landscapes and New York City's preeminence as the

Garden of the Ford Foundation, Dan Kiley Landscape Architect. Courtesy of Kevin Roche John Dinkeloo and Associates, LLC.

corporate center of the United States. Distant agricultural sites and the inner biological frontiers of the City began to become equated.

Initially, the continual replacement of plants proved to be the most economical solution to maintaining the foundation's garden.[22] However, with the trees dying, the landscape technician in charge of the garden wondered which trees were actually most appropriate for this space. Everett Conklin, the first manager of the Ford Foundation landscape, hypothesized that the landscape was akin to a tropical climate and that the light and pollution levels demanded the replacement of the American woodland plants with more hardy tropical species. Expressing frustration, Conklin explained, "[W]hat we are attempting to do is to grow these southern temperate zone trees and plants in what amounts to a tropical or semi-tropical environment. The lowest temperature ever recorded in these gardens is 63 deg. F and this for probably not more than three or four hours. The relative humidity averages about 25% in the winter months but is higher during the rest of the year."[23] By the early 1980s, Conklin's company gradually replaced the magnolias with *Ficus benjamina,* a tree that was native to semihumid tropical jungles but that gave the appearance of a more temperate tree and thus maintained the aesthetics of Kiley's original scheme. The ficus flourished in the space and remain in the garden, where only one of the original magnolias survives from the original planting scheme. Whereas Kiley originally interpreted the indoor air of an office building as a specifically Eastern North American form of climate, the technicians of the garden imagined the indoor air of an office building to be more like the geographic zones at the peripheries of the Western world. Its climate was more akin to the tropics than to anything found in the symbolic ancestral landscapes of the United States.

Whatever the ultimate species and climate, the Ford Foundation demonstrated how the atmosphere of the office building could be understood as something with geographically representative qualities. Although the garden was a mixed success, its implications were significant for the shift in nature production in Manhattan. The project suggested that the environment of the office building could be recalibrated for growing nature inside the City. It demonstrated that areas with numerous office buildings could effectively become areas with concentrations of urban nature, but it also suggested that an office building's environment contained possibilities outside human comfort. That environment could be oriented toward the maintenance of a wider range of urban material. Soon after it was completed, the Ford Foundation garden inspired the authors of New York City's zoning documents by shifting the production of new public spaces in this area of the City from the type of exterior plan-

Garden detail, Ford Foundation. Library of Congress Prints and Photographs Division, Carol M. Highsmith Archive (LC-DIG-highsm-12997).

ning evident in the Capitol Street and Urban Design Manhattan Plans to the development of a string of indoor "plazas" that effectively mimicked several of the features of the Ford Foundation idea. In 1970, the planning board approved a code that would encourage a similar series of rooms in the City, particularly in the area that became known as the Special Fifth Avenue Zoning District—the core of Midtown East. The code offered an incentive that linked the development of these spaces to variances for increased height and bulk in office construction. The new zoning code, developed by the innovative Office of Midtown Planning and entered into law in 1970, enabled enclosed pedestrian spaces attached to office buildings to receive building bulk allotments of eleven square feet for every one square foot of covered pedestrian space, and fourteen square feet for every one square foot of air-conditioned enclosed space. Owners of existing office buildings that could not take advantage of the new codes also built large climate-controlled, plant-filled spaces to better compete with the new towers and their plazas rising in the area. The developments at the Ford Foundation, the implementation of codes that encouraged epicenters of indoor office gardens, and the larger, lingering desire to bring office workers into select areas of the City resulted in a significant number of proposals for these types of spaces in Midtown East. Between 1970 and 1982 (the year the special zoning incentives were eliminated), more than twenty similar spaces were proposed in Midtown East, with about twelve of these receiving zoning bonuses.[24] Using the Ford Foundation as its model, the new construction activity tied the provision of a new type of indoor nature to the development of both office buildings and the remaining undeveloped areas of the Midtown East neighborhood.

INSTITUTIONALIZING THE OFFICE GARDEN

Although there is evidence that the Ford Foundation Building inspired the future gardens of Midtown East, the codes for the indoor plazas that were legislated in the 1970s never stipulated that the new spaces must be used for the growing of plants and trees. The Ford Foundation certainly convinced developers and architects of the possibilities of growing vegetation in office buildings, but the proliferation of interior atrium garden rooms within Manhattan's corporate skyscrapers can be traced to pronounced and specific institutional alignments taking place within Manhattan as well as various disciplinary factors within the field of architecture. In the late 1970s, the corporate greenhouse rose as an urban typology incorporated into office and commercial spaces. In the catalog of his 1979 survey exhibition, "Transformations in Modern Architecture," at the Museum of Modern Art, curator Arthur Drexler included a section on late-modern "greenhouses." Drexler traced the corporate reinvention of this typology to the Ford Foundation but further linked it to buildings such as Pennzoil Place (Philip Johnson and John Burgee, 1976), the IDS Center (also by Johnson and Burgee, 1974), the Rainbow Center Garden (Cesar Pelli with Victor Gruen, 1975), and the interiors of John Portman and Associates. According to Drexler, the greenhouse signaled one of many tendencies that a new generation of architects positively used to think past high modernity. But the greenhouse also marked the troubling rise of the aesthetics of the "private community" within public spaces, something Drexler believed evoked a surprising range of nineteenth-century institutional architecture, from greenhouses to opera houses.[25]

Drexler's analysis of urban greenhouses was located between additional sections in his catalog that examined the use of mirrored glass and hybrid architectural buildings. Programmatic hybridity, mirrored skins, and verdant interiors ultimately became a key corporate assemblage within the office buildings found in the central business districts of many American cities. They also emerged as the key features of what Fredric Jameson would ultimately identify as a "postmodern" interior sensibility, illustrated via his analysis of John Portman's Bonaventure Hotel in Los Angeles. This vision of postmodernism, more ahistoricist compared to the semiological and historicist one of Charles Jencks, emphasized specular and kinetic effects within insular worlds: interiorization of plants and light, and the "rejection" of the city. Jameson saw these interiors as technologically spectacular analogues to a globalizing economy that rejected the integrative clarity of the city. Curiously, in their intense analyses of these interior planted rooms, neither Drexler nor Jameson addressed the pronounced environmental transformation within these spaces. These spaces were atmospheric and environmental spectacles as well in the downtowns of Houston, Minneapolis, and New York City.

The greenhouse atria of Midtown East entangled with these important and larger disciplinary shifts, but they also emerged from an equally critical and local institutional set of alignments. In concert with new codes and the disciplinary interests advanced by figures such as Drexler, Johnson, and others, we should also consider the largely undocumented and critical efforts of the New York Botanical Garden to explore the potential and challenges of growing plants and trees in the indoor environment of office buildings in Manhattan. Within this particular effort, we can identify additional political, aesthetic, and institutional agendas that further elaborate the corporate garden's role in the restructuring of New York City. In the late 1970s and early 1980s, very few individuals had any expertise in growing large-scale landscapes in the indoor climate of an office building. By the late 1970s, fewer than a half-dozen articles were written on the subject, and only a few books provided any type of guide. Within this increasing knowledge vacuum, technicians from the New York Botanical Garden applied their knowledge to the realization of gardens in the City's office building interiors. The Botanical Garden was effectively an institution charged with the exhibition and production of greenery for the public of New York City. The office buildings of Midtown East would become one more arena in which this institution would test the production of species of plants; but through its work in this context, the New York Botanical Garden reoriented its public role toward the corporate sector,

further changing the parameters of the office building's interior, the types of expertise brought to bear within it, and the economic alignments of the City's historically public institutions.

In the late 1970s, the Botanical Garden explored both architectural and organizational strategies to expand its public mission. Its 1974 plan "Toward the Year 2000" emphasized the Botanical Garden's financial troubles while simultaneously and surprisingly proposing an expansion of its mission and infrastructure within its existing grounds. In addition to a proposed restoration of the garden's original conservatory, the garden's leaders proposed a new "House of Plants and Man," a large exhibition greenhouse designed by Edward Larrabee Barnes Associates. The project would tell the story of plant life in an expansive global context and serve as an "educational tool to serve the needs of scientists, students and the public."[26] The architectural proposal featured numerous nested, hexagonal "biomes" of Corten steel and glass that represented alpine, tropical, and desert landscapes. The mechanical engineering firm Lehr Associates proposed a sophisticated climate system for the building that not only would filter atmospheric pollution but would also pull heat from one biome and use it in another. The project suggested an integrated architectural ecology that nonetheless represented completely different ecosystems. Representationally, the House of Plants and Man aligned concepts of environment found within the space-frames of Fuller's and Went's work—the

Model of House of Plants and Man, Edward Larrabee Barnes Associates, 1974. Courtesy of the Edward Larrabee Barnes Archive, Harvard Graduate School of Design.

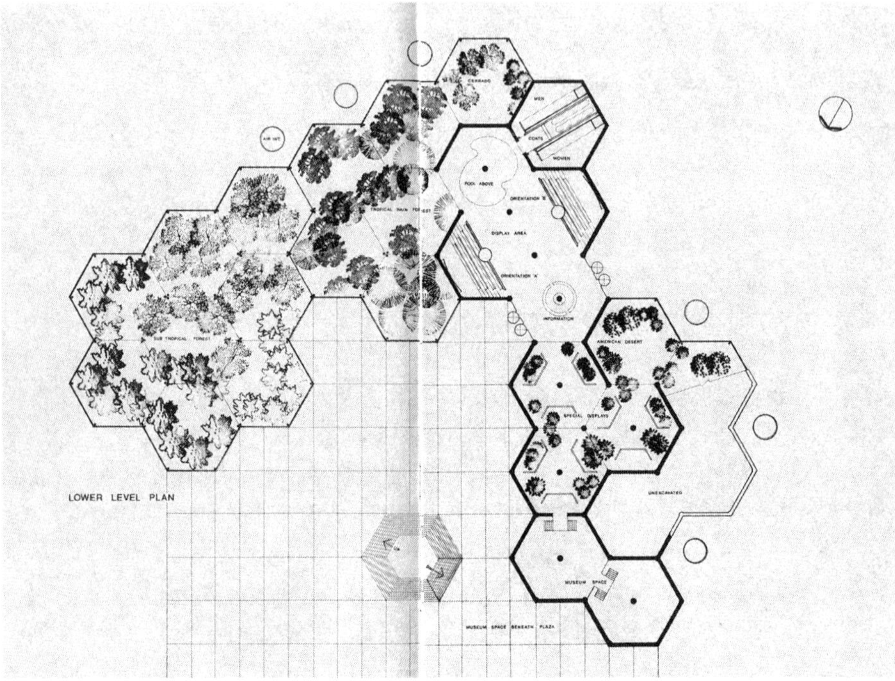

Plan of House of Plants and Man, Edward Larrabee Barnes Associates, 1974. Courtesy of the Edward Larrabee Barnes Archive, Harvard Graduate School of Design.

Model of House of Plants and Man. Courtesy of the Edward Larrabee Barnes Archive, Harvard Graduate School of Design.

hexagonal environmental matrix—with an emerging late-modern expressionism. The House of Plants and Man's modules and sloping roofs recalled the aggregations of historical form that were a continual interest of Barnes's. His earlier projects, such as the complex at the Haystack Mountain School of Crafts, in Deer Isle, Maine, combined vernacular forms and materials, such as shingles, into modern assemblages. The tinted glass and steel of the House of Plants and Man render the project's modules without the material sentimentality of the Haystack complex. Like Roche and Dinkeloo's interest in antiarchitecture and amonumentality, this project emphasized expressionistic effects of glass and environment.

Although it was a public-relations success, the House of Plants and Man was scrapped because of financial cuts (the conservatory would eventually be restored in the early 1980s as the Enid A. Haupt Conservatory). Not only did the financial cuts halt future development of the garden's original grounds, they also, more drastically, forced the Botanical Garden to reduce its operational budget, maintenance staff, and public mission. The garden's annual report of 1975–76 noted that "the most serious problem besetting the Garden during the year was the pervasive impact of the reductions in city support of the Garden's horticulture and maintenance staff."[27] The New York Botanical Garden's municipal funds, along with those of most other public institutions, were stripped in the late 1970s as a result of the citywide bank strike. In exchange for loans to the City, the City's chief banks demanded restricted municipal funding for a host of urban services, including the City's public-park system. At the Botanical Gardens, these cuts resulted in the deterioration of gardens and the elimination of fifty staff members. By the late 1970s, corporate funding permanently replaced much of the municipal funding, and the largest corporate funders included the very banks—Citicorp and Chemical Banks—that had engineered the bank strike. Equally significant, these banks financed several of the new real-estate investments that reshaped the physical context of Midtown East, including the Citicenter and ChemCourt plazas. The Botanical Garden was entering into a new corporate relationship with economic powers, remaking the physical landscape of the City.

Intrigued by the development of the Ford Foundation garden, responding to the desire to "green" office buildings, aware of the new codes reshaping Midtown East, and responding to the interests of their corporate funders, the New York Botanical Garden shifted its emphasis away from projects such as the House of Plants and Man. Instead of pursuing such ambitious master plans within more explicitly museological contexts, the institution examined the office building's potential role in the production of a new indoor environment particularly suitable to the growing of plants and trees and to educating the public. Reaching out to both corporations and larger urban needs, the Institute of Urban Horticulture was initially founded at the Botanical Garden's Cary Arboretum facility to disperse its institutional knowledge outside the confines of the Botanical Garden. Through the institute, which would eventually be located at the main facility, in the Bronx, the Botanical Garden worked with horticultural explorers, scientists, office planners, and developers to rethink the uses and locations of nature in the City. In the literature announcing its public mission, the institute included images of the Ford Foundation garden, a potential strategy for introducing additional plant life into a now-struggling urban economy.[28]

In forming the institute, a group of distinguished landscape architects—Lawrence Halpern, Dan Kiley, Ian McHarg, and Paul Friedberg—and scientists—David Karnosky and Thomas Elias—explored ways "to introduce, test, develop, and distribute new species and cultivars," "to deal with the peculiar problems of interior landscapes (plant selection, environment, cultural procedures)," and "to define environmental factors influencing culture and how they can be modified."[29] Like the planners of the Ford Foundation garden, the scientists and researchers of the institute viewed indoor plants and trees as producing a counterenvironment to the polluted environment of the City. The Institute of Urban Horticulture was concerned with the devastating effects of urban air pollution on the trees and plants that formed the most visible nature of New York City. Its reliance on an indoor strategy to steward the verdancy of the City was, in many ways, a response to the apparent hostile exterior atmosphere of the City that was destroying urban nature. In 1982, as the City began climbing out of financial difficulty, the institute sponsored a study of air pollution that involved the location of plant matter in test chambers in select locations throughout New York City, including the roof of the World Trade Center. In addition to conducting work on the effects of pollution on urban greenery, the scientists from the institute also explored the importation

Cover from a publication of the Institute of Urban Horticulture showing pictures of the Ford Foundation garden in tandem with other urban landscapes. Courtesy of The New York Botanical Garden.

Model of IBM Building and garden, Edward Larrabee Barnes Associates. Photograph copyright Louis Checkman. Courtesy of the Edward Larrabee Barnes Archive, Harvard Graduate School of Design.

of species of plants that could best survive in the interiors of urban buildings. The institute's 1982 literature mentions two trips to China and the Soviet Union in search of species of plants suitable for use in indoor gardens. These efforts were not isolated. In the 1980s and early 1990s, literature from the field of indoor landscaping mentions informal expeditions to discover new cultivars in the tropical world that were suitable to the inside of office buildings and other commercial applications.[30] Like Went, Kiley, and Roche and Dinkeloo, the institute treated the interior of the office building as a geographical zone, but one requiring more intense scientific study.

Horticulturalists from the New York Botanical Garden, using its growing research on the growing of plants in interiors, also participated in the development of the IBM and ChemCourt gardens, the two most prominent indoor gardens the organization realized in Midtown East. Edward Larrabee Barnes, the architect of the IBM headquarters building, invited specialists from the New York Botanical Garden to collaborate with his firm on the design of a garden plaza in front of the building that was based partially on his firm's defunct greenhouse concept for the Botanical Garden's Bronx campus. The IBM Building, completed in 1983, consisted of a green-stone, glass-ribboned tower with a series of chamfered edges. Barnes extended then-contemporary interests in perceptual ambiguity and aesthetic dissonance that were evident in numerous mirrored towers. At IBM, he designed the crystalline-shaped building so that "you will never quite realize what the form is" and, further emphasizing its antimonumental relationships, broke with the paradigm established by the Seagram's Building of pushing slender towers back away from the street.[31] Instead, Barnes sited the tower directly against the site's northwest corner and located the greenhouse atrium of glass and white-steel frame on the opposite corner.

Barnes, his mechanical engineers, and the consultants from the New York Botanical Garden extended some of the environmental concepts that Barnes's team explored at the House of Plants and Man. If for that project they attempted to link radically different geographically specific ecosystems into one atmospheric and environmental system, here they attempted to join the interior atmosphere of the office building—the comfort zone—with the verdant environment of the greenhouse. The en-

Interior garden of the IBM Building, Edward Larrabee Barnes and Robert Zion, 1984. Copyright Norman McGrath/ESTO.

gineers conceived of this indoor garden as a specialized environment, an air reserve that would siphon off exhausted air from the enormous office building, presumably recirculate oxygen from the plant-filled atrium, and eventually recirculate it back into the office above, a system quite different from that used in the Ford Foundation Building with its reliance on purely recirculated air. The mechanical engineers from Loring and Associates, writing to the horticulturists at the New York Botanical Garden, communicated that they intended the garden "as a building relief air outlet" that operates "with 0% outside air."[32] Within this sealed environment, the landscape architect Robert Zion, of Zion and Breen Associates, and Robert Hebb and Robert Lees, both employees of the Botanical Garden and involved with the Institute of Urban Horticulture, debated the best possible plants. Zion originally wanted American magnolias, but Hebb agitated for a species of palm, *Paurotis wrightii,* that could survive both the office building's climate and the variations in that climate caused by the constantly opening and closing doors of the structure.[33] Averse to the palm, Zion eventually settled for a Chinese species of bamboo that survived but did not initially thrive in the environment. After great care and experimentation, the sweeping interior of bamboo culms grew to a substantial size in the room and became one of this garden's most enticing features. To complement the bamboo plantings, the Botanical Garden developed rotating displays of tropical plants in large planters that were set around the room.

The institutional alignments between the corporate tenants of Midtown East and the Botanical Garden's specialists extended into work at ChemCourt, within sight of the IBM garden. There, in 1983, Chemical Bank Corporation and its architects constructed a glass-enclosed, climate-controlled room over the existing urban plaza in front of the company's building in the name of revitalizing the preexisting decrepit space.[34] No zoning bonuses were given for this space; rather, the official motivation was that the plaza flooded frequently and contained dying trees and plants. In an extreme manifestation of the logic of the Ford Foundation, the glass skin of the corporate office building and the building's HVAC system would salvage the plaza by creating a zone for the production of

ChemCourt garden enclosure, Haines Lundberg Waehler, 1983. Hepler Associates. George Cserna Collection, Box 3, Folder 9, Avery Architectural and Fine Arts Library, Columbia University.

indoor nature—"a gift of greenery," the Chemical Bank's press release proclaimed.[35] At ChemCourt, the glass-skin design, by Haines Lundberg Waehler (HLW), telescoped out and over the original entryway of the 1960s-era office building. The original square columns that framed the entry, and that were now within the greenhouse, were sheathed in large, circular aluminum tubes. With layers of glass and aluminum columns, the greening of Midtown East's interiors was entangled with the corporate turn toward late-modern aesthetics—the resheathing of buildings in a seemingly more populist, monumental, and "environmental" image of modernism.

In the interior of ChemCourt, specialists from the New York Botanical Garden developed a powerful display of horticulture. The organization filled the interior with rotating displays of four thousand flower-bearing plants of fifty different tropical varieties, many related to popular domestic species. Several of these were developed from new cultivars by the Botanical Garden to specifically thrive within this context.[36] Here, the plantings were positioned to completely overwhelm the interior. If the Ford Foundation and IBM gardens demonstrated the possibilities and pitfalls of growing plants and trees in indoor office-building environments, the botanists working on the ChemCourt project attempted to demonstrate the comparability of corporate indoor gardens to the outdoor gardens and plazas that formed a staple of an earlier generation of office buildings. The ChemCourt Building's tropical plantings were vibrant, and the thriving of these indoor plant species demonstrated that, given the right circumstances, the office building's interior could be used for the growing of a new indoor nature. In her review of the space, the garden editor of the *New York Times*, Joan Faust, was surprised at how well the plants did in an office context where the availability of fresh air, rain, and light was clearly limited.[37] Unlike the plants at the Ford Foundation or even at IBM, the plants in ChemCourt grew to considerable sizes, necessitating forklifts to move them in the garden's annual rotations. The density of tropical plants and trees in ChemCourt, and their healthy growth in the

Interior of the ChemCourt garden, 1983. Hepler Associates. George Cserna Collection, Box 3, Folder 9, Avery Architectural and Fine Arts Library, Columbia University.

space, suggested a fecund milieu within the office interior. In developing continuous rotations of plant displays, a practice repeated in the nearby Park Plaza, the garden at ChemCourt also suggested something akin to a museological setting, in which nature had become integrated into an expanding cultural industry.[38]

The efforts of the New York Botanical Garden linked the production of trees and plants in office buildings with the historical mission of the institution. Among its roles, the garden stewarded the growth of exotic vegetation for public enjoyment within New York City, and it promoted greenery as a positive addition to the health of the City. By entangling these goals with the indoor gardens of Midtown East, the Botanical Garden aligned its investigation of global greenery and its use of horticultural science with the production of late-modern corporate space. In this effort, the Botanical Garden also extended the long-standing relationship between the production of verdant spaces and the development of real-estate wealth in New York City. The gardens at IBM and ChemCourt were, in part, functions of a speculative real-estate market in which amenities such as gardens increased the value of space and commanded higher rents. But, in aligning plants with late-modern corporate space, the Botanical Garden also transformed plant life into something akin to an empty sign. If the Botanical Garden transformed the meaning of its institutional mission within this context, it also transformed the ultimate meaning of plants in this city. Within the indoor gardens of the Ford Foundation, IBM, ChemCourt, Park Plaza, Citicorp, and the many other gardens in the City, plants did not hold their historical role as physically beneficial to the industrial city, nor was their role counter to the industrial city.

In coming to grips with the new ornamental and real-estate alignments of urban verdure, the Botanical Garden convened a 1985 symposium, "Improving the Quality of Urban Life with Plants and Trees." At this conference, David Karnosky acknowledged the clear benefit of trees and plants increasing the value of property, but he also argued that the use of indoor plants in urban spaces emitted chemicals into the air of buildings that "lower blood pressure" and "increase serotonin levels."[39] Such scientific claims moved through the conference, attempting to align, however tendentiously, future nature production in New York with its historical role as a source of health. In many ways, these efforts radicalized the ideas of environment first explored in the garden at the Ford Foundation. If the introduction of significant vegetation inside office buildings at the Ford Foundation provided an alternative to the dying vegetation outside the garden and humanized the monumentality of New York's offices with a *representation* of environment, here the representational project is suspended. The office environment becomes naturalized—and vegetation is imagined as optimizing the office environment as a site of labor and economy.

THE REACH OF THE INDOOR GARDEN

The New York Botanical Garden's successes with IBM, ChemCourt, and the larger distribution of indoor greenery in the area continued to influence the verdant turn of Midtown East; taken together with the Ford Foundation and the lucrative codes encouraging atrium construction, the indoor-garden form would become the dominant "public" space built in the rapidly corporatizing neighborhood. By 1985, verdant indoor air-conditioned gardens were so numerous in Midtown East that the *New York Times* could publish a map of these spaces as a type of interconnected park network extending in an almost twenty-block matrix from the southern end of Central Park to the United Nations Building. In 1985, Midtown East contained twelve air-conditioned public spaces that housed gardens of substantial species, six of which were classified as indoor parks. The use of public forms of indoor greenery, in addition to these explicit containers of plants, stretched throughout the lobbies of buildings in Midtown as well as office spaces upstairs. The increase in indoor gardens corresponded with the virtual remaking of the neighborhood into a zone that contained most of New York City's six hundred thousand financial workers and a large portion of its commercial real-estate wealth. Numerous buildings in midtown Manhattan employed a gardening service such as John Mini, which planted the ChemCourt gardens, or Conklin Landscapes, which planted the Ford Foundation garden.

Within New York City, the scale and quantity of the gardens of Midtown East appeared to bring the most distant nature of the world into a relationship with everyday metropolitan experience; as Joan Faust wrote in one of her many reviews of these gardens, "Tropical trees. Hanging vines. Cooling waterfalls. Are they far away? Not for New Yorkers who can wander through midtown and find them. . . . [S]uch intimate contacts with tropical foliage can be found in the public areas of many of the city's commercial buildings."[40] Such statements reflect a long and modern historical narrative in which life from great distances is brought to cities, reaffirming the City's position as a metropole and providing indexical counterpoints to modernization. In other words, although such plants contrast with the literal modern material of the contemporary city, its modern and industrially produced space, they merely reinforce the trade systems and political relationships that underpin the modern experience. Whereas Faust viewed the presence of so much exotic greenery as a positive addition to the City, other critics viewed this as a recalibration of nature and public space for the enjoyment of the ever-dwindling number admitted into the City's new interiorized public sphere. Dan Graham and Robin Hurst argued that the new indoor parks of Midtown East were "corporate arcadias" that glossed over the contradictions of helping nature grow in the "urban" city by growing it in office buildings. For these authors, the corporate Acadias were zones of institutional control that fetishized and suburbanized nature in New York City for workers frightened of the "crime and drugs" of the City.[41] In their continued writing on these forms, Graham and Hurst argued that the form of the indoor garden launched in Midtown East had initiated a general rethinking of the interior that stretched from museum interiors, such as the Guggenheim Museum (built much earlier than these gardens), to the interiors of hotel lobbies, such as John Portman's Peachtree Plaza in Atlanta. In one of their more striking observations, they argued that this corporate reconstruction of gardens had affected more historical forms of garden design, evident in the botanical gardens of Emilio Ambasz in San Antonio that were built in the early 1980s.[42] The critic Michael Sorkin also wrote critically of the gardens in Midtown, concentrating on the interiority, lushness, and fetishization of nature found in the Ford Foundation garden. More pronounced were his arguments that the Ford Foundation's garden was analogous to U.S. "strategic hamlets" that eliminated otherness and political strife.[43] Although this group of critical writings is part of a broader literature engaged with the corporatization and "interiorization" of cities, we might further consider the more literal transurban implications of these office buildings as a site for nature. The critics in particular, in their ascription of loathsome properties to these spaces, ironically further fetishized the objects (such as tropical plants and trees) within them. Despite the neo-Marxism of Graham, Hurst, and Sorkin, they failed to ask a simple yet significant materialist question about this indoor, lush environment: where did its nature come from?

As the architects, botanists, and landscape architects operating in Midtown East transformed the way plants and trees were grown and maintained in the City, their efforts began to entangle with larger structural and historical processes surrounding the cultivation and maintenance of urban nature. Through the increased consumption of tropical indoor plants in office buildings in the 1970s and 1980s, the office environment became a nature form that more forcefully entangled with the histories and economies of distant agricultural landscapes. We have already witnessed how horticulturalists and the scientists at the New York Botanical

Dan Graham and Robin Hurst, ChemCourt Building, New York, 1989. Courtesy Dan Graham Studio.

Garden sought out tropical plants from distant regions that could grow well in the indoor gardens planned in Midtown East. Such activities became amplified with the increasing use of ornamental horticulture within modern office interiors.

In the 1980s, Central and South America emerged as important production sites of ornamental horticulture for American markets, for several reasons: these countries' economies already contained established networks of trade with United States urban markets; enormous regions in these nations were devoted to market-driven ornamental agriculture; and, in this specific case, these nations contained climates that were ideal for growing the types of plants that best thrived in North American commercial and domestic interiors—with average temperatures of approximately 68 degrees and approximately 50 percent humidity.[44] Growing areas within Costa Rica, Colombia, and Mexico (among many other places) were situated within climates parallel to the "human ideal" of the comfort zone established in New York and other cities' office buildings. The conceptual and material form of the comfort zone reached from American office epicenters such as Manhattan to the plantations of the global South to the agricultural areas of the United States that contained average temperatures of roughly 70 degrees and similar levels of humidity. Plants and trees for indoor use were grown overseas as small "plantlets" on enormous plantations, where, depending on the species, they were either further raised as mature plants or shipped to Southern California, Texas, or Florida, where they were stewarded for the U.S. commercial market.

We can see the geographical connection of an office epicenter such as New York and a growing region such as South America as a type of spatial extension of the climatic parameters to grow plants. Such connections between space, economy, and biology have been examined in architecture in the writing of Keller Easterling on vegetable production in Europe.[45] Such a logistical perspective is useful in understanding some of the interactions between metropole and antipode. However, in the case of ornamental horticulture, developed specifically for use within buildings, the relationships between flora and space are more complex geographically and can be reinterpreted through a more complex representational and historical framework.

From a logistical perspective, the relationship between New York City and the global South was not entirely linear. The office environment was not simply a metropolitan form that set a series of parameters for the production of ornamental plants elsewhere in the world. As ornamental-plant plantations emerged in the tropical zones of the world, these zones were further peppered with fragments that represented the interior of office buildings. As indoor-plant orders increased, growers used a technique known as acclimatization to literally breed the plants for the conditions inside office buildings. In early plantings, plants from the outside were simply brought indoors "to fight it out," as Dan Kiley once proclaimed.[46] Beginning in the late 1970s, indoor plants were taken from their nursery or plantation and raised in intermediate spaces with more limited exposure to sunlight and open air for a period of five weeks. This acclimatization made the plants more likely to survive as they became accustomed to the actual conditions within office buildings. This practice had become the norm by the 1980s. In Asia, South America, and the southern United States, those plants destined for the indoor-office market were placed in acclimatization settings both indoors and out. These rooms slowly transformed (over a series of weeks) the climate of small plants from the conditions found in a plantation greenhouse to those found in modern urban interiors. Gradually plants were weaned off full sunlight to make them more accustomed to the actual sunlight in a building's interior. In special and expensive custom plantings, reproduction rooms were developed to more accurately portray the environmental features of a particular room's indoor atmosphere and light conditions. In the Mojave Desert, for example, a desert-palm-growing company received plantlets from Mexico and then created a room in plastic that roughly matched the interior of Cesar Pelli and Associates' Winter Garden, under construction in the mid-1980s in downtown Manhattan.[47] Not only were the interiors of office buildings providing an environmental framework for developing agriculture, but also representations of the office environment partially appeared in remote agricultural settings. From an architectural perspective, the interiors of office buildings became represented, in completely environmental terms, outside any recognizable system of architectural signification.

More significantly, as the gardens of Midtown East engaged with this seemingly postmodern and data-bound conception of nature, they actually reconnected to systems of representation, signification, and geography that extend back to much earlier economic relationships of a modern Western city. In nineteenth-century England, for example, companies funded expeditions to islands in the tropical zones to satisfy the desire of the metropole to consume exotic species of plants, primarily in the home but also in institutional settings and markets. These species were brought back to England, where they were fostered in greenhouses, studied for their optimal growing conditions, and then reintroduced into their original sites. These institutional studies impacted how these species would be developed in British colonies to further metropolitan industries and economies. Common indoor species such as *Monstera deliciosa, Yucca elephantipes,* and *Dieffenbachia amoena* came from eighteenth- and nineteenth-century expeditions to South America and Africa. Not only were they purchased for their beauty, they also affirmed the modern city and home as a site for the cultivation and preservation of species originally found in the antipodes. We tend to consider these processes historically, but rarely do we consider these metropole–antipodean webworks as they relate to our aesthetic experience of the contemporary city. The practices in Midtown East extended these earlier relations into a new economic era: the postindustrial. In the late 1980s, the production of indoor plants in the United States connected the commercial real-estate center of the country, New York City, with those ornamental-horticultural plantations, primarily in Central and South America, that could grow plants and trees for use in indoor gardens and offices. Here, the consumption of plants and trees in office buildings established a parallel form of international trade and nature production established along the old commercial lines.

The scale of the entire indoor ornamental-horticultural market is difficult to comprehend. As a commodity, indoor plants and trees are highly visible, but as a form of crop production, they do not figure prominently in the public understanding of what foreign and domestic agricultural centers produce. For example, in the late 1980s, precisely corresponding with the rise of indoor gardens in urban corporate sectors, ornamental-horticultural exports replaced bananas (in dollars) as the chief export from Colombia.[48] The overall demand for nonflowering indoor plants increased 23 percent between 1981 and 1984, involving 231 million square feet of growing area in the United States.[49] Between 1980 and 1986, the total consumption of indoor plants in the United States increased from $329 million to $521.4

million.[50] These processes demonstrate how the interior of urban office buildings became immersed in an expansive agricultural geography.

With the development of indoor gardens, these relationships entangled with more spatialized economies even as they continued the ongoing aestheticization of the global South within cities. Most significantly, the interior gardens of Manhattan affirmed the conduits and networks of the metropole as a space that sustains world life. The fabrication of indoor vegetation in office buildings restructured the more hierarchically spatial and economic metropole–colony relation of old into a seemingly more amorphous yet intelligible postindustrial form. In a uniquely late-modern manner, the commodification of plants more directly entangled with the commodification of the spaces that maintained them in the City. The office now joined a larger group of spaces that, since the nineteenth century, had entangled with biological reproduction. The gardens of Midtown East reaffirmed and re-aestheticized the antipodal presence of nature in the experience of the City; and although the old forms of economy were replaced with new representations, this process nonetheless resurrected aspects of the older material reality. In this sense, the maintenance of distant forms of nature, however exotic, is a thoroughly modern and urban experience of nature.

CONCLUSION

As indoor plant use in offices continued to increase in the 1990s, surprisingly, within New York City, the public expression of the indoor garden decreased. Corresponding with the transformation of the area, the rise of office populations in Midtown East, and a lack of interest from the municipality to press companies to provide public benefits as an aspect of real-estate development, many of the indoor gardens in Midtown East were converted, had their vegetation removed, or were simply demolished. In 1995, the owners of the IBM Building explored options to remove the bamboo grove; it still remains, but the plant displays managed by the New York Botanical Garden ceased.[51] In 1994, the owners of ChemCourt, one of the most publicized indoor gardens, demolished the glass enclosure that had revegetated the plaza in front of the Chemical Bank headquarters.[52]

The plaza was reconstructed as an open space, similar to its original form. Citicorp Corporation removed most of the plantings in its indoor garden because of the expense of maintaining them, and on a recent visit, the entire interior of Park Plaza was devoid of vegetation. In one sense, these spaces, which once exemplified a new corporate transformation of nature in the City, appear to be far more innocent and perhaps naive gestures of what the architectural environment could foster; the great and conspiratorial critiques of them generated in the 1980s do not register with their current reality. In another sense, we might understand the processes embedded within these spaces to have extended to the whole of Manhattan. With the revanchist agenda of Mayor Rudolph Giuliani and the more corporatist spatial agenda of Michael Bloomberg, outdoor areas of Manhattan have become analogous to interior corporate spaces. The nature found outside in New York City has been partially remade in the image of the nature fostered inside the corporation, utilized as an enhancement of real-estate economies and office and managerial labor. Such a viewpoint is similar to the theorizations of Manhattan nature by Matthew Gandy, who has argued that the management of Central Park via a conservancy board has made the park an analogous extension of the Metropolitan Museum of Art that sits within it.[53] Of course, the extension of corporatist mentalities regarding nature within cities has troubling implications for nature as a public form. This is not only because of the literal corporate reimagination of public space, where nature is generally experienced in cities, but also because of the potentially more disturbing reconfigurations regarding the ultimate meaning of nature in cities. Nature continues to be emptied out of its historical function, in which it has a dialectical relationship to the development processes of urbanization, something we witnessed with the development of gardens in the literal environment of office buildings but now is extended out to the City at large.

In this latter sense, we might ultimately understand the indoor garden as a brief formation that indexically naturalized the office building as an essentially socionatural form stewarding nature in a troubled moment in New York's history. We see this in the Ford Foundation garden and the realization of gardens in the IBM Building and at ChemCourt. The indoor gardens were a specific form of nature realized through the alignment of architectural aesthetics, codes, and the constituent features of the air within buildings. The realization of plantings in these spaces not only restructured the natural landscape of Midtown East but also revived spatio-economic relationships that underpin the global modernity of the contemporary city. With the indoor gardens of Midtown East, the production of the office environment entailed far more than the fabrication of a distinct indoor milieu separated from the outside; the parameters of the office building's environment were being employed as a climate to steward a new type of nature related to the redevelopment of an area of the City. In developing this new type of indoor garden, the planners positioned the atmosphere of office buildings as an interpretive framework for reconsidering the conditions for horticulture in the City. If the architects and landscape architects of Midtown East interpreted the environment of these late-modern buildings as a type of climate, in the next chapter we see how the atmosphere of the museum was interpreted as a site of conservation and preservation within Manhattan's critical cultural economy but was used in a similar process of city building, spatial restructuring, and urban maintenance.

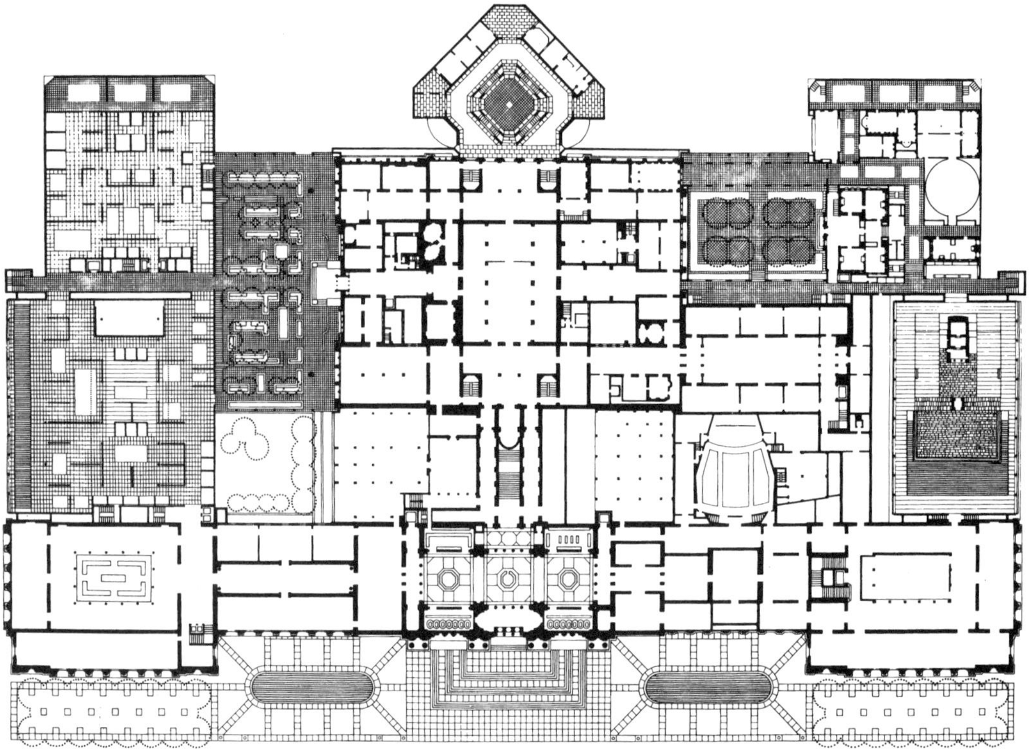

Plan of the expanded Metropolitan Museum of Art, 1970. Image copyright The Metropolitan Museum of Art. Image source: Kevin Roche John Dinkeloo and Associates.

3 PRESERVATION

Territories of Culture at the Metropolitan Museum of Art

IN THE ATRIA OF NEW YORK CITY, architects, engineers, landscape architects, scientists, and corporate managers explored the architectural environment as a representational geography within which to rebuild nature within this city. They used the productive capacities of late-modern architecture to tie the experience of office buildings with urban forms and experiences of nature. This form of environmental production and maintenance, employed in the office interiors of Midtown East, was also oriented toward the housing of works of art and employed in the spaces of the City's burgeoning cultural sector. Throughout the 1970s and 1980s, numerous New York City museums engaged in sophisticated expansions of their institutions to provide more exhibition space, improve visitor circulation, enhance their real estate for capital leverage, and draw larger audiences to their collections. Such projects reflected not only the wealth of the City's museums but also the critical position of New York City within larger economies of world culture. Among the rebuilding projects, such as the Museum of Modern Art's expansion and residential tower (Cesar Pelli and Associates, 1980–84) and the Guggenheim Museum's North Annex (Gwathmey Siegel Architects, 1988–92), the expansion of the Metropolitan Museum of Art (Kevin Roche John Dinkeloo Associates, 1974–88) vividly illustrates how late-modern space and its attendant indoor environment were used to further the cultural and spatial goals of museums in postindustrializing New York and to expand the concepts of maintenance as a new type of urban power. When completed, the Sackler, Rockefeller, Lehman, and American Wings of the Metropolitan Museum housed spectacular global artifacts protected from the air pollution outside in large, often cavernous spaces that were visually and technically alluring.

The ensemble of new spaces enabled the Metropolitan Museum to rival the scale and visitorship of other very large museums in emerging global cities, such as the Louvre in Paris and the British Museum in London. Both the Louvre and the British Museum would also undergo reconstructions after the Metropolitan Museum, with a similar use of late-modern aesthetics that also emphasized museums as containers of conditioned space.[1] The Louvre's entry and subterranean areas were reconstructed by I. M. Pei from 1984 to 1989, and the British Museum was repurposed with an enormous glass enclosure by Foster and Partners (1994–2000). Both renovations expanded existing exhibition space, improved mechanical systems, and reworked the way large crowds circulated through these museums' interiors.[2] These structures contribute to our understanding of the way urban museums transformed within the context of postindustrializing global cities and also of their emergence as a type of specialized late-modern environment. In developing its own late-modern expansions, the Metropolitan Museum powerfully argued for the role of specially engineered museum environments—conditioned, filtered, and pollution free—in the significant expansion of its collections, the movement of cultural relics from distant places; the reconstruction of public space in the City; and the consolidation of its own cultural institution as a global presence. The new spaces of the museum enhanced the discursive and material role of the Western museum as an environmental refuge in cities. This role has always been an aspect of urban museums, but it suddenly took on a new level of significance at the Metropolitan Museum. This related to both the structural transformations staged in New York City and the lingering image of the City's degraded environment, explored in earlier chapters. In visibly enacting an environment for the acquisition of cultural material, the museum developed interiors that represented, for many critical commentators, the way New York had achieved cultural ascendancy in the United States and a power over cultural objects circulating within a global cultural economy. The expansions of the Metropolitan Museum into Central Park lent this cultural institution a new form of power in configuring the socionatural experience of the City, a form of production that commingled an indoor architectural environment, natural material, and cultural objects into an ascendant, urbanized image of an American urban museum.

The expansions of the Metropolitan Museum of Art represent an important aspect of the postwar cultural rise of New York City. In the 1960s,

New York City emerged as the art capital of the United States, if not the entire West, and, by the 1970s, a major cultural competitor in the international drive for tourists and the acquisition of cultural objects. This cultural ascendancy, like the City's corporate ascendancy, is one of the defining features of its postindustrial urbanization and one of the significant factors in the City's restructuring and redevelopment. In the 1970s, the employment in art-related occupations in New York City rose alongside the City's corporate and service-sector employment. By the late 1970s, it represented 30 percent of all arts employment in the United States, and the revenues from the City's museums were 25 percent of those from museums throughout the United States. Approximately 50 percent of visitors to New York City claim that they come for the "cultural attractions."[3] The tourist dollars raised from this influx of culture seekers are considerable, but the ascendancy of cultural power in New York also affects the value of property, the circulation of capital, and the spatial structure of the City as a material, aesthetic form. Each of these features relates to the other, as the legibility of cultural power is expressed through development both within and outside a museum. Not only do cultural institutions such as the Metropolitan Museum of Art visibly hold valuable property and sit on valuable property, but also their cultural capital often translates into increased real-estate value for those investors in the museum's immediate surroundings. These processes have even translated into more typically corporate forms of investment. The Metropolitan Museum of Art brazenly transformed its cultural capital into real capital in its 1985 sale of $45 million of bonds to fund new construction projects. Credit analysts Standard and Poor's and Moody's gave the museum's bonds one of their highest ratings, "AAA," based on the worth of the museum, which in recent figures has topped $2 billion. In its acquisition of objects, expansions, and capital, the Metropolitan Museum of Art is central to the way cultural institutions have become major spatial players in cities and, to some degree, the world.

As the Metropolitan Museum influenced the surrounding urban space, it also impacted the socionatural politics of the City's spaces and more distant arenas of sociopolitical change. Of course, all museums impact the literal situatedness of urban landscapes and environment through their construction, particularly in the case of the Metropolitan Museum of Art, which was built in Central Park. And, as we shall see, the movement of an entire edifice often entails very real environmental destruction. But more generally, since the nineteenth century, the construction of museums has been intimately bound up with the museum's role as a refuge from the environmental deficiencies of modern urbanization. Since the early nineteenth century, museums have been engaged in a form of urban-environment production that aligns them with other biopolitical forms, such as hospitals, prisons, and schools. In 1850, for example, the directors of the National Gallery in London, Michael Faraday and Charles Eastlake, wrote of the museum as a counterpoint to the surrounding city.[4] Faraday and Eastlake developed their conception of a museum in an industrial city as a refuge from the industrial processes in that city. The directors developed a ventilation scheme for the National Gallery that protected the museum's assets from industrial pollution and that is still referred to in the contemporary literature on indoor museum environments. The early structures of the Metropolitan Museum of Art followed this example. The builders of the museum worked with the City to acquire a site in Central Park, and the museum was outfitted with one of the earliest, though primitive, air-conditioning systems as a way to further protect the collection within. In the past twenty-five years, museums have begun to expand their role as counterurban environments engaging with much larger geographic space-times. Today, rather than solely offering environmental counterpoints to their surrounding cities, museums are increasingly becoming a counterpoint to the most distant environmentally disastrous sites and to other seemingly pollution-ridden cities.[5] The Metropolitan Museum's administration argued that its expansions reproduced the destroyed ecosystem of ancient Egypt; offered a stable atmosphere for indigenous Pacific Island works of art that would crumble in the South Pacific climate; and provided a refuge from the destructive pollution of American cities. The reconstruction of the Metropolitan Museum's interior as a site to maintain culture that could otherwise not be maintained not only informed the spatial and environmental role of the museum within its host city but also, as we shall see, informed the relation of the museum to spaces and environments in the most remote areas.

Among the large gallery additions at the Metropolitan Museum of Art, the development of the Sackler Wing for the Temple of Dendur best illustrates the intersection of these processes. All the wings of the Metropolitan Museum demonstrate the way the museum wielded forms of spatialized power over objects through the production of indoor environments, and the Rockefeller and Sackler Wings both encompass specific concentrations of carefully engineered atmospheres. But the Sackler Wing, which was one of the first wings to be completed, specifically illustrates how this museum interior emerged as an environmental form used for cultural empowerment in New York City and how it tied the City's growing cultural power into a larger museological and developmental arena. The debates surrounding the space for the temple bring the particular refashioning of the late-modern architectural environment in New York into focus, and features of this gallery eventually informed discourses on the other spaces of the Metropolitan Museum. The development of the space for the Temple of Dendur was a formative moment in New York's competition for global artifacts, in discourses on protective museum environments, in the acquisition of cultural objects from distant lands, in an ongoing metropolitan entanglement with antipodal and colonial "auras," and in the right of institutions to concentrate things and spaces so as to further their own institutional presence.

NATURE, ACQUISITION, AND ENGINEERING

The Temple of Dendur, which now sits in a late-modern, climate-controlled, glass-curtain-walled space, is one of the spectacular centerpieces of the Metropolitan Museum of Art's late-twentieth-century expansions. The space that holds the temple represents one phase in a long historical process of moving precious cultural objects in the name of transforming space both in New York City and in the most distant landscapes. The United Arab Republic of Egypt first offered the temple inside this room to the United States government's Kennedy administration in 1963 in exchange for funds to develop its Aswan High Dam Project. The president of Egypt, Gamel Abdul Nasser, offered four Roman-era Egyptian temples and numerous ancient Egyptian artifacts in exchange for funds to rework sites around the dam—moving, among other objects, the statues of Abu Simbel from the Nubian Plain. The Aswan High Dam Project would replace an earlier dam from the British colonial era and would generate significant amounts of electricity. Four Augustan-era temples, the Temples of Debod, Dendur, Ellysea, and Saffeh, which were then periodically flooded, would be permanently flooded by the dam project. But more significantly, the project would displace fifty thousand people and destroy one of the world's ancient ecosystems. Although it was a significant modernization effort, Nasser disentangled the preservation of cultural heritage from a larger concern with socioenvironmental preservation. Using UNESCO as the international broker, Nasser worked with the governments of the United States, Spain, and Italy to acquire more than $36 million to hire crews and import machinery to disassemble, move, and reassemble various ancient objects well below the dam. For the countries offering assistance for the dam project, the temples would be a significant acquisition, par-

The Temple of Dendur before disassembly, mid-1960s. Image copyright The Metropolitan Museum of Art.

ticularly at a time when nations and their cities were beginning to hedge their economic futures increasingly on tourists in search of the display of important and spectacular cultural objects. There was some symmetry to the investments these nations would make: in helping Egyptian industrialization, they would in turn be offered cultural objects that took on new forms of value in a culturally productive, postindustrial urban economy. But the transfer of the temples and the industrialization of the Nubian Plain also intersected with a wider geopolitical phenomenon. Through the discourse of preservation and world cultural heritage, the United States and other Western powers found a way to involve their nations in what was a largely Soviet-funded and -backed Egyptian project.[6]

Doubts about moving the temples appeared with the earliest arguments to save them and transfer them to the West. Despite a long history of displaying buildings and building fragments such as the Pergamon Altar and Gates of Babylon in Berlin, and the Elgin Marbles in London, many critics doubted the merits of moving the Egyptian temples outside their original context and climate. Some of the dissent was based on the temples' artistic and historical merit, and some of it focused on solely environmental issues. Illustratively, a dissenting archaeologist wrote, "With the possible exception of Dendur, these are the less interesting of the Nubian temples. . . . Outside of their natural setting they will not look like much. And probably they will not hold up well away from a desert climate. . . . An ideal site would be the Arizona desert, except there no one would see it."[7] Such skepticism and environmentally determinist attitudes about the location and interpretation of cultural objects would move through arguments surrounding the future location of the temples, becoming part of a more general discourse on the location of world cultural treasures.

Although representative of the experience and economies of postcolonial modernization and postindustrial urbanization, the actual movement of these Egyptian artifacts would revive an activity that is deeply bundled with the material reorderings that constitute core aspects of modernity. The movement of exotic colonial objects has always held an important role in political relations between metropole and colony and in the reordering of urban space and nature; and the movement of Egyptian objects, in particular, holds a fascinating and central role in sociotechnological and socionatural experiences of the Western city. The centrality of Egyptian objects in Western cities is symbolic of new economic relationships between the West and East as well as of the endless movements of capital and machinery that remake both sites. It is also part of an aesthetic trope that maintains the aura of modernity within Western centers via a focus on displaced, exoticized, and distant cultural objects. The moving and raising of Egyptian obelisks, for example, entangled cultural and technological spectacles that recentered urban spaces and experience, often around the power of emerging institutional forces. The raising of the obelisk in the Place de la Concorde was used by the newly empowered French republic to demonstrate colonial acquisitional power and the theoretical power of mechanical sciences to literally move massive objects and develop new concepts of space in cities. The republic used a technology that symbolized state maintenance of thermodynamic forces and showed that "the guidance of the state now truly enabled man to conquer nature."[8] Even in New York City, the acquisition and movement of "Cleopatra's Needle" into Central Park incorporated the spectacular movement of this ancient object into the City via a rail network. This simultaneously related a modern technology to the ancient feat of moving obelisks and bolstered the role of the monopoly capital of the Vanderbilts (partially acquired through railway enterprises) that brought it into such a significant symbolic space in the City. For the scholar Antonia Lant, "[B]ringing home an obelisk . . . could bestow on this society the status of ancient Egypt, the status of a founding civilisation, eternally present through its magnificent monuments and mummified bodies." Additionally, bringing home an obelisk often represented newly formed trade relations and investments that transformed the colonial state in the name of the metropolitan economy.[9]

In addition to the actual movement of Egyptian objects, the experience of the modern city entails many complex relations between various Western sociotechnical cultural formations and the engagement with Egyptian aesthetics. The 1851 Crystal Palace in London was one site where ancient Egyptian imagery was entangled with the production of a modern engineered space. Within this space, the apogee of British iron-and-glass technology, the exhibitors re-created an "Egyptian" tableau replete with reproductions of the monuments of Abu Simbel and verdant tropical vegetation that actually related little to the upper Nile's ecosystem but that generated a unique, orientalist image of nature. Within the Crystal Palace, the exhibitors produced a wish-image of cultural expropriation that mirrored the actual movement of Egyptian objects that is part of the history of the development of Western cities. The movement of Egyptian artifacts aligned old and new technologies, but it also lent the old monuments an odd suspension of their own historical space and time. The new architecture of the Crystal Palace, like its latest variants, appeared to aggregate and reorganize elements of the world.

The development of the spaces at the Museum of Metropolitan Art belongs to this historical lineage in several ways. It emphasized aesthetics of geographical and cultural distance—the experience of an ancient Egyptian artifact in a Western tableau—to reimagine a late-modern techno-

Philip Henry Delamotte, Egyptian Display, Crystal Palace, 1851. The Getty Research Institute, Los Angeles (93.R.37).

logical assemblage of space, sealed and air-conditioned, that constituted an emerging and critical environment in New York. At the Metropolitan Museum of Art, the spectacle of actually moving the massive Temple of Dendur to New York City, so important to nineteenth-century technical imagery, was downplayed and the creation of environments to preserve the temple enhanced. In a move unlike earlier efforts that involved moving cultural objects from the East, the museum and its architects chose to reify and monumentalize environmental technology and transformation over mechanical technology. The galleries presented an aesthetic of environmentalized space over the mechanization of space. Nevertheless, this environmentalism still linked the appearance of culture to those spatial aesthetics that were being used to remake the City. That is, just as the late-modern architectural environment appeared to be a tool of urban transformation in apartment and office buildings, the cultural sector also explored how this new urban form might be used to develop new experiences and relationships to the cultural objects that also define late-modern urbanization. The Metropolitan Museum was certainly not the first museum to build gallery spaces with both a corporate curtain wall and air-conditioning; important buildings such as the Berlin National Gallery, by Ludwig Mies van der Rohe (1962–68), preceded this gallery. But the galleries developed by the Metropolitan Museum were the first to align this vision of space with the older form of Western spectacle and capture described earlier.

COMPETITIVE ATMOSPHERES

Although the Temple of Dendur is currently housed in New York City, its home was determined through a prolonged process that involved a large, transurban competition resting on the power of museums to produce the most "appropriate" engineered environment for the preservation and safekeeping of the temple. Debates about environment, preservation, and urban development moved through specific cities' and museums' arguments. Beginning in 1965, the Johnson administration began to solicit proposals on the future location of the temple in the United States. In that year, Johnson created the Committee Formed to Make Recommendations to the President of the United States concerning the American Location for the Temple of Dendur, chaired by John Gardner, a bureaucrat with the National Endowment for the Arts. Numerous cities competed for the temple; it would be an enormous asset to cities generally, but especially at a time when many American urban municipal governments were beginning to compete as centers of cultural production and tourism. The applications presented to the committee primarily highlighted a particular city's ecological and climatic suitability for the temple, whether this "suitability" would be produced or was a natural aspect of the city's environment. For example, the city of Albuquerque, New Mexico, claimed that its municipality would pay for an outdoor site where the climate of the city would be the most appropriate for the temple's preservation. The initial bid made by the Trustees of the Smithsonian contained a proposal to create a replication of the Nile environment on the banks of the Potomac River that would immerse the temple in an outdoor setting that was both representational and linked to the other great "classical" monuments of the symbolic city.[10] The Metropolitan Museum of Art was unique in its proposals in that the museum argued that the environment of late-modern architecture was the most suitable for the preservation and potential interpretation of the monument.

The Metropolitan Museum of Art worked with the architects of the recently completed Lawson Library (the museum's research center) to extend that building's Miesian vocabulary for an enormous climate-controlled "vitrine" for the temple. In his memoirs, the Metropolitan Museum's then-director, Thomas Hoving, wrote, "I had concluded that we had to put the entire temple and its pylon and podium under a huge glass showcase. . . . The night scene, showing the golden sandstone shimmering under floodlights, was as captivating as the Taj Mahal would be during a *son et lumiere*. Everybody was impressed. . . . So what if it looked like a two-foot-long glass case—blown up? . . . I was willing to bet no other city or institution would come up with anything like it."[11] Hoving claimed that the museum would re-create aspects of the temple's original environment. The proposed glass case contained a water concourse, Nile reeds, and strong lighting mimicking the Egyptian sun. The museum's proposal joined the numerous others in what was labeled the "Dendur derby," a nationwide competition to acquire the temple as a central urban

Proposal for Temple of Dendur Pavilion, Brown, Lawford and Forbes Architects, 1967. Image copyright The Metropolitan Museum of Art.

artifact. Mirroring the Metropolitan Museum's proposal, Southern Illinois University worked with Buckminster Fuller, who held a professorship at the institution from 1959 to 1975, to develop a potential interior for the temple that would be competitive with the Metropolitan Museum's vision. Fuller proposed reassembling the ideas explored in the geodesic dome he designed for the 1967 Montreal Expo, recalibrating it to contain an enormous interpretive re-creation of the Nile valley in a climate-controlled chamber. The Johnson administration did not seriously consider the latter proposal, but both proposals reveal how a more normative and corporate conception of modern space and Fuller's spatial conception were both conceived as viable interior locales for the reconstruction of environments. Frits Went, the botanist examined in chapter 2, turned to Fuller's spatial concept to recreate natural ecosystems, and one might argue that this conception, the sphere, has emerged as the more dominant space in which ecologically replicated worlds are re-created, from Epcot in Florida to the Biosphere facilities of the American Southwest. This reality only makes the Metropolitan Museum's proposal, its investigation of a spatial conception largely associated with the American workplace or with the assembly of crowds as the site for the staging of an environmental re-creation, that much more intriguing from a historical perspective.

Fragments of the Temple of Dendur were eventually provided to the two most competitive bidders: the Smithsonian and the Metropolitan. The U.S. government asked these institutions to analyze how their proposals would impact the surface of the temple's engravings and its general long-term preservation. In the government request to the museums, the committee wrote that the "cementing problem" (disintegration) of the stone "would probably be aggravated by the dissolved gas contaminants of city or industrial atmospheres," "thaw cycles," and "wind abrasion." In its guidelines, the committee wrote that "an application should show what steps will be taken to protect the temple from deterioration" and "ensur[e] its permanent safety."[12] The Smithsonian determined that the temple would be saturated with moisture from Washington's humid climate and that this moisture would freeze inside its stones in the winter, effectively crumbling the surfaces of the stones that contained most of the visual artistic interest. The Smithsonian worked with the Texas Refinery Company to develop a preservative that would essentially seal the surfaces of the temple: Pencapsula, briefly explored as a stabilization agent in historic preservation. In its aggressive efforts to acquire the temple, the Smithsonian flirted with science-fiction imagery as Richard Goodwin, a major agitator for a Washington-based Dendur, talked of "surrounding the temple with an invisible shield, a 'field of force,'" to protect the temple from the city's climate.[13] In addition to this concept, the Smithsonian collaborated with the National Park Service to develop a far less fantastic dome similar to the Southern Illinois University proposal. The team from the Metropolitan Museum of Art worked with research scientists at Konstadt Laboratories to analyze both the optimum conditions for the stones and the existing conditions in the museum's most technologically sophisticated galleries. The museum and Konstadt successfully countered the Smithsonian by arguing that the climate control proposed in their Dendur

Gallery was both a source of human comfort and a medium that effected a chemical transformation in the air by removing pollution. In their final application to the committee, the scientists wrote, "These reports show that in those galleries where air-conditioning has been installed an exceptionally pure atmospheric condition is maintained. The area of the new wing for the Temple of Dendur will have the same high degree of protection against air pollution as those mentioned in the Konstadt report."[14] The notion of conditioned space as being protected from pollution extended the interpretation of air-conditioning evident at the Washington Bridge Apartments and the Ford Foundation Building. Within a museological context, the interior architectural environment now arrived as a more scientific system of architectural preservation.

The debates regarding the future home of the temple almost exclusively remained within the discourse of environment, climate, and protection from the various invidious forces of American cities. In 1965, the editors of the *Washington Post* wrote, "[I]t seems to us that the logical home is Washington. . . . The chief problem of placing the temple here is the humidity, which could erode away the elaborate carvings in sandstone. But the temple could be protected within a transparent shell constructed around it. It could be given a site on the Potomac that would duplicate its present setting on the Nile. . . . [B]y providing a suitable home for this temple, the way could be opened for possible acquisition of other relics now threatened by the rising waters of the Aswan Dam project."[15] Katherine Kuh, a significant art critic of the time, pressed for a New York–based temple, again intertwining the scholarly reputation of the Metropolitan Museum with climatic arguments:

> There has been some talk of locating the temple in Washington on the banks of the Potomac. From every point of view this plan seems unfortunate. The sandstone structure decorated inside and out with handsome reliefs was built in the reign of Augustus, during the Roman occupation of Egypt. Seen as an isolated example of late Egyptian architecture, it would unquestionably be interesting, but far less so than were it located in chronological context and surrounded by related objects.
>
> If the Temple of Dendur finally comes to the Metropolitan Museum, it would find a sympathetic home where some 5,000,000 visitors a year could see it and where numerous graduate students of Egyptology from nearby

> institutions would welcome it. . . . The museum is also prepared to invest $1,500,000 toward a proper indoor setting for the temple. The plan is to erect an extension to the Egyptian galleries where artificial light could reproduce the brilliance of an African sun, and where visitors could examine the building from both ground and balcony levels.
>
> But far more important, ultimately, than correct lighting and comfortable viewing facilities is the preservation of a fine example of late Egyptian architecture. Because the building is made of highly porous and friable aeolian sandstone, it demands an indoor setting. To expose it to Washington's damp climate and dirty air would constitute a risk even more serious than the dangers of possible vandalism. At present no chemical or plastic exists that can harden the surface of porous stone and yet protect it from air pollutants and weather. Dendur's pink stone was created by windblown sand, not by the usual mineral deposits, and hence is extremely fragile. Laboratory experiments show that it can even be abraded by talc—the softest of all minerals. In a few years, if exposed to an outdoor urban onslaught, the temple's subtle color would deteriorate and its crisp reliefs disintegrate.
>
> Egypt's hot, dry climate coupled with high dunes of blown sand protected the temple over the centuries. In its original setting, an intense southern light gave tonal vitality to the reliefs, which were carved with a deliberate understanding of the environment they were to inhabit. To locate the temple amid Washington's historic, albeit youthful, American monuments would be both meaningless and inept.[10]

The Metropolitan Museum's and Kuh's arguments represent an extension of the parameters developed by the International Institute for the Conservation of Museum Objects (IIC). The group's charter and atmospheric regulatory guidelines, developed in 1950, provided aids to assist museums in the management and preservation of objects. Initially, the development of the IIC helped establish parameters for museums to determine what objects could be displayed within a museum's existing environmental conditions, but the Metropolitan Museum of Art used its ability to achieve the organization's ideal set of environmental standards on a large scale and with absolute precision to advance its position over other museums competing for the Temple of Dendur. Such tactics, which used these guidelines for acquisitional power, continued with the development of guidelines by the International Council of Museums in 1966 in New York City. These guidelines further established regulations governing humidity, temperature, and pollutant levels in museums, but they argued for the centrality of technically advanced spaces in the preservation of objects.[17] Ultimately, it was the Metropolitan Museum's arguments regarding the scale and precision with which it could achieve the agreed-upon environmental parameters for conserving the temple that convinced the more technically oriented concerns of the Washington, D.C., committee. In the committee's official report, it decided to cede the temple to the Metropolitan Museum, because "there was no way of guaranteeing the preservation of the temple out-of-doors and . . . the museum obviously had the financial resources to maintain it properly."[18] Although numerous factors went into the committee's final determination of the location of the temple—the Metropolitan Museum's level of expertise in Egyptian antiquities, various political connections of its board of trustees, and its ability to secure long-term funding[19]—the museum was able to justify a location of the temple with a mixture of architectural and scientific concepts.

THE ARCHITECTURAL ENVIRONMENT OF PRESERVATION

From its arrival in New York City, the Temple of Dendur was housed in specially developed structures that produced specific indoor climates and that further enhanced the role of the museum and modern architecture as protective sites of ancient culture. These features appeared with the permanent additions, but they also appeared in the several temporary shelters developed for the temple by the museum's in-house architects and hired technicians. After shipping the disassembled temple from its temporary transit site in Egypt to New York City, the museum housed it in an enormous inflatable structure while plans to build a more permanent structure were developed. Walter Bird, the engineer of the U.S. Atomic Energy Commission Pavilion, the Arctic "Radomes" (with Buckminster Fuller), and mobile hospitals for the Vietnam War, designed the structure, which was built by his company, Birdair. Hoving had used Birdair's inflatables before; as the director of parks, he asked Bird to provide such structures in Bryant Park in 1966 as a way to house people in temporary spaces, which also lent the park's activities the aura of futuristic aerospace technology. This spectacular use of temporary architecture was a specialty of

Hoving's and drew people to what were coined "Hoving's Happenings." Bird's inflatable structures, and inflatables more generally, oscillated between the utopian and the institutional in their imagery. Throughout the 1960s, inflatables were used in military installations and were appropriated by various "experimental" architects of the late 1960s, generally with more counterinstitutional aims. Bird's Arctic Radomes provided the postwar nation with a new sense of the American militarized frontier. The transportable inflatables developed by Bird for both the Vietnam War and for American backyard swimming pools only furthered the "pneumatic imagination" that emerged "out of the military and recreational realms in the late fifties."[20] In developing designs for the Metropolitan Museum, Bird, with his inflatables, provided the museum with a more thoroughly instrumental display of preservation technologies aligned with cold-war technologies.

Bird's technicians installed the 29-foot-high, 100-foot-long, and 60-foot-wide structure adjacent to the Metropolitan Museum's North Wing. There, park- and museumgoers could observe the unassembled temple stones in a shelter that the museum claimed "was necessary to prevent expansion or cracking by moisture."[21] The inflatable conveyed the sense of urgency the museum wished to project regarding its preservation of the temple and its role as a counterenvironment within New York City. As one reporter observed of the inflating of the shelter and the movement of the stones into it, "The fork-lifts scurry like beetles between them, sorting out a jig-saw puzzle, hurrying to get the stones under shelter before they are destroyed, corroded by the New York air."[22] The "iron lung," as one critic dubbed it,[23] provided a visible way for the museum to preserve the temple, and the powerful contrast with the existing Beaux-Arts building made high drama of the museum's salvaging efforts.

The planned permanent wing for the Temple of Dendur was part of a Comprehensive Architectural Plan for the Second Century by Kevin Roche and John Dinkeloo and Associates, architect of the Ford Foundation Building, and was under the managerial supervision of Thomas Hoving, who remained the director of the Metropolitan Museum of Art throughout the 1970s. Impressed by Roche Dinkeloo's vision of an interior world at the Ford Foundation Building, Hoving hired the architect to develop a series of monumental indoor galleries for the Metropolitan. In addition

Metropolitan Museum of Art before expansion, ca. 1968. Birdair Pavilion is visible in lower left. Photograph copyright The Metropolitan Museum of Art.

Birdair Pavilion holding Dendur stones, 1968. Construction on the museum's wings is under way in foreground. Image copyright The Metropolitan Museum of Art.

Interior of Birdair Pavilion holding Dendur stones, 1968. Image copyright The Metropolitan Museum of Art.

to a wing for the temple (the Sackler Wing), Roche Dinkeloo worked with Hoving on a wing for Pacific Island art (the Michael C. Rockefeller Wing), a gallery for collections of European masterworks (the Robert Lehman Wing), and the American Wing for American art and architectural fragments. Roche Dinkeloo's responsibilities also included the renovation of the museum's Fifth Avenue facade and the reworking of the museum's circulation spaces. All of the new construction provided various environmentally and/or culturally "appropriate" settings for the museum's recent acquisitions, formed through mixtures of complex engineering and the incorporation of greenery, pools, and other indoor nature-matter.[24] In addition to addressing the museum's room for the vulnerable Temple of Dendur, the museum's literature describes the fragility of the Pacific Island artworks, the significance of the Rockefeller Wing's mechanical systems in preserving them, and the methods used by Roche Dinkeloo to save various architectural fragments of American masterpieces in the American wings. In Roche Dinkeloo's initial designs, themes of preservation, conservation, and the stewarding of nature became highly aestheticized.

In developing the forms and structures of these buildings, Kevin Roche claimed that he was inspired by the British iron-and-glass architecture developed by Joseph Paxton and others for greenhouses. Not only did these types of spaces operationalize the production of interior worlds, in a manner reviewed earlier, but also Roche believed they were easily integrated into the surrounding Central Park landscape.[25] Roche Dinkeloo's architectural vocabulary also abstractly evoked nineteenth-century architecture such as the Second Empire aesthetics of the original Richard Morris Hunt and McKim, Mead and White museum structures. Roche Dinkeloo's slanted, mirrored-glass additions emphasized symmetry and reinforced the Beaux-Arts planning of the original buildings by Hunt and McKim, Mead and White. Large, mirrored walls of glass had been used throughout late-modern architecture since they were first developed at the Bell Labs by Eero Saarinen (a project designed by Roche and Dinkeloo when they were at the firm), but here they took on another historically representational dimension: evoking the roofs of the Metropolitan Museum's original historicist architecture, Egyptian architectural forms, and British imperial greenhouses. In addition to these abstract historical invocations, the large expanses of mirrored glass also related to specific environmental and museological goals. Because of the ability of mirrored glass to mitigate the impact of ultraviolet radiation within interior spaces, it became reoriented within this context toward the goals of museological preservation. Taken together, the mirrored-glass expansions simultaneously referred to an earlier American and European era of collecting, while suggesting the interior as the site for the production of novel museological environments.

Like Roche Dinkeloo's earlier work at the Ford Foundation Building, the master-plan proposal contained various landscaped spaces within it. The spaces potentially offered the museum's curators the opportunity to present works of art in indoor abstractions of outdoor settings, particularly in the Sackler and American Wings. In this sense, the building's architectural forms and the proposed plantings marked a transition within Roche Dinkeloo's architecture from an environmentally inflected late-modern architectural grammar evident at the Ford Foundation to an emerging but still not explicit postmodern one. In evoking historical greenhouses, proposing various interior tableaux as abstractions of historical landscapes, Roche Dinkeloo further suggested the neohistoricization or potential postmodernization of "environment" within architecture. As it had done at Ford, Roche Dinkeloo transformed the otherwise biophysical aspects of an architectural interior environment into something more visually representational. In his commentaries on Kevin Roche's career, the theorist Jeffrey Inaba argues that Roche Dinkeloo's architecture from this period also began to transform modern space through the use of dramatic lighting, mirrors, and mirrored glass.[26] As I have discussed in chapter 2, such specular effects became a type of dissonance that suspends the monumentality of earlier modern architectural conceptions and the integrative clarity of the modern city. Although such effects are not in full force within the museum proposals, specular effects (reflections, abrupt lighting changes, and exaggerations) appear as emerging aspects within Roche Dinkeloo's work for the Metropolitan Museum.

As the museum developed these spaces with the architects, museum administrators used themes of preservation and stewardship to publicly argue for the expansion of the museum's structure into Central Park. These arguments were primarily presented in local papers and press releases and to potential funders of the wings. Despite the museum's stated

Model, Temple of Dendur Room, Kevin Roche John Dinkeloo and Associates, 1970. Image copyright The Metropolitan Museum of Art. Image source: Kevin Roche John Dinkeloo and Associates.

Model of museum expansions, Kevin Roche John Dinkeloo and Associates. Image copyright The Metropolitan Museum of Art. Image source: Kevin Roche John Dinkeloo and Associates.

benevolence in carrying out this work, the expansion of the museum was vigorously criticized on grounds of park "encroachment," cultural "centralization," and even "imperialism." Most immediately, the proposed expansion of the museum into Central Park would entail dismantling a popular playground and would bring the museum almost directly against the carriage path to the west. The expansion of the museum and the criticisms of it are far more complex than simply seeing architectural development as encroaching upon nature. The expansion of the museum suggested larger political and economic shifts: recalibrations of City resources and values and a new shift of cultural wealth and power within New York from outdoor public sites such as the park to interior, institutional ones. Thus, the controversy became less a debate about building over a playground and more a generalized struggle over a shift in the concentration of wealth and space.

In numerous public appearances before city, parks, and community review boards, the museum's administrators attempted to mollify the critics of the expansion. Rather than simply argue for the validity of "culture" as a public resource, the museum positioned itself as a new force in the production of urban nature. In one review meeting, Hoving claimed, "We have to be of the utmost sensitivity. . . . Anything we build will be in some manner, a sympathetic extension of the park. We would be very lacking in sensitivity not to solve the problem that way." In the development of the museum expansion, Hoving and Roche Dinkeloo stressed that "the new plans would be a blend of landscape and building." And Hoving made continuous reference to the fact that "work in progress in other parts of the country by the Roche-Dinkeloo firm shows an unconventional synthesis of these elements, a factor that was influential in its selection by the museum."[27] The earliest plans for the proposal show a pronounced use of vegetation that would not appear in the final scheme; the museum appeared laced with green spaces that mixed art, trees, and other plantings. In subsequent arguments for the expansion, Hoving claimed that the new project would actually add land to the park by replacing existing parking areas with "53,700 square feet" of new "indoor" park. But in placing the terms of the argument solely on the quantity of natural material, Hoving missed some of the key concerns of the museum's critics.[28]

In addition to the tendentious nature of building in the park, commentators attacked the general consolidation of the Metropolitan Museum into an even larger, single spatial entity devoted to the fine arts. Rather than the museum encroaching on parkland, a variety of newspapers, community groups, and art critics claimed that the Temple of Dendur (among other museum acquisitions) should be relocated to another area of the City or repatriated with its nation and culture of origin. In place of material preservation and cultural interpretation, these critics argued for the diffusion of artifacts to enable social and urban transformation. A New York City community group, Harlem CORE (Congress of Racial Equality) stressed that the Temple of Dendur was the product of a Nubian-African culture and should be located either in a neighborhood in the City that could claim a population culturally and nationally related, ultimately suggesting Harlem or Bedford-Stuyvesant. Extending the museum's own discourse of environmental appropriateness, the group stressed that these neighborhoods were the most "ethnically" linked to the temple. A "Harlem Dendur" would provide a cultural centerpiece to bolster a neighborhood entering an uncertain future in postindustrial New York City while symbolically repatriating the object with an "African" social aggregation.[29] The editors of the *New York Times* mirrored these arguments when they wrote, "What is raised [by the museum's expansion] is a much larger and more important issue—the way in which the Temple of Dendur could be used to enrich the City far beyond making it one more jam-packed treasure in Fifth Avenue's awesome supermart of art. To use it as a city-planning tool, a cultural focus and point of beauty for any one of the many parts of New York that need it far more than Fifth Avenue and Central Park, is a challenge that should surely be explored."[30] For the editors of the *Times*, the location of the temple should be used to develop a new cultural marker in New York City. The editors argued that the temple's deployment would be used to enact an urban transformation, in the manner of City Beautiful–era planning.

The arguments surrounding the museum's expansion extended for several more years. In 1970, Bernhard Leitner, a frequent architectural critic for *Artforum*, examined the tapping of Roche Dinkeloo architects, their corporate associations, and late-modern aesthetics as they would relate to the development of the museum's new expansion and the proposed natural enhancements of the museum in Central Park:

> When Mr. Hoving, the Director of the Metropolitan Museum, selected the architects Kevin Roche, John Dinkeloo and Associates to prepare the new Master Plan, he accepted—maybe even wanted—what is the hallmark of Kevin Roche and Co.: simplicity of form and monumentality of scale. It is design reduced to the simplest, immediately comprehensible, objective, geometrical shapes—but subjectively exaggerated and forced into gigantic dimensions suggesting a certain lust for power. It is the kind of architecture which is difficult to reconcile with respect for the individual.[31]

Leitner further questioned the development of interior parks spaces in an existing and important public park:

> It is difficult to overlook the new spirit. The Master Plan provides for two interior parks, enclosed with glass, climate-controlled with green trees twelve months a year. Both will have a most welcome entrance from Central Park. An artificial park within a museum within a park might help to smooth the transition between nature and art. . . . An artificial year-round green park within the natural year-round Central Park is like an aquarium in the ocean: Perhaps a touch of surrealism but certainly extremely effective, an unforgettable impression—nature *de luxe*.[32]

Considering the large degree of artifice in the park itself, Leitner's criticism is ironic, if not historically uninformed. But in addition to Leitner's piece, the debates over the architectural expansion of the museum and the massive acquisition of objects it represented produced a key text of critical museum studies: Leon Golub's article "Regarding the Lehman and Rockefeller Gifts to the Metropolitan Museum," of 1970. Golub provided the most incisive criticism, linking the production of the museum's spaces with the museum's new role as both local and international reorganizer of space. He wrote that opposition to the Metropolitan Museums of Art's proposed expansion was "largely concerned with the protection of Central Park, decentralization, city financial responsibilities, etc." "However," he continued, "one can question the means and ends taken for granted in the acquiring of vast art collections and the centralizing of these collections in American museum custody."[33] Golub linked the museum's expansion to a larger symbolic and material process of cultural disenfranchisement:

> Americans collect art in massive expenditures of surplus wealth (aided by governmental tax policies). The collecting of art, the aggrandisement of cul-

> tural choice, can be considered as surplus dividends to the exalted existence of the dominant west. As one notes in the Lehman Collection, the collecting of art continues to function as an imperial preserve in respect to the quasi-deification of the collector.
>
> The power governing the acquisition and distribution of art is a distillation of the acquisitions and distributions of economic and strategic resources. Boards of Trustees of major museums are powerful cross-sections of American international economic power. The assets of art are as equally well protected as the assets of oil, uranium, or cobalt. Characterologically, the collecting of art on vast scales illustrates in a highly sublimated manner the consumption patterns and fantasies of American power manias.
>
> A museum is an agency to centralize the holding of artifacts and art objects. These must come from somewhere. This *somewhere* is typically the nations that cannot protect their arts for one reason or another. Just as it is an assumed American prerogative to take possession of (what is estimated to be) 60–70% of the world's resources, it is, also, our privilege to take possession of much of the world's art. . . . Our cultural imperative is one with our strategic and territorial imperative.[34]

Although the entire history of the politics surrounding the acquisition of objects such as the Temple of Dendur and the Rockefeller Collection of primitive art was probably unavailable to him, Golub effectively linked aspects of the museum's expansion, the acquisition of objects, and the remaking of space both abroad and in the United States. But in connecting cultural intensification with the intensification of resources, Golub also entered into critical dialogue with the very factors that brought the Temple of Dendur to New York City. Golub's criticism was essentially Marxist in that he argued for redistributing the uneven distribution of cultural and material resources as a form of social and cultural justice.

Finally, the museum's impending expansions in the park engaged with aesthetic debates in the writings of Robert Smithson, forming a core portion of his "Dialectical Landscape" essay of 1973. Smithson wandered Central Park considering the constant mediation of city and nature through its landscape. He noted the irony of the "ecological graffiti" on the boulders that surrounded the site of the future museum expansions—graffiti protesting the museum's impending confrontation with the nature in the park. Smithson recounted what this graffiti, sprayed on natural elements, proclaimed:

"Concrete and trees do not mix."

"Let's not turn Central Park into an Asphalt jungle."

"Save the Park."

"The Met is not good for trees and other flowering things."

"Does the Met smell as nice as a tree?"[35]

For Smithson, the graffiti illustrated the larger and ineluctable dialectic of city and nature represented by the park itself. Smithson wrote that the structures that formed in the park must be understood as part of a process set in motion by the very tendentious concept of an "urban nature." The park, for him, was a place where the contradictions of nature and urbanization were assembled, "like having an orchid garden in a steel mill, or a factory where palm trees would be lit by the fire of blast furnaces." However, although critically engaged with this dialectical conception, Smithson oddly reiterated a view of the park's designer, Frederick Law Olmsted, who viewed the museum as one of several "subtractions" from the park and thus, by implication, outside its dialectic of nature and society. Such a view was reinforced with a photograph by Smithson of a construction barrier for the Dendur Room that accompanied his essay. Smithson's photograph showed the barrier covered with graffiti and brimming with a pile of dirt. Hoving and Roche clearly wished to amend Smithson's interpretation that the museum was an intrusion, or at best a "subtraction," from the park.[36]

In light of the critiques and insights of Leitner, Golub, and Smithson, we might more accurately understand the work of Roche Dinkeloo and the museum administrators as attempting to entangle the museum in the historical "dialectic" of Central Park while reconfiguring these very dialectical processes into a far more complex form of interchange. The area immediately outside the museum already contained mixtures of plants, water, and an ancient artifact, "Cleopatra's Needle," an object performatively moved from its original site and resituated within the park landscape. But, if the earlier Egyptian relic was *naturalized* into its urban setting via the material aesthetics of the nineteenth-century picturesque, the Temple of Dendur was primarily *environmentalized* into its new location via the material aesthetic of late-modern architecture. Roche Dinkeloo's design

View of construction of the Dendur wing, early 1970s. Image copyright The Metropolitan Museum of Art.

extended and intensified a long-established activity of geographical cultural relocation. But he employed a particularly late-modern assemblage. Mirrored curtain wall, indoor verdure, lighting effects, and the environmental engineering of indoor air established a protected setting for the Temple of Dendur within New York City yet visually connected it to a historically significant landscape.

In simultaneously opening the museum to the urban nature of the park, developing an engineered environment that would inarguably relocate the temple from the Nubian Plain into the museum, and partially evoking the technologies of the corporate city to accomplish this, the constructions of Roche Dinkeloo and the museum suggest even more complex interfaces between nature and the City than those imagined by Leitner, Golub, and Smithson. Rather than simple natural mimesis, in the ways described by Leitner, or an explicitly dialectical synthesis between nature and the City organized in pastoral or counterpastoral forms, as outlined by Smithson,

Photograph by Robert Smithson of a construction wall outside the Metropolitan Museum of Art, 1973. Photograph copyright Estate of Robert Smithson. Licensed by VAGA, New York, N.Y.

or the naked expression of colonial reorganization, described by Golub, the development of the space at the Metropolitan Museum can be understood as staging a new type of territorialization of culture in and through the aesthetics of environmental production, representation, and maintenance.[37] The processes that set the temple free and resituated it in New York City were structured around governmental and institutional conceptualizations of conservation and preservation, actualized through a complex corporate, museological, and late-modern conception of space and technology. The production of the Dendur Room differed from the strategies of other cities that argued for their particular correspondence or innate natural equivalence to the Nubian landscape and climate. Through Roche Dinkeloo, institutional management, corporate space, and preservation were conjoined through the production of a space and its vaporous atmosphere that might situate ancient artifacts unhinged from their original sites.

Construction did not begin on the various wings until 1972, after eighteen months of particularly aggressive lawsuits brought by the Municipal Art Society and the Parks Council of the City of New York. The Lehman Wing, housing European masterworks, was the first of the wings to be completed, in 1974; this was followed by completion of the Sackler Wing, in 1979; the Michael C. Rockefeller Wing, for primitive art, in 1982; and the remaining wings by 1988. When finished, the wing housing the Temple of Dendur was one of the most technologically sophisticated spaces built in any Western museum. Not only did the space employ the latest hygrographic systems, developed by Severud and Associates, but the entire complex was devoted to environmental object preservation. A special temporary chamber was housed underneath the enormous temple platform (what would eventually become an indoor staff garage) that contained "the country's first museum environmental chamber, designed to condition art objects brought to the Metropolitan whose materials might be sensitive to climatic changes."[38] Once this space was completed, the temple blocks were moved out of the inflatable room and into the staging area underneath the Dendur Room, awaiting reassembly. Inside the temple space above, limestone pavers surrounded a pool that evoked, to some degree, the Nile setting of the temple, although they could just as easily have evoked the types of pools lying within one of Roche's atria or the

Dendur Room under construction, 1977. Image copyright The Metropolitan Museum of Art.

podia of an immense sculpture. The pool makes the temple appear as if it is floating in the surrounding space, visually connecting it to the surrounding park but objectifying it within its new space.

Preservation and the generation of an engineered environment appear as a visible aesthetic form and experience within the room. When the room was completed, in 1978, numerous critics were befuddled at the massive size of the room when compared to the small temple. The monumental space seemed out of scale relative to the temple. But what one witnesses in this room is not just the temple itself but also the production of a protective and museological environment for it. The ceiling becomes completely sublimated within a diffused spotlighting system (a reconstruction of corporate panel lighting), the sloping walls connect to a series of air registers at their base, and the location of the HVAC's return, in the very rear of the temple, becomes a monumental moment in the

Completed Dendur Room, 1978. Image copyright The Metropolitan Museum of Art. Image source: Kevin Roche John Dinkeloo and Associates.

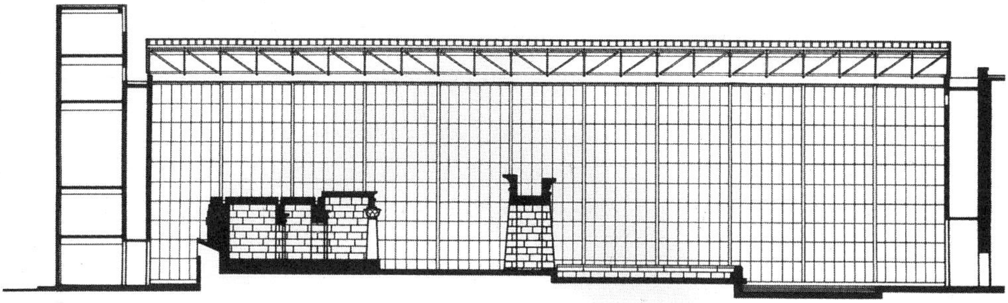

Section of the Dendur Room showing air plenum underneath temple, 1970. Image copyright The Metropolitan Museum of Art. Image source: Kevin Roche John Dinkeloo and Associates.

design. Here, the architects and mechanical engineers designed a large air-supply plenum into the rear of the temple's base to provide conditioned air for the temple space and the staging area below. The plenum also resolves the difference in topography between the original Egyptian setting of the temple and the new room by replicating the slope on which the temple originally stood. The plenum quite literally replaces the ground (a more traditional zone of territorial dispute) with a hollow topography built to deliver the specialized atmosphere of the temple space. Given the discourse on native and constructed environments moving through the arguments that brought this space into existence, the room presents us with an aesthetic experience of museological maintenance as much as the experience of things maintained.

TOWARD THE GLOBAL MUSEOLOGICAL ENVIRONMENT

By the mid-1980s, the Metropolitan Museum's expansions provided the institution with an emerging form of power with which to collect and reconfigure the experience of cultural objects. The tactics developed by the museum and the architects of the Dendur Room extended to the other wings of the newly refurbished museum. The planning of the museum's Rockefeller Wing is one example of an approach that expanded the environmental stewardship pioneered in the Sackler Wing. The critic Grace Glueck praised the "spectacular" wing, which was equal in size to the entire Whitney Museum of American Art, as a "conservator's dream." One curator at the Metropolitan claimed, "Never has so much expensive high technology been lavished on a display of 'primitive' art." Like the Dendur Room, the Rockefeller Wing employed sophisticated displays of modernity in the name of cultural preservation. The museum's press releases boasted that "[n]early an acre of sophisticated, temperature and humidity-controlled glass cases" were "painstakingly built to display the 2000-odd objects."[39] The production of atmosphere and the museum's global position as a center of world culture became ever more solidified.

As the initial expansions were completed, the Metropolitan Museum was literally bounded by spaces that enabled it to engage with a new dis-

The largely completed museum expansions, early 1990s. Image copyright The Metropolitan Museum of Art. Image source: Kevin Roche John Dinkeloo and Associates.

course on the power of indoor space in the development of the museum as a cultural center both in New York City and among other international centers of culture. The museum was expanded in the name of cultural preservation, but the expansions had sparked legitimate debates regarding the museum's appropriation of the City's existing park spaces, the further centralization of cultural power in the City, and the implementation of forms of power over poorer, primarily developing nations. But the case of the Temple of Dendur is significant in that it represents how these various aspects of metropolitan and antipodal cultural exchange can still be interpreted as extensions of earlier, equally interrelated processes. The movement of the temple into the Metropolitan Museum in Central Park represents interconnected processes related to ideas of development, culture, and the position of postindustrial urbanism relative to developing cities. As with the indoor atria examined in chapter 2, the advancement of maintenance as an institutional and experiential form operated with a transurban scale and geography. The environments developed by Roche Dinkeloo and the museum administrators at the Metropolitan Museum are partially in the service of those processes outlined by Golub—American and metropolitan cultural centralization and empire—but in a far more complex webwork of interaction than that traced by either Golub or Smithson. More specifically, like the atria, the spaces at the Metropolitan Museum of Art involve the fabrication of new socionatural urban forms—a carefully engineered indoor environment, forms of architectural and urban representation—that more adequately serve the particular transnational and transurban relationships being staged within this city. And it is in this latter role that the Dendur Room is the most revealing: ultimately, the development of the Dendur Room reveals how architecture and urbanization undertaken in the name of conservation and preservation deterritorialized and reterritorialized culture within a specifically globalized architectural and metropolitan milieu. Although the spatial and environmental transformations that followed the movement of cultural objects to New York City register most intensely in the transformed landscapes of the developing world, they also appear in the environments moving through this museum, whose spaces and surrounding landscapes were refashioned to offer a site of stability and concentration. Such phenomena mark transformations in an emerging culture industry in New

York City, but more significant are the shifts of environmental production being staged here—toward the maintenance of the subjects and objects of an emerging political economy. These features that registered in the atria of Midtown East and in the Metropolitan Museum of Art will only become more pronounced in the iterations of maintenance-oriented environments in the City's financial sectors, the subject of the next chapter.

4 EXCHANGE

The Communication Environments of Finance

WE ARE WITNESSING the interrelationship between the late-modern architecture and interiors of New York City, the environments of those interiors, and the City's overall transformation into its contemporary state. The prominent new architectural environments in the City became new material forms that suggested links between the subjects and objects of the City. The co-mingling of "protection," "growth," and "preservation" is one of the more alluring and unexplored features embedded within late-modern environments, and it reveals the particular role of the architectural environment as a new urban reality. These environments are such a core aspect of everyday life in Western cities that we hardly realize the authorship that underpins contemporary relationships between such mundane things as glass walls, indoor air, greenery, and art, nor do we fully realize the urban and supra-urban geography of this mixture. Having explored the interiors of apartment buildings, the spaces of the indoor atria garden, and the contemporary museum, we now turn to the monumental spaces of financial labor in Lower Manhattan, what are referred to as "trading rooms" or "trading halls." Historically within the collective spaces of trading halls, young men surrounded by an array of computers aggressively and boisterously moved shares of companies and governmental bonds between their respective clients. This activity, within this space, formed the core structure of "the market" in New York City.

In addition to their noticeably high-pitched level of activity, trading rooms, like indoor atria and museums, were always marked for the massive expense and the artifice that went into the constituent features of their interiors: the forceful use of cooling, lighting, and sound control that maintained trade, as both an activity and a space. Those journalists, reporters, and critics who examined life in the trading halls often described the immense electrical loads of the air-conditioning and computer equipment through analogical comparisons: "enough power to electrify Guatemala," "Schenectady," "a small city."[1] In addition to their pronounced scale, trading rooms produced new material concepts regarding the production of interior spaces and environments, and regarding the relationship of these to the work that constituted the financial-services economy. If we understand the architectural environment in these rooms as an emerging type of urban socionature, then the trading rooms of Lower Manhattan represent how this socionature intersects with the literal trade that is an integral aspect of a postindustrial and global urban economy.

Most analyses of the "environment" or "nature" of Lower Manhattan concentrate on the privatization of the green spaces that often surround its office buildings, such as those found at the World Financial Center's Winter Garden.[2] Indeed, the park spaces surrounding or within financial-services sectors in New York City illustrate how the City's emerging economies restructure traditional forms of urban "nature." The meaning and use of trees and verdant lawns in these business centers shift what and where we understand nature to be in a city. In addition to its obviously more interiorized and privatized form, nature is also released from any ecological role within the City. We might notice trees in such areas as solely visually oriented effects, afterthoughts, or simply reiterations of a building's spatial composition and order. But lurking within urban trading precincts are other, much more hybrid forms of socionature that fulfill a city's historical role as a place that builds biophysical environments for its citizens, however perversely. Indeed, the production of socionatural environments has transformed in ways not often explored in these precincts. In this chapter, we go inside, exploring how the production of an atmospheric environment for financial trading stitches workers' bodies, computers, the neighborhood of Lower Manhattan, and cities into a webwork of connections. In trading rooms, the architectural environment cooled machines and bodies, becoming a type of hybrid environment of financial communications and fiscal crisis management. As this environment rose in significance relative to the City's global economy, architects fashioned it as a new monumental form in and against the historical City.

Contemporary Lower Manhattan contains most of the trading halls located in the New York City metropolitan area, but the development of Lower Manhattan into a center for financial services stretches back to the

City's earliest history. Mythically originating under the shade of a buttonwood tree, the New York Stock Exchange became one of the City's and the nation's first financial-services centers. From the eighteenth to the early twentieth century, the stock exchange moved and expanded, eventually establishing a permanent space in 1902. Throughout the immediate pre– and post–World War II period, the stock exchange continued to expand, when it was joined by additional large-scale peripheral trading rooms during the financial-services boom of the late 1970s and 1980s. During this boom, the number of stockbrokers and dealers in New York City increased from fifty-six thousand to ninety-nine thousand, becoming core members of the City's "young urban professionals" that transformed Wall Street's staid image into one of an exciting, frenzied landscape of collective and individual acquisition.[3] Although Midtown East was expanding into a business sector at this time, many financial-services firms chose to build in Lower Manhattan. Not only did this area hold the City's financial-services infrastructure via the existing New York Stock Exchange, but also the underdeveloped financial district offered cheaper rents for the large-scale spaces required by this particular industry.

The corporate owners, developers, and managers of trading halls viewed the gathering of traders in Lower Manhattan and the building of trading rooms as enacting a transformative effect on the demographics and ultimate real-estate values of the surrounding area. The New York Stock Exchange was rebuilt in the early twentieth century during the rise of the post–Spanish War "imperial era" in the United States. The stock exchange was a City Beautiful monument that boosted Wall Street's image as a capital of American capitalism. The building contrasted with the peripheral industrial and underdeveloped residential areas that characterized most of industrial-era Lower Manhattan. Further construction, in the 1960s and 1970s, of financial-services operations contrasted with the area's increasingly mixed reputation. Although some areas of Lower Manhattan (such as Coenties Slip and the Fulton Fish Market) were vibrant centers of artistic and working-class life, some commentators saw them as out of place in contrast to the trading halls.[4] The physical disjunctions that characterized Lower Manhattan formed the basis of various real-estate schemes, and they fueled artist practices that sought to illustrate and seize the peripheral areas of the business neighborhood. The commentary on the disjointed precinct extended from the 1960s into the 1970s and 1980s with discussions surrounding the construction of the World Financial Center. This latter development, whose sleek design seemingly beckoned to an earlier era of skyscraper construction in Manhattan, would hold several of the City's largest trading halls and was built on top of a complex postindustrial landscape: a landfill site for impromptu artist performances, exhibitions, and rallies.

If the exterior of the trading halls offered potential counterpoints to the surrounding neighborhood, within the trading halls, the environments operated to support the remarkably boisterous activity and subjects of financial services. Connecting the calm, early twentieth-century neoclassical New York Stock Exchange and the late-modern mirror-glassed World Financial Center were interiors of frenzied traders and sophisticated, engineered atmospheres built to enhance their work. Our understanding of these people's screaming, running, and gesturing, as well as the environment they worked within—the heat and noise levels inside trading

Water Street, Wall Street, New York, 1978. Copyright Thomas Struth.

rooms—emerges through writings by various authors, engineers, architects, and commentators who attempted to capture this unique interior culture. From the earliest examinations of these rooms to contemporary accounts, authors have described traders as monstrously boisterous and animalistic in their manner, at work in often oppressive conditions. Edwin Markham wrote as early as 1912 of the New York Stock Exchange as a space promoting near-animal-like behavior. Markham used terms such as "hawks" and "wolves" to describe the traders in the New York Stock Exchange, and more common terms including "bullish" and "bearish" refer both to the market and to the animalistic personae traders often acquire. In a 1982 analysis of trading-room design, David Ellingson, in the magazine *Industrial Design,* claimed that "traders are animals—and generally proud of it—so putting bulls and bears into the pits requires some deft human factors as stock markets around the world call for more space and improved communications." In the same article, Ellingson quotes Charles Kinsey, a designer of trading-floor systems: "'[T]rading people are really animals, absolutely chimpanzees,' because of all the fierce frenzy meant to prevent individuals and companies from losing millions of dollars on paper within seconds. 'You have to design the place to be indestructible.'"[5] Carolyn Iu, the designer of Merrill Lynch's trading rooms at the World Financial Center, also noted the roar of the traders, as well as the endless consumption of food to fuel their activity.[6] Such observations are critical, and they leave a troubling sentiment: if traders are animals, then trading becomes a type of force of nature that taps into some internal, transhistorical impulse.[7]

Within the larger context of neighborhood transformation, urban counterenvironments, and the emerging subjects of financial markets, the trading rooms of Lower Manhattan emerged as veritable eyes in the storm of an initially industrializing and then deindustrializing city. As we shall see, engineers, financial managers, and traders fostered new forms of architectural environments as facilitators and protectors of the market's boisterous subjects and dynamics. Through their spatial, acoustical, and atmospheric design, trading rooms were calibrated in ways that focused the subjects of trade and the activity they conducted into spaces of communications networks. The work in these rooms was primarily, if not solely, completed by young men, and the gathering of these male, gesticulating bodies into trading spaces was predicated on maintaining their bodies and voices as active producers of the market. The separation from the City outside and the ability to scream, to yell, to listen, and to maintain this level of activity emerged as a chief project of environmental production in these spaces. As Caitlin Zaloom, an anthropologist examining trading halls, has noted, "[H]and signals and shouts conveyed prices and dealing offers, placing the body at the centre of traders' dealing strategies. Floor trading was taxing physical labor. To take full advantage of the markets a trader stood for hours a day among throngs of competitors jostling each other for advantage. For the interim trading floor to work, it had to provide a certain level of physical comfort for the traders and allow them to hear and see the sounds and gestures of their trading partners and the markets as a whole."[8] In addition to their interactions with one another, traders entangled themselves with telephones, acoustical amplifiers, tickers, and other machines that promoted the transfer of capital essential to the functioning of the market.

Developers, corporate directors, managers, and engineers viewed the production of the architectural environment as a pretext for the trading activity within these spaces. For example, from the late 1970s to the late 1980s, studies on indoor air in trading halls argued that the positive quality of indoor air increased workplace productivity by as much as 18 or 21 percent.[9] These studies of productivity often focused specifically on trading rooms, where researchers imagined that the quality of indoor air could have a palliative effect on the stresses unique to the trading environment. Engineers such as Harold Lorsch and Norman Kurtz envisioned cool air as actually promoting and prolonging the frenzied activity of market makers. Studies by environmental engineers suggested that increased cooling and humidification, in addition to cooling human bodies, increased the efficiency of computer equipment as well.[10] In the most simplistic sense, both the active young men and the computers inside these spaces generated heat, and engineers demanded specific cooling loads that facilitated the intense concentration of machines and people in these spaces. Such a literal and frankly instrumental interpretation of these environments actually contains more conceptually rich connections and concepts: in linking the cooling of the financial-services-workers' bodies and the computer equipment used by them, engineers, business owners, and other financial-market makers realized a physical socionatural milieu that formed an integral and concrete aspect of the vast and largely virtual territory that constituted the world financial markets. In recent architectural writing, markets emerge as virtual spaces—"networks" or organizational concepts such as "logistics" and "protocols."[11] But moving through the networked market is an environmental form, an atmospheric stratum of coolth, that negotiates the new transurban relations between the people that work within the environment, the machines they use, and international trading networks. This environmental form is more than just a setting for the market; it is tied to its labor and financial dynamics, and it became a material shaped by architects as a potential urban form within New York City.

BUILDING THE ATMOSPHERE OF TRADE

From their appearance in the City, trading halls were experimental sites in the production of indoor environments, particularly in the use of ventilation techniques. The large, prominent trading halls of Lower Manhattan were central in the economic and urban debates surrounding this production process. One of the first fully functioning air-conditioning systems in the United States was installed in the New York Stock Exchange to cool the active bodies of the traders inside. In 1902, on Wall and Nassau Streets, the architect George B. Post and the engineer Alfred Wolff resituated technologies used for the production of coolth from cold-storage rooms into the central trading hall of the New York Stock Exchange headquarters. Cold-storage rooms were one of the most intense locales for the production of cold indoor air in late nineteenth-century cities, used primarily for the storage of animal goods. The scientist Ogdern Doremus referred to the proposed "technology transfer" from cold storage to trading hall, claiming that "if they can cool dead hogs in Chicago, why not live 'bulls and bears' in the New York Stock Exchange?"[12] The stock-exchange engineer Alfred Wolff incorporated innovations from cold-storage rooms and other smaller-scale installations. In his previous installations, Wolff developed a set of techniques for the control of coolth, humidity, ventilation, and the filtering of air for cleanliness. The New York Stock Exchange was unusual, as it was the first setting in which to bring these parameters together into a total system. This setting was also one of the first whose mechanically produced environment suffused the entire structure and its systems: "[A]ir was taken in at roof level, drawn down a shaft to the basement, and went through a filter of 5,400 square feet of cheesecloth hanging in a zigzag pattern. Exhaust generators that supplied the building's lighting system powered the refrigeration equipment. Brine from a basement tank was chilled and then passed through coils located between the cheesecloth filters and the blower."[13] Architecture was more than a container for environment; its interior spaces were reconfigured for the generation of this new environmental form. As a contribution to technological history, the stock exchange was an early large-scale installation of air cooling oriented toward work and outside industrial applications.[14]

In addition to having engineering significance, urbanistically the stock exchange was one of the first systems that directly addressed the production of a type of atmosphere to entangle with the physical and psychological effects of the enervated crowds of the City. The system at the stock exchange was not the first cooling system for large groups of people; earlier air-conditioning systems such as the one Wolff designed for Carnegie Hall and the system designed for the Chicago Auditorium building also cooled crowds. Yet, unlike the system at the stock exchange, these other early cooling systems cooled crowds at rest. The enervated crowd, as historians Jeffrey Schnapp and Matthew Tiews point out, is one of the key constructs of urban modernity, yet one that is rarely imagined or visualized inside.[15] In this sense, the stock exchange's system produced coolth in a building whose interior generated significantly more heat than external pressures. Today, this is what environmental engineers call an "internally loaded" building. With the exception of the auditoriums already mentioned, most early nonindustrial air-conditioning systems reacted to heat stresses *outside* of a building caused by radiation from direct sunlight and convection from neighboring structures. Whether we examine apartments, hospitals, museums, or other emerging institutions in the industrial city, the developers of these buildings often isolated their interiors as a response to the socionatural environment outside the structure. The production of air within them offered a counterpoint to the surrounding city. The engineering of the stock exchange presented a more complex relationship between body, interior, and city; interior space was both

Interior of New York Stock Exchange, 1910s. Library of Congress Prints and Photographs Division (LC-USZ62-94123).

counterpoint to the surrounding city and counterpoint to itself. As Cecil Elliott notes, "In New York's hot and muggy summer weather, the expanse of windows that opened into the trading room of George B. Post's design was responsible for about 25 percent of the heat in the room. But this was a small matter when compared with the heat generated by the bodies of around 1,000 anxious traders in the market, which contributed, at maximum condition, at least 66 percent of the design load."[16] More significantly, the environment generated in trading rooms was imagined as both a counter to the boisterous activity that occurred within trading rooms and as a facilitator of it. For their managers, workers could more easily maintain the stressful maneuvers required on the trading floor with the aid of comfort-conditioned air. In an era when collapsed traders became frequent on the trading-hall floor, the production of cool air supported the financial worker's labor.[17] Proponents of indoor-air engineering imagined this new form of urban environment as promoting efficiency, productivity, and, in many respects, "gentility" via the removal of sweat, the calming of nerves, and the promotion of individuality.[18] In other words, this produced environment generated a countersense to the enervated crowd's typical manifestations.

This interpretation of the stock exchange's interior environment must be seen in partial contrast to the maintenance of labor explored simultaneously in the European and American factory environment; in this latter effort, workers were maintained as "motors" limited by the exhaustive actions of repetitive tasks. Managers used ideas from Fordism, Taylorism, and the physiological sciences to propel a mechanistic image of the human body to ever-greater degrees of productivity and efficiency. As the historian Gail Cooper has noted, cooled environments were employed in the development of the human motor, keeping the factory and its products conditioned in temperature and humidity.[19] At the stock exchange, air systems were used to maintain workers' bodies, but these bodies were not conceptualized as machines. Rather, in the realm of financial trading, the workers of the stock exchange functioned as important facilitators of *communication* in financial markets. Their bodies were maintained to facilitate the smooth flow of information. The environmental innovations of the stock exchange promoted information flow between the communicators that formed the structure of market interactions. Such a concept would transfer, fifty years later, into the computer machinery that would form the new nodes of the international market in the 1970s and 1980s.

The image of the New York Stock Exchange as a space of uncanny activity matched with an attendant supportive interior environment continued more forcefully with the renovations of the hall in the 1940s and 50s, and in the proposals for a new and extensively renovated hall from the 1960s through the 1990s. By the 1960s, the trading floor required extensive renovation and rethinking as the New York Stock Exchange outgrew its original headquarters, and after several upgrades, its environmental systems required significant reengineering. In various proposals to both move and expand the stock exchange, the lively activity within the large space was increasingly presented in counterpoint to the surrounding neighborhood.[20] Reflecting tendencies in postwar modern architecture, the architect Richard Adler reinterpreted the trading room of the stock exchange as an arena-like space amid more neutral office buildings. I. M. Pei and Skidmore, Owings and Merrill both developed visions for the stock exchange in the early 1960s as large, open, Miesian spaces with office development above. In later proposals, such as Hardy Holtzman Pfeiffer's of 1996, the trading room was likened to the air-conditioned gardens and atria of Midtown East. In both types of proposals, the trading room appeared as a stable epicenter within an area of the City with an unpredictable financial future.

Whereas the renovations and proposals of the 1960s responded to the surrounding neighborhood, the renovations of the 1980s primarily responded to the increased crowding of traders and the increased computerization of trading. Not only did computers require physical space for their processors, cabling, and monitors, but they also produced excessive heat, adversely affecting the mechanical systems of the stock exchange. Such uses of computer machinery extended into other forms of office works as well, but trading was unique in the number of computers and monitors used by each financial-services worker. By 1980, the indoor environment of the New York Stock Exchange had reached a new level of intolerability because of the crowding of people and trading equipment. As Tim Carrington, a reporter for the *Wall Street Journal,* noted, "Traffic on the floor of the New York Stock Exchange is fast approaching gridlock. . . . As volume has crept upward, more traders and more machines have crowded the floor to handle it all. With space strained to capacity, executing a trade has become, as never before, a boisterous obstacle course. . . . Big Board officials are nervously scrambling to alleviate congestion and make the exchange ready for trading days when as many as 150 million shares could change hands."[21] A trader, William Higgins, noted ironically, "We don't protect our environment here like an industry does. . . . [W]e don't know about noise, light, air." In response to the often-intense heat of the trading floor from the activity of computers and traders, a floor messenger noted the specific health issues surrounding this form of work: "It's pushing and shoving and stamina. . . . In the summer, the squad population went from 110 to 85. . . . Our absentee rates were just atrocious."[22] Trading was cast as a fundamentally physical activity, adding to its ambiguous position and imagery as a type of labor. In addition to the environmental problems that accompanied computerization, the stock exchange was also losing vol-

Mock-up of computerized trading station, New York Stock Exchange. Copyright Bettmann/CORBIS.

ume to "off-site" computer trading conducted in neighboring buildings and corporations. The rise of trading outside the stock exchange was due to policies of deregulation during the presidency of Ronald Reagan, who worked with the U.S. Congress to enact laws that ceased oversight from a centralized trading market. The deregulations corresponded with a new level of development in New York City as the financial crisis of the mid- and late 1970s began to abate. The rise in the City's economy, the dispersion of trade, and its increased computerization helped set the conditions for the number and intensity of corporate-owned trading rooms concentrated in Lower Manhattan.[23]

COMPUTER ENVIRONMENTS

By the early 1980s, the frenetic activity of financial exchange had extended to the numerous trading halls being built throughout Lower Manhattan by financial-services companies. These new trading rooms, often located in monumental buildings or assemblages of buildings, were epicenters of computerized trading and large-scale cooling and data systems. Corporate managers, such as Ivan Boesky, located their trading operations within buildings with the largest floor plates, carving them out of vast building interiors that were not purpose-built for this activity, and thus often these programs were at odds with the interior architecture. The large number of traders was one issue, but the overhead air-conditioning systems that cooled computer machinery and the under-floor cabling systems that connected computerized trading forced companies to either squash floor heights down to intolerable levels or demolish floor plates.[24] Many of the postwar buildings in the Wall Street area contained massive floor plates by New York standards. Skidmore, Owings and Merrill's Chase Manhattan Bank (Gordon Bunshaft designer, 1963) was one of the first of these very large postwar buildings built in the Wall Street area. This building loomed over the much smaller prewar buildings in the area. Seven World Trade Center was also large and held floors of 48,000 square feet. But both buildings contained relatively narrow floor-to-floor heights; in November 1989, Solomon Brothers signed a lease with the developer Larry Silverstein to rebuild several floors of Seven World Trade Center as one of the first "very-large" trading rooms. Solomon Brothers worked with Skidmore, Owings and Merrill's architects to demolish several concrete-and-steel floors to create three new double-height trading rooms. Another center for the financial-services industry, 75 Park Place, contained 38,000- to 47,000-square-foot-office floors and additional rooms devoted to fiber-optic, microwave, and satellite communications. The computer-operations center for Shearson American Express had two-acre-size floors in the eight-story building for its computer operations center, which provided data links for American Express's financial-services division.[25] In the early 1980s, Merrill Lynch purchased the Skidmore, Owings and Merrill–designed One Liberty Plaza from American Steel Corporation, an iconic, massive tower completed in 1973. The building was intended as a showcase for steel construction and contained wide structural bays. But the managers of Merrill Lynch quickly realized that, to satisfy their trading-room needs, the raised floor and lowered ceiling would diminish the critical sense of site and acoustical quality that also form key aspects of trading floors.

The potential spatial problems were intimately related to the intense computerization of these spaces, but computerization also presented new problems in the atmospheric engineering of offices. Computers generated heat and required different combinations of cooling and humidity than people did. According to Paul Glickman, president of Glickman Design Group and a designer of trading rooms in the early 1980s, "Space isn't the only nettlesome problem that computerization has brought. . . . A personal computer generates about the same amount of heat as one human. As computers arrive at more work stations, the heat and air-conditioning load rises, often above the capacity of the existing cooling and electrical systems."[26] Though computers began to appear throughout offices in Manhattan in the late 1960s and 1970s, because of its concentration in trading centers, the financial-trading industry was one of the first industries to realize the scope of multiple computers installed in relatively low spaces. Glickman was asked to explore the cooling system for Bear Stearns & Co.'s 20,000-square-foot trading room in Lower Manhattan. The space was used by three hundred people and contained a heavy load of computer equipment. The firm was forced to add forty tons of air-conditioning equipment just to keep the trading room habitable, an unprecedented load and engineering expense in the early 1980s. Carl Hastrom, a trader at Bear Stearns, proclaimed, "[M]ost first-class office buildings that were built 10 years ago don't supply enough electrical power or air-conditioning (to accommodate wholesale computerization)."[27] In both spatial and environmental terms, earlier modernist spaces could not easily accommodate this emerging office labor; the trading room demanded a partial rethinking of interior office architecture.

As trading rooms demanded reassessments of office design, they also demanded reconsiderations of interior environments and the parameters used to measure them. In addition to assessment of the overall load requirements for air-conditioning people in trading rooms, these spaces also demanded unique parameters for the cooling and humidification of computer equipment, independent of its human operators. As we explored in chapter 2, the comfort zone of 70 degrees and 40–50 percent humidity was an ideal perpetuated throughout the American office building. The comfort zone was hypothesized as the optimum temperature and humidity for clerical work. Because of the intense activity of trading, this work was not strictly clerical, as defined in engineering literature; additionally, computers in the 1970s and early 1980s often required colder temperatures to operate properly, and some, surprisingly, required higher levels of humidity.[28] Via trading rooms, the "subject" of air systems would shift into a more hybrid form, away from a sole orientation on human comfort toward a mixture of human and mechanical. This conceptual problem necessitated increasingly coordinated forms of expertise; both the intense heat generation of computers and the hybrid needs of people and machines necessitated more precise connections between data engineers and climate engineers. Between 1980 and 1987, mechanical-engineering firms such as Flack and Kurtz worked with new telecommunications firms to rethink the indoor atmosphere of their financial-services-clients' trading rooms, effectively building the indoor atmosphere of computerized trading. Early studies established more concrete connections between data and atmosphere, but they also resulted in the reconstruction of the indoor atmosphere of buildings to be better aligned with the market itself. Because computer activity was higher within spaces and times of intense trading, the comfort zone was partially rethought. Instead of conditioning the air relative to the number or density of occupants or the seasons, the conditioning of the air also had to be aligned with the peaks and valleys in daily trading activity reflected in the intensity of computer use.[29] Thus, the traders inhabited an environment within which they were but one of its objects and subjects. The atmosphere within buildings was always a material artifact and a representation of optimum human comfort and performance. Now, this atmosphere was transforming into a representation of the dynamics of the market itself.

Finally, the notion of the trading room as a type of late-modern computerized and environmentalized space extended into attitudes about its interior organization that further influenced its potential architecture. Compared to the office interiors designed earlier by Skidmore, Owings and Merrill, among others, the interiors of trading rooms were not envisioned as spaces of hierarchical organization. Skidmore, Owings and Merrill's hallmark interiors of the 1960s, such as those for the Union Carbide Building in Midtown Manhattan (1964), typically entailed a large secretarial "pool" surrounded by executive and managerial offices. These surrounding spaces generally became shaped through modular construction systems to further enable hierarchical distinctions between executives. According to Adrian Forty, the computerization of office work in the 1960s actually led to an increase in the hierarchical interior architecture of office buildings. Cubicles in the 1960s arose to house computer analysts and other computer-using nonexecutive managers within the former secretarial pool.[30] But within trading rooms, hierarchical expression was eliminated in favor of a more flattened interior architecture. The Latourian sociologists Daniel Beunza Ibáñez and David Stark analyzed the new spatial formations of trading rooms in Manhattan and called this formation a new type of office "heterarchy" that enabled communication to move quickly and expeditiously throughout the space. This heterarchical space became shaped through the open architecture of its rooms and the desk, which was envisioned as a continuous, almost isomorphic flat space upon which traders operated computer machinery. Within such a space, "a sharp contrast to the conventional environment of corporate America[,] . . . information roams freely."[31] The trading rooms' environmentalization appears not only in the openness of the space and the intensity of atmospheric engineering within it but also in the interrelationships of traders within this space that suggest the heterarchical absorption of traders within the market.

The links between these spaces' interiors (as architectural and atmospheric forms), the function of financial markets, and their potential urban meaning appears most vividly in the design of the trading rooms within the World Financial Center. The World Financial Center, designed by Cesar Pelli and Associates (1982–88) and developed by Olympia and York, consisted of four very large towers of varying heights, each composed of a stone-curtain-wall base and mirrored-curtain-wall upper floors and all crowned with an iconic, geometrically abstract top. The towers were joined together via sky bridges, and at its center the complex contained the Winter Garden, a large indoor atrium similar to those in Midtown East except for its much larger size. The project reworked earlier master plans for the site by the New York State Planning Commission and was partially based on Pelli's sleek, silver-skinned, megastructural competition entry for an office complex in Vienna, Austria. The World Financial Center would become a symbol of corporate postmodernity as well as of the new scale of the financial-services industry in the City.

Before the complex was fully complete, American Express, Solomon Brothers, and Merrill Lynch began using the towers' spaces. They installed new high-tech trading floors filled at times with more than one thousand traders within its various towers. These interiors contained significant residual areas for telecommunications and environmental technology within spaces filled with traders in constant contact with each other and with various international economic centers. Reflecting broader trends, American Express, Merrill Lynch, and Solomon Brothers spent approximately one-half of their budgets on various technical services, an enormous

World Financial Center, 1987. Courtesy of Pelli Clarke Pelli Architects.

shift from the build-outs of earlier corporate-interiors projects. The new expense was due partly to the actual costs of telecommunications equipment and partly to the corresponding increase in cooling loads to keep computer equipment running within acceptable temperature ranges. Both Merrill Lynch and American Express relied on assemblages of technologies that both provided the raw material of trading and promoted their traders as being at the forefront of financial-information exchange. The spaces provided by Olympia and York, Cesar Pelli and Associates, and interior architects Skidmore, Owings and Merrill and Swanke Hayden Connell Architects specifically enhanced these types of financial institutions. Pelli's office developed buildings uniquely suited to the financial-trading sectors; they contained enormous floor plates—40,000 square feet, on average, far more than the more normal 25,000 square feet in New York City development.[32] This enabled the gathering of huge numbers of traders in one space, which corporations preferred. Several of the floors contained 25-foot-high ceilings, which further facilitated the ability to stack trading desks in large rooms in theaterlike arrangements. The amount of power and refrigeration necessary to cool these floors was significant; not since the development of the World Trade Center had such an energy-intensive interior scheme been devised in New York City. Although the adjacent World Trade Center comprised much larger buildings, the telecommunications equipment at the World Financial Center forced the provision of an additional 2 million cubic feet of refrigeration, far more than any other office building of the time.[33]

Of the interiors in the World Financial Center, those developed by Merrill Lynch best illustrate the new shifts. Merrill Lynch occupied buildings 2 and 4 (also known as the North Tower) at the World Financial Center, and its presence there drew additional tenants, as the company was the United States' largest brokerage house. In 1986, at the commencement of the firm's term in the World Financial Center, the 102-year-old brokerage company was the biggest dealer in commercial stock, with trades totaling $60 billion; the leader in municipal securities; and the manager of the world's largest mutual-fund portfolios. Its total revenues in 1986 reached $10.9 billion. And it was "the only firm that literally trade[d] 24 hours a day because of its seats on the pivotal New York, Toronto, London, and Tokyo stock exchanges." The interior design for Merrill Lynch at the

World Financial Center reflected the various superlatives of the company; it totaled 4.2 million square feet, making it the largest single corporate-interiors project in the United States and "the most complex in terms of technology and management."[34] The nerve centers of the new "twenty-four-hour" interiors developed by Merrill Lynch's designers—Skidmore, Owings and Merrill—were the trading rooms, built on raked floors stacked above areas of almost equal size that contained the various necessary telecommunications networks and refrigeration equipment. The scale of the corporate trading rooms at Merrill Lynch's World Financial Center were unprecedented and quickly became dubbed as a new type: the "Mega trading room."[35]

These trading rooms are on the fifth, seventh, and ninth floors of the North Tower. Only recently decommissioned, in 2009, after Merrill Lynch's Bank of America takeover, they have nonetheless become icons of American office design because of their scale, simplicity, and late-modern aesthetics.[36] Skidmore, Owings and Merrill built these spaces primarily to emphasize the presence of computers and the sight lines, and to satisfy the wiring demands and refrigeration loads of the spaces. The interiors were almost gallerylike in their height, abstraction, and internalization, with deep external walls that deemphasized the surrounding urban views and a mute color palette repeated on the walls and the ceiling of recessed fluorescent lighting. A partner at Skidmore, Owings and Merrill commented that the noticeable height of the room had a palliative effect: "When the activity becomes frenetic, a large volume helps to dissipate the kinetic energy."[37] Reflecting the general "heterarchy" of late-modern trading rooms, the interior structure that surrounded the work spaces was rendered as a stable background to labor rather than a more forceful representation of the dynamics of changeability in corporate offices. The room appeared to be a container for labor instead of a "system" that either represents differences in power or responds to its dynamic transformations.

The sense of architectural calm within this space contrasted with the significant amounts of wiring and environmental controls that laced the interior together. *Engineering News Record*, a journal of building technology, noted that the Merrill Lynch trading rooms contained seventy-five thousand miles of copper wire and two-hundred-thousand-line-capacity telephones—the equivalent capacity of a small city. The needs of telecommunications alone made up 20 percent of the total budget, and cabling was 20 percent of the construction budget. The cabling and chiller needs were so intense that internal cores measuring fifteen by twenty feet (about the area of four elevator cabs) were filled with data and chiller pipes.[38] On the trading floor, each trader sat at one of fourteen hundred trading stations that were rendered as continuous units extending through the space; each trading station contained "conglomerations of up to eight different screens, phones and jumbled wiring." Each trader was provided with a veritable command center that included "a British Telecom Centel 13" touch screen with 40 telephone numbers per screen page; a hands free communications device, based on the European Erickson equipment, that connects the Merrill field offices of the trader (eventually London will be included); two handsets; a speed calling program with direct private lines to the exchange floors, and a 9-pac Rich video switch and monitor display

View of main trading room, Merrill Lynch, Skidmore, Owings and Merrill, 1988. Photograph by Peter Aaron/OTTO.

Typical trader desk at Merrill Lynch, 1988. Photograph by Peter Aaron/OTTO.

system operated by a single keyboard that allows traders access to a total of 8 market information services such as Quotron, Reuters or the Merrill Lynch data library."[39] These descriptions are mentioned at length in order to convey the novelty of such a large amount of technology concentrated in an individual worker's space. Merrill Lynch positioned its traders' connectivity as a factor in the corporation's ascendancy and resilience in the shifting financial markets of the City. The company claimed that the technology and custom connectivity to various infrastructural systems helped it retain profits and traders during dips in the markets and the deregulation of the United States' financial markets.[40]

In addition to the details already mentioned, each console also contained its own air-conditioning equipment in order to reduce the load to the climate system of the trading-floor interior. At Merrill Lynch, industrial and interior designers reconceived the office desk as a global command station integrated into the building's environmental systems. Where most office interiors' mechanical systems produced atmospheres for human comfort, the technologically rich spaces of Merrill Lynch and American Express were unique in that the mechanical engineers who designed them built them to keep the telecommunications equipment as stable as the human occupants in the building. Expenditures on such systems were most apparent in the Merrill Lynch building, where an entire floor was devoted to telecommunications equipment. And each floor featured what was then the novelty of having telecommunications centers replete with their own climate systems, in addition to the more traditional mechanical "cores" that were more standard features of office buildings.

In an interview, the mechanical engineer Norman Kurtz noted that the interface between telecommunications engineering and HVAC engineering formed the technological conditions that facilitated these massive trading halls. As a result, "[m]echanical systems had to be upgraded to handle heat rejected from the crowded technology and trading floors. The equipment alone consumes 12 to 20 watts per sq ft, plus 2 watts per sq ft for lighting, compared with a total of 4 watts per sq ft in an ordinary Merrill Lynch office. Chillers for an additional 2,250 tons of cooling capacity found a penthouse home on the tower's roof. Keeping them company is a 7,500-kw emergency generator system that has already kept trading operations alive during a brownout."[41] Thus, building on the role of trading halls as central sites in the production of sophisticated interior environments, the new trading halls of Merrill Lynch more specifically positioned the generation of coolth as a significant aspect of the communication flows that form market activity. If in earlier chapters we witnessed a variety of urban actors positioning the architectural environment as a form entangled with our understanding of space and objects, in the trading rooms we see the architectural environment used to promote the physical conduits of information flow—people and computers—that form key aspects of the international financial network.

These links between architectural environment and financial networks are significant, and they further counteract any lingering notion we may have regarding the "immateriality" of the international financial markets. In her work on "global" cities, the critic Saskia Sassen has noted that markets are made of matter and labor; they are composed of underground communications networks and various other built forms made in and through human work, like earlier economic forms.[42] Through the analysis presented here, we might additionally understand the market as something that contains built socionatural forms. This is not necessarily hidden from us, but, like the communications networks of the market, it also requires a historical geography to describe. The seemingly ephemeral market of late-modern New York was rooted in an increased engineering and industrializing of building structure and interior space, manifested in a type of climatic form. Via an understanding of the trading-room environment, we realize that the market is hardly ephemeral; rather, it involves the production of environmental epicenters in global cities such as New York, London, Tokyo, and Frankfurt that are physically and urbanistically prominent.

SPLINTERED ATMOSPHERES

The activity and environment within the trading rooms in Lower Manhattan became increasingly legible to the City's public on October, 19, 1987, "Black Monday," when the Dow Jones Industrial Average (DJIA) dropped in one of the most dramatic profit losses in the history of the American and international stock markets. At a loss of 22.68% of the DJIA overall value, the drop was, at that time, the second largest in the history of the U.S. stock market. In addition, markets in Hong Kong lost 45.8% of their value, followed by Australia, 41.8%; the United Kingdom, 26.4%; and Canada, 22.5%. The crash of 1987 tested the new technological trading-floor assemblages and their ability to respond to market crises and panics. In the financial reporting that forms the core impression of trading floors, these spaces and their predecessors were often imagined as sites where society produced, responded to, and often resolved financial crises. New York City stock-market panics of 1792, 1837, 1857, 1865–69, 1873, 1884, 1893–95, 1901, 1907, 1929, and 1962 often revolved around depictions of trading-floor activity and its ability to manage enormous sell-offs quickly and expeditiously.[43] Additionally, the functioning of these spaces in times of extramarket crises—riots, blackouts, and natural disasters—also forms core images of a city's and a region's financial stability. For example, the critical maintenance of the New York financial sector's electrical network first emerged during the blackout of 1981, the first major blackout since the inception of computerized trading. That blackout hit lower New York City during a day of exceptionally heavy trading, testing the ability of computers, traders, and mechanical engineers. As a building manager for the financial services conveyed, "Computers are difficult to maintain in a blackout not only because they draw heavy amounts of electricity themselves, but also because their sensitive natures require a steady stream of air-conditioning to keep them from becoming overheated."[44] As a result of this blackout, engineers developed backup computerized data systems and "hardened" air-conditioning systems that would respond to a variety of infrastructural, natural, and economic challenges. Engineers proclaimed that the indoor environments they produced in response to the event overcame the crisis, or at least participated in the mediation of the crisis.

The 1987 panic was unique in that it was the first cataclysmic market event in the age of complete computerized trade. Where earlier panics were hypothetically allayed with a steady flow of information from the financial media to buyers and sellers, the panic of 1987 engaged with the need to maintain flows of information and the health of computer equipment and the environmental systems used to maintain it.[45] Yet discourse on the panic of 1987 was further complicated by debates regarding whether the smooth flowing of machinery had mitigated the panic or caused the panic. A middle-class American public with increasing amounts of investments flowing into trading centers like lower New York questioned whether computer programs that automatically sold shares with little human intervention caused the collapse of the market's value. Investment companies argued that such automatic trades, called "program trades," enabled their traders to more instantly respond to the demands of their clients, keeping financial-trading companies profitable during tumultuous market activity. The panic of 1987 was the first where the ability to simultaneously maintain digital flows, the traders' environment, and the necessary environment for computer performance was advanced as a critical project by the financial-services industry.

Because of the challenges of maintaining their computer operations, financial-services companies in New York City such as Merrill Lynch argued that the complexity and internationalism of computerized trading demanded a new relationship between their operations and the City's infrastructural systems. As the World Financial Center was being constructed, Merrill Lynch demanded that the City facilitate custom regional relationships that would enable its operations in the World Financial Center to enjoy an unequal level of "premium" infrastructure provision. This would further the connectivity of its workers to global communications, and would mitigate natural and economic disasters. As Merrill Lynch was the largest trader of New York City's municipal securities, the development of custom infrastructural links merely mirrored other economic benefits the firm reaped from its existent relationships with the municipality. Both Merrill Lynch's and American Express's corporate negotiators demanded additional services for data, power, and climate-control equipment from the City that would further aid the companies' development as world leaders in financial trading. As *Interior* magazine's profile of the firms' new technologically outfitted interiors noted,

> Since financial institutions literally run on power—power to fuel communications and data processing systems—one crucial demand was to build in a power supply that was clean, continuous and reliable in the event of a black out. At the same time, the cost of the huge power load should be as economical as possible. Both buildings [towers 2 and 4] were upgraded . . . by installing six 950kv generators in the North Tower, a UPS system to keep

> power clean, and the addition of cellular deck to the rest of the North Tower. Refrigeration capacity for 2 million square feet was installed to supplement O&Y's central plant. One benefit, which lowers unit price and reduces main-duct size is the 13,000 volts that Con ED supplies to the WFC—instead of the usual 480 volts. Two telephone systems using fiber, NY Telephone and Teleport Communications, a Merrill Lynch subsidiary, provide a 50% communications redundancy at no additional cost.[46]

These sites of customized and intensified infrastructure were connected to other similar sites, particularly the trading centers in the financial districts of London and Tokyo. Such interconnections and customizations both ensured protection against the potential problems of these cities' infrastructural systems and enabled a never-ending, twenty-four-hour trading cycle between these cities and these cities' hierarchy within world markets.[47]

In the 1990s, the geographers Stephen Graham and Simon Marvin examined the infrastructural transformations staged at World Financial Center. They included this building as exemplary of a larger phenomenon they labeled "splintered spaces." These are precincts of cities that have customized and isolated infrastructure. For Graham and Marvin, splintered spaces reject modernist concepts of urban totality and integration; infrastructure and space become scaled, relative to the quality of infrastructural connections and the relationship of space to a surrounding city.[48] At the World Financial Center, a "premium" level of infrastructure is used to maintain the computer equipment and the traders who form the essential elements of the world financial market. Such hierarchical distributions of infrastructure typify the splintering of urban space: at the financial center, we see the intensification of air and communications equipment, but such partitioning of infrastructure can reach an intense cruelty when it extends to far more urgent needs, such as the quality of or access to urban water in cities.

Linking the ideas of Graham and Marvin with additional concepts on the urban development of socionature, we might see the trading rooms of the World Financial Center as something more than just a splintered space. Rather, we witness a form of splintered atmosphere (or environment) that facilitates the efficiency and protection of market subjects and objects. Like the parks that exist outside financial-services companies, this splintered atmosphere offers financial workers an experience of urban socionature unhinged from the immediate city. Yet, unlike these parks (and Graham and Marvin's own analysis of air-conditioning), this form of socionature provides more than just a bubble of human comfort in the city. This atmosphere was more than simply the environment outside brought inside. As we have seen here and in the preceding chapters, the construction of these seemingly disconnected environments represents a reconstruction of environment itself that ultimately links the conditions of subjects to the patterns of global economic trade. Extending and radicalizing the earliest transformations of urban air staged in the New York Stock Exchange, the environments developed for trade both situated workers within a rebuilt atmosphere that better enabled them and the machinery to perform the communications work of the market, and insulated them from the environmental and financial stresses that acted upon the City.

THE MONUMENTAL ATMOSPHERE

The splintered atmospheres of the World Financial Center also entered into more specific and representational urban dialogues with the original (and important) conditions of its surrounding landscape. The World Financial Center was built on a portion of a large strip of landfill that the conspiratorially minded anthropologist Robert Fitch claimed "buried" the working-class industrial harbor under the soil excavated from the construction of the World Trade Center.[49] In the mid-1970s, this stretch of land was nicknamed "the Beach" for its sandy and barren character. Numerous attempts to develop this site failed, and from the mid- to late 1970s, it was used as an impromptu beach and a site where demonstrations against nuclear arms were held, as well as displays of experimental forms of art and urban dance. By the late 1970s, this undeveloped and contentious site had effectively become a people's park where arts performances and various political demonstrations were staged. In both its state as a type of urban nature and in the activity that was staged there, it could not have been more different from the municipal plans for the area. State officials working for the Battery Park Authority labeled the Beach a "barren desert." Such a name emphasized its empty, undeveloped quality as well as the dust from the Beach, which often transgressed its urban lot.

As the World Financial Center moved toward completion in the late 1980s, the mirrored-glass walls of these new buildings and their interiors emerged in sharp contrast to the windy and dusty spaces of the remaining stretches of the desertlike beach. The two visions of the City and its future environment could not be more different.[50] By the late 1980s, when the center was complete, the remainder of the Beach to the north and south was considered a veritable wasteland. To the south, where it remained unsodded, it created dunes and dust storms, much to the torment of the people who recently moved into this area of Lower Manhattan and/or who worked at the World Financial Center.[51] The interior of the World Financial Center rose above and against this landscape, and if it offered a splintered environment that supported the City's position in world trade, it also offered a more symbolic counterenvironment to its particular surrounding

Battery Park landfill in mid-1970s. Battery Park City Authority.

Rock Steady performance, Susan Rethorst and Dancers, Creative Time's Art on the Beach, New York City, July 1982. Photograph copyright Robin Holland.

historical landscape. The Beach presented a uniquely late-modern form of environmental pestilence, the literal atmospheric production of a prime yet completely undeveloped Manhattan site. In contrast, the World Financial Center contained an atmosphere of pure capital productivity.[52]

The potential urban relationships and meaning of the World Financial Center's splintered environment also appear within the architectural grammar of the buildings themselves. The buildings contained powerful rhetorical architectural elements that articulated ideas about the autonomy of their environment, the historical City, and the architecture of economic markets and financial globalization. These included the smooth curtain wall of mirrored glass and stone wrapping the interiors, which narratively emerged from a more historicist base; the Winter Garden, the glass-and-steel public space at the center of the development, which evoked nineteenth-century gallerias and housed two rows of palm trees;[53]

and, finally, the iconic pyramidal and domed mansard and ziggurat tops that completed the towers. For some, the architectural language of the World Financial Center typified the postmodernization of the skyscraper; the iconic tops of the buildings, on top of more abstracted towers, illustrated rapprochements between the representational legibility of traditional architecture and the more abstract language of modernist corporate form. The roof forms and the massing of the towers clearly evoked the architectural language of earlier skyscrapers, such as the Woolworth Building and its image of American corporatism.[54]

For Mario Gandelsonas, who examined the World Financial Center and the Pacific Design Center (Los Angeles, 1972) in an essay for Cesar Pelli's 1990 monograph, Pelli's World Financial Center represented the ascendancy of the spaces of the global market in a struggling and deindustrializing city. In his writing on the World Financial Center, Gandelsonas wrote that the historicist glass-and-stone skins were a series of "'jackets'

World Financial Center under construction. The remnants of "the Beach" can be seen at left. Photograph copyright Brian Rose.

. . . exhibiting, undressing: . . . [u]nveiling the representation of the basic [grid] system implied by all the facades of the building." These grids reveal the endless abstract space of the floors of the complex and hence the structure of abstracted corporate space. The tops were a provisional system of representation, a momentary cap to contain the potentially infinite space of the global market symbolized by the towers' immense size: these tops are "caps that stop the buildings" in their vertical movement. "Why does the movement need to be stopped?" Gandelsonas asked. "Because the towers inside imply an infinitely tall building."[55] Gandelsonas argued that the architectural grammar of enormous, abstract, gridded spaces situated within "the financial center of the world" enable us to experience the "colossal" reach and scale of "globalization." Evoking the philosophy

The World Financial Center in dialogue with the City's architecture. Library of Congress Prints and Photographs Division, Carol M. Highsmith Archive (LC-DIG-highsm-15610).

of Derrida, Gandelsonas argued that the colossal sense of the World Financial Center is a "qualification" of something otherwise unseen—in this case, the economy of the global city. Gandelsonas further argued that the World Financial Center links this colossal aesthetic to the mechanics of urban restructuring. Unlike those of the earlier, equally massive World Trade Center, Gandelsonas argued that the roof forms and tower shafts of the World Financial Center suggested ways to bring the potentially monstrous and abstract space of globalized financial office labor into a dialogue with the unique and historical grammar of Manhattan's early twentieth-century skyscrapers. Pelli's buildings allude to the stepped and crowned language of Manhattan's historical skyscrapers, they suggest the march of these skyscrapers into the abandoned and once industrialized waterfront, and they also suggest a symbolic waterfront "gateway" into the financial heart of the global financial capital. For Gandelsonas, the World Financial

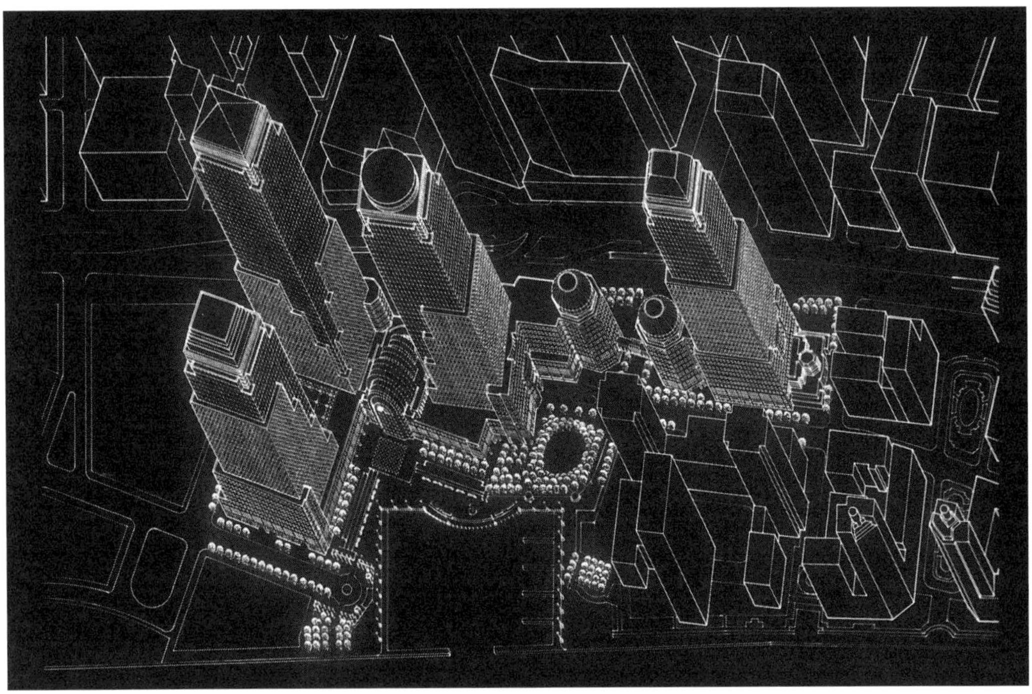

Axonometric drawing of World Financial Center, Cesar Pelli and Associates. Courtesy of Pelli Clarke Pelli Architects.

Center situates an immensity of space within systems of urban legibility and transformation.

But in interpreting these buildings' representational grammar, the trading rooms within them, and their largely splintered urban relationships, we must note one final and seemingly more simplistic aspect of them. Turning to the literal, material content of the tops, we realize that the most pronounced and visible elements of the World Financial Center—the dome, pyramid, mansard, and ziggurat—house machinery, the enormous air-conditioning chillers that cool the trading rooms within these buildings. The dome and ziggurat of the Merrill Lynch buildings contained rooms that briefly held some of the largest air-conditioning plants on corporate buildings in Manhattan.[56] These large housings, in tandem with the skin of glass that emerged from its more traditionalist base, and set against the surrounding and strange landscape, envision a monumental representation of environmental production within this city as much as spatial legibility and historicization. Reflecting on the design of these buildings, Cesar Pelli wrote, "The grid of stone expresses the modular nature of the undifferentiated office space. . . . [T]he crowns are enclosures of mechanical equipment, expressing thus that they are not of the same nature as the office space."[57] And for Pelli, modern interior space is also conditioned space, as he wrote in the same essay: "[B]uildings today are not just shelters but are complete containers of controlled environments requiring continuity of the enclosing environment."[58] In effect, Pelli's seemingly postmodern towers actually entail the aims of modernist legibility but exaggerate them into a late-modern effect. For Pelli, the towers are neither solely historicist representations nor purely empty signs that simply stop a seemingly endless space; they carefully articulate an environmentalized modernity. Aligning the material reality of the tops with Pelli's statements and Gandelsonas's careful analysis, we might understand the towers as a representation of production; the colossal postindustrial atmosphere that emerges from the tops of the buildings captures and restructures an important socionatural site of this city.[59] Thus, in addition to providing a planning grammar for the global city and its interior spaces, we might also understand the World Financial Center as giving form to a system of production intimately related to the aims of Manhattan's globalization. Here, at the World Financial Center, the late-modern

The distinctive "tops" of the World Financial Center. Photograph by Peter Aaron/OTTO.

atmosphere becomes reified—literally given ideological and instrumental shape—within a specific, reurbanizing postindustrial landscape. Physical maintenance, communications, and stability move through an atmosphere that enables "trade" and that becomes a monumental presence in Manhattan.

CONCLUSION

Returning to some of the theoretical concepts that move through this book, recall how cities generate environments oriented toward the maintenance of specific formations and the political economies that move through these institutional structures. In the context of Manhattan's history, this process extends from the creation of the City's water network, a site of health and investment, to the types of interior environments examined throughout this book. In the trading halls of lower Manhattan, the development of environments in trading rooms might be one of our most concise illustrations of the socionatural forms that emerge from financial epicenters. Most examinations of the socionatural environments surrounding these corporate spaces concentrate on privatization, the passing of previously public parks or green spaces into the purview of the corporation and the resulting forms of control and surveillance this process entails. Instead of focusing on this particular phenomenon in this chapter, we went inside, reflecting on how the production of the indoor environment—its atmosphere—entangles with key aspects of financial trading and its representation: ideas of workplace health, architectural expression, new ideas regarding workplace technology and systems, the interaction and structure of global markets, and the crises that often grip financial-market centers. Financial-services trading rooms were built to specifically link aspects of human productivity with the specific agenda of financial trading.

In previous chapters, we witnessed how the production of architectural environments interacted with transformations staged within New York. They appeared as forms of protection, stewarding the growth of plants and the preservation and conservation of objects. And in each, we saw how these aspects of the architectural environment link a particular form of socionature with a particular institutional force and an emerging and older economic order. In the trading rooms, we continue to see how the City's environments become remade in relation to emerging economies and crisis particular to New York City and yet oriented toward the maintenance of key subjects and objects of late-modern urbanization and globalization. Through their indoor architectural environment, the trading rooms link the desire for human comfort and the ideals of communications that structure market interaction. Here, we see the literal atmosphere of these spaces as a physical understructure to the flows of capital that centered here in the 1970s and 1980s and that moved from city to city. Finally, the centrality of this environment, the manner in which it sits at the center of the financial theater of globalization, became integrated into forms of architectural and urban representation. At the World Financial Center, historicist architectural grammars that appear to refer to Manhattan's economic history actually further articulate environmental relationships and instruments of late-modern environmental and geographical relationships. For Mario Gandelsonas, the towers extended the City into the previously untapped spaces of its waterfront, thereby signifying the ascendancy of postindustrial corporate space over the former industrial space of the harbor. But, in understanding the forms of atmospheric production in these spaces, we can further understand this conquest of space as a socionatural one as well. Here, a powerful postindustrial environment supplants an earlier industrial and postindustrial "barren" landscape in the City. If the World Financial Center was a gateway of the global city, it was also an immense site in which this global city's architectural environment announces itself as the socionatural support of "the financial center of the world."

EPILOGUE

Reimagining Maintenance Environments

THE MAINTENANCE ENVIRONMENT was far more than a passive background of support to New York City's financial and physical restructuring. Throughout this book, we have witnessed how the maintenance environments of New York helped negotiate specific environmental pressures acting on this city while ushering in the geographical and economic relationships, objects, and even subjects of the City's emerging global, urban spatial order. Such a relationship did not simply bypass the older and important forms of nature that were produced in this city; it often reengaged, reworked, repurposed, and expanded them. As architecture took on these roles, its late-modern interior took on a new representative quality. Within the megastructural and air-rights projects of the 1960s and 1970s, architects, developers, and municipal leaders reworked the socioeconomic manifestations of gentrification into an environmental analogue. The interior environments of architecture evoked both notions of protection and the potentially more hostile external urban environment within a context of transforming urban governance. Within the corporate atria of Midtown East, more literal forms of urban nature became newly aligned with the biophysical qualities of emerging corporate spaces yet simultaneously reawakened older metropole–antipode relationships. The interior environment of buildings suggested a new geographically representative quality that was evoked by the exotic plants within it. Museums became elaborate sites of capture within which their environments became reimagined as the safe haven for objects of world heritage. In the case of the Metropolitan Museum of Art, these new museological maintenance spaces also became entangled with the older politics of nature production in the City. Finally, the trading halls of the World Financial Center rose over the old industrial-era landscape of labor, producing a new atmosphere for a form of labor tied to Manhattan's role as a global financial center.

Within these spaces, institutions, architects, and landscape architects linked something as simple as the air within buildings to concepts and concerns moving through the transformations of this city: physical protection from pollution, the future growth of nature, the aggregation and conservation of cultural objects, and the communication of markets. Architects fashioned this new atmosphere and the silvery skins of the late-modern architecture that contained it into a spatial grammar for an environmentalized vision of a present and future New York. The monumental architecture that rose in Central Park and along the former industrial harbor of the City was often a monument to the environments within it. All of the spaces examined in this book suggest complex dialogues between acts of maintenance, the historical role of nature production and architecture in this city, and a postindustrial, emerging global sociocultural economy. When we consider the physical artifacts of emerging global epicenters, we must also consider the particular presence of these types of interiors and their particular power. When we consider the particular power and representative quality of the monumental buildings that rose in New York City during its restructuring, we must now also consider a certain environment that appeared with that restructuring, an environment that further illustrates architecture's alignment with fomenting contemporary urbanization.

New York City was the urban epicenter of postwar postindustrialization in the United States, but, as the case of New York City's interiors demonstrates, what we understand as a "postindustrial" city, its spaces and architecture, may be anything but. Postindustrialization suggests a lack of industrial forms of management and material that, if present, appear in the hardware and physical dynamics of the equipment, largely computerized, that illustrates the larger economic turn. Nevertheless, other, dissenting views of postindustrialization suggest additional possible ways to interpret the economic shifts of this era and its physical manifestations and interconnections. In his reflections on the 1960s and 1970s and their emerging postindustrial economies, the economist Ernst Mandel theorized the pervasive industrialization that underlines the experience of a presumably postindustrial urban society.[1] Mandel wrote that late capitalism engendered a "generalized" and "universal industrialization" in which various aspects of industrialization extended into more and more productive territory. Under late capitalism, the management of time, intense specialization, and parcelization of the space of labor now extended far outside the sites of commodity production, where they were once based. As one example, Mandel cited the reconstruction of agriculture as an arena that became more intensely industrialized in and through the "green" revolution of the postwar era with the introduction of chemical engineering. Here, the transformation of living matter into an increasingly datafied and biologically reworked form illustrates an invidious industrial mentality.

This Mandelian sense of pervasive industrialization offers one final lens through which we may understand maintenance as an architectural and environmental form. Meta-industrialization extends well past the industrial production that goes into the spaces we have examined, their literal incorporation of products of industry—aluminum skins, mirrored glass, and mechanical equipment—their seemingly vast interiors, and the presence of labor. It extends as well into the conception of specific forms of environmental space that move throughout this book. As we have witnessed, the interior architectural environment increasingly became a totalizing system of production as it was reworked physically and representationally into the socioeconomic structure of New York City. Various programs became laced into these environments. Such productions extended well past a "comfort zone" into new alignments between the parameters of interior environments and the specific agenda of New York's municipality, institutions, and corporations. As we have witnessed, this expansion of modern management into the interior climate of buildings had further implications for urban antipodes. The development of agriculture, culture, and labor also became remade in and through the fabrication of late-modern interior environments.

Thus, the expansion of maintenance environments not only entails their reproduction in the architecture of contemporary global cities but also involves other, less clearly connected phenomena, such as the way they become ensnared in the intensification of agricultural development and the displacement of cultural treasures in the global South. Through Mandel's concept of hyperindustrialization, we are left with a historical understanding of the maintenance environment as something that involves a reworking of all environments. Rather than simply being troubled by the sheer ubiquity of these spaces, as some architects urge, we might more carefully examine how this environment becomes endlessly reshaped as a representation of power, an expansive environment with urban implications that stretch outside architecture that is nonetheless linked and concentrated within specific urban sites and urban economies. The maintenance environment suggests a pervasive refashioning of space, labor, and culture both within and outside its literal interiors.

As these environments become a dominant form of socionatural production, governments, architects, and institutions have developed responses to these environments as an urban reality. Today, in cities such as New York, Chicago, Tokyo, and London, responses to these spaces extend to new urban and extra-urban crises such as the impacts of global warming, depletion of energy resources, environmental exposure, and terrorism. Buildings have become as much a reexamination of the architectural environment, in environmentalist, green, and health-based critiques concerned with sick-building syndrome, as they were once reexaminations of earlier forms of urban nature. Contemporary critiques of the pervasiveness of these environments are not just concerned with instrumental problems or health; they also appear within disciplinary writings examining the very status of global architecture. Neophenomenologists such as Kenneth Frampton bemoan the loss of climatic geographical connection within global forms of architectural space, whereas the architect and theorist Rem Koolhaas, who operates from a completely different theoretical viewpoint, critiques the pervasive, conditioned environment that moves through what he calls "junkspace."[2] These authors share a view that these environments appear to be a type of all-consuming space with impacts on the City as a site of public activity. In his essay "Junkspace," Koolhaas examined the ubiquity of the conditioned interior, its often monumental scale, and its commercial orientation that, by the late twentieth century, had become the dominant architectural experience of every global city. Commenting on the spread of massive office towers, global museums, convention centers, and the interiors of enormous airports in Asia and Europe, he declared, "Air-conditioning has launched the endless building. . . . Because it costs money, is no longer free, conditioned space inevitably becomes conditional space."[3] The environment within buildings is a representation of a rampant late-modern capitalization of space and its subjects. But if the environment within buildings has become a Mandelian, hyperindustrialized site within which the socionatural project of the City is now staged, then its problems extend past issues of isotropic internalization, disorientation, and commercialization.

As I have mentioned, in contending with these environments' contemporary urban form and ubiquity, municipalities, architects, and engineers appear compelled to reexamine these environments as the support systems they have become. Within these reexaminations, we witness new politics that only continue to highlight the particularly urbanized quality of the late-modern environment and its continued role as a form of urban socionature that requires much more intense examination. Among the numerous examples of urban refashionings of maintenance environments, in recent years global cities such as New York City, London, Frankfurt, and Chicago have become epicenters of an environmentalist rethinking of the large-scale architectural interior. Such reconceptualizations supported by both municipal governments and nongovernmental organizations address both the scale and the intense energy usage of air-conditioning and lighting systems within a city's office and apartment buildings.[4] These responses also address many of the types of criticisms launched by Frampton and his followers; they often entail a turn toward some site-specific reality. Those who both pioneered and continue to explore an environmentalist reconsideration of large-scale buildings demand a reconstruction of the often-sealed skins of office buildings and the mechanical machinery of cooling and heating systems with more "passive" systems that draw on existing environmental features of sites (such as wind and sunlight) and that also rely on renewable forms of energy.[5] The architects and engineers who theorize, develop, and help draw up urban codes for this work—William McDonough, Arup, Guy Battle, and Atelier 10, among others—imagine relating large-scale building programs to the climates of cities via a generalized set of strategies. They see their work as both humanizing this architecture and participating in a more equitable use of world resources.

As compelling as these shifts may be, we should consider that these mechanical systems mostly offer lower-energy representations of established environments and discourses about interior environments that were formulated years ago. As a type of critical analysis of maintenance, the politics of an urban-architectural environmentalism also are limited.

For example, even if the most ecologically responsible global museum were built, such as the recent interiors of the renovated British Museum in London, by Norman Foster, and the Acropolis Museum in Athens, by Bernard Tschumi, such a realization still would not come to any spatial reckoning with the particular power of the museum's interior climate in localizing culture.[6] As the ongoing battle between these museum sites over the Elgin Marbles demonstrates, environmentalism cannot easily inform the more globalized and urbanized politics of maintenance and the architectural environment.[7] Similarly, consider the recent environmentalist discourse on optimizing the health of interior air systems to "increase worker productivity" in office buildings. In conjoining environmentalism and worker output, we realize that some of the goals within contemporary architectural environmentalism are little more than the most crude realizations and rhetorical formulations of the brute power of maintenance in furthering a corporate conception of the subject.[8]

In addition to responding to various forms of environmentalism, the municipal governments of New York and Chicago have developed responses to various illnesses and deaths caused by heat exposure and the lack of access to air-conditioning by opening cooling centers for the urban poor and elderly.[9] These activities mirror earlier efforts such as the provision of heat shelters for the homeless in the 1980s and 1990s in New York City. What is particularly interesting about this development is the recognition by municipal governments both that individuals have a right to a particular and relatively sophisticated atmosphere that circulates in contemporary cities and that such an environment is hardly as ubiquitous as architectural critiques such as Koolhaas's and Frampton's make it appear. As with earlier efforts to provide people access to urban nature, today the constituents of cities consider that a citizenry has a right to protective and sustaining environments. In a much more incidental but ultimately similar example, in 1993 the Metropolitan Museum of Art permitted the Sackler Wing, which houses the Temple of Dendur, to be used as a temporary classroom for New York City schoolchildren who were evacuated out of their school building because of asbestos. Somewhat aware of the tendentious nature of these spaces and their technological sophistication in comparison to other spaces in the City, the museum attempted to use them to fill in some of the inequities related to the maintenance of health in New York City. One striking image, which nonetheless speaks to new sites of maintenance in the contemporary City, is of the evacuated children sitting in the Dendur Room safe from the asbestos-laden classroom of their crumbling school building.[10] We might understand this approach as attempting to provide a more even distribution of sophisticated architectural environments in the face of their uneven distribution.

As interesting as such distributionist approaches are, there is an equally troubling and continually evolving vision for splintered interior environments that are nonetheless explored in the name of public health. Following the attacks of September 11, 2001, several studies emerged in both New York City and London to consider the protection of the interiors of the cities' buildings from a biological attack. Firms such as Arup Security Consulting, with offices in almost every major global city, specialize in both protecting buildings from chemical and biological attack and environmentalist engineering.[11] A *New York Times* article published soon after 9/11, titled "Envisioning an Expensive Future in the Brave New World of Fortress New York," illustrates the general responses. The author, David Barstow, invited nine security and terrorism experts to envision various possibilities for the Times Square Business District, which became a focus for these types of studies as well as for green building in a Mayor Giuliani–led effort to clean up the area. Security experts imagined Times Square's buildings armored with "air-conditioning systems . . . with devices that neutralize chemical and biological agents with pulsing ultraviolet light. . . . They would build 'shelter-in-place areas,' large, secure rooms with air-lock entrances that commuters could dash into should chemical or biological agents be detected."[12] In another article on the protection of New York City buildings, an engineer linked environmentalist goals within architecture and bioterror armoring when he claimed that the City was well prepared for any bioterror attack, as advances in building engineering "have grown out of mundane needs like filtering small particles for the air to prevent 'sick building syndrome.'"[13] In 2004, the Department of Homeland Security began what it termed an "urban dispersion project," a study of the dispersion and movement of air in various urban sites, including Times Square.[14] The study involved examinations of the outdoor and indoor movement of air and the potential ability to map the flows of air with sophisticated computer equipment. One aspect of the study entailed a computer-simulated biological attack in which an aerosolized weapon was detonated in Times Square and then the distribution of contaminants mapped, to better understand how it would move in and against the surrounding buildings. The images of this project, in their chilling and stunning beauty, appear to bring us back to a Victorian era in which reformers mapped the airflows of London and New York to better understand disease. In tandem with the studies, the Department of Homeland Security also released a series of guidelines for architects, developers, engineers, and building managers to better protect their structures from atmospheric terrorism.

These links between architectural environmentalism and counterterrorism are disturbing, but such strategies also continue in less obvious ways through the "greening" of once environmentally questionable sites. For example, Battery Park City was one of several sites where workers and residents reported health impacts after the collapse of the World Trade Center and the building fires and demolitions that followed that attack; but this particular neighborhood is also an epicenter of green architecture in New York City. The advertisements for the Solaire apartment complex in Battery Park City (designed by Pelli Clarke Pelli Architects, the most recent iteration of Cesar Pelli's firm), which is located within one-quarter mile of the former World Trade Center, promised future residents "filtered air" and protection from "random air filtration." Such amenities appear to be critical within a context known, immediately after the World Trade Center attacks, for its profusion of unhealthy dust.[15] Curiously, as the City became increasingly criticized for its inability to either manage the cleanup of the World Trade Center disaster site or protect nearby residents from its toxic aftereffects, architecture began to fill this governmental lacuna.[16] In this sense, the types of architectural strategies that we see in this more contemporary context are materialist responses to perceived withdrawals of governance and governmental oversight. We have witnessed the formation of such thinking in the EPA's early-1970s analysis of the Washington Bridge Apartments, a site where some glimpse of this present reality appears to be staged. This more recent iteration is global architecture at its most literal, an architectural agenda existing in the gaps of a nascent, potentially post-state space—architecture understood in the most basic environmental terms. Within this context, architecture becomes laced with the historical agenda of a state bureaucracy, including its ability to manage the distribution of health.

Within these recent activities—distributing cool spaces throughout the City to contend with urban heat, using museum galleries as shelters, protecting and sealing spaces off from the City outside in fear of terrorism or disease—we witness emerging politics of environmental maintenance. The interiors examined within this book have become an integral aspect of cities in that they are simultaneously distributed, splintered, and urbanistically represented as stable sites. Although the politics of private and public space have shifted somewhat from forty years ago, we have nonetheless returned to very modernist politics of inside and out. Here, we witness the further entanglement of the maintenance environment with a type of power over life. But this form of power now becomes spatialized anew, within the context of weakening municipal governance and its infrastructural tissues and more militant visions of urban governance.[17] Within these latter and more extreme scenarios, the maintenance environment evokes notions of a more rudimentary and potentially chilling variation of Foucauldian bio-power. This involves the notion of life at its most basic and unsupported, evoked through the distribution of a life-supporting power.[18] The global cities of the world may not, in fact, be sites of evaporating health and increasing danger, but several buildings evoke this particular reality.

Despite the weakness, cynicism, and intense scientism that mark contemporary engagements and rethinking of these environments, a project clearly remains to reimagine and reconstitute the particular power of architecture's maintenance environments. Through this study, we realize that the project of the architectural environment is an urban one, constituted within and through specific urban realities.[19] But if a future, more critical and explicitly urban project for the maintenance environment remains, how will we get there? This is more than just a practical question; it is a disciplinarian one as well. This book is a work of both architectural-historical and geographical analysis. What I call the maintenance environment is a geographical category of architecture; it is spatial, with power concentrated in certain urban locations and spatial relationships, but it is also architectural-historical, with power wielded within work that figures in specific periodizations, architectural practices, and material realities.

For urban geographers, the final words of a book often provide opportunities to consider various spatial alternatives to the power that their work charts, excavates, and examines. They offer an opportunity to find forms of action or new geographical practices within cities that articulate outsides, oppositions, and reworkings of power within those cities. Within architectural history, such a forceful relationship between historical analysis and the present inevitably becomes a problem, as that work becomes "operative" within contemporary architectural practice. For many architectural historians, the power of architectural history for practice lies in its forceful disconnection from its concerns.[20] By pointing out worlds other than our own, architectural history becomes political by understanding instruments of a historical time that are not our everyday reality.

In understanding how to further interpret, critique, and develop the category of the maintenance environment, we might turn to a representational project that both reifies maintenance anew and examines the possibility of the architectural environment unhinged from its current biophysical and instrumental roles in the City. We have seen how the architectural environments of New York City became reimagined as sites of protection, biological nurturing and growth, and preservation and communication that entangled with specific visions of this city. From an instrumental perspective, many of these efforts were more successful as *representations of maintenance* than as actual sites within which plants, people, or art could be properly maintained. If technically deficient, these spaces remain haunting and potent from a representational perspective. The remaining project is not a technical one (a better alignment between representation and technique) for this city or any other. In the face of this difference, the problem is not how to make maintenance more technically proficient but, rather, to contemplate what else this architectural formation can represent. In exploring this question, we might continue to consider the way maintenance operates geographically and historically as well as considering its potential ability to appear as a more overt aspect of architectural representation.

We have observed an architecturally situated form of socionature that potentially supports subjects (nonhuman life), gives objects their historical status (factored into the development of a late-modern city), and serves as a politically complex and powerful object on its own. Historically, we can continue to lift the veil, excavating the maintenance environment in specific cities for what it is and does: a historicizing, urbanizing, and politicizing form. Although seemingly climatically overdetermined, the types of architectural environments rising in the new cities of the global South have a visually and urbanistically prominent character that has been little examined in contemporary literature. Geographically, we also might consider what it means to consider maintenance as a more democratic form. One can understand those architects, both institutionally aligned and critical, who imagined urban possibilities in constructing maintenance environments. One can further imagine how their architectural-representation project, the production and shaping of environment, might continue anew. In 1970s New York City, maintenance appeared as a silvery and monumental architectural apparition rising in and against the historical fabric of this city. It visualized New York City as an environment to be resisted and reworked. A future project must address the maintenance environment in all its vaporous and material representations—how it appears as a site of support and such a site's relationship to a surrounding city. Thus, the type of power wielded by various architects, institutions, and municipal leaders within New York might be reimagined within different contexts, scenarios, and forms. But, in considering all of these factors, we can also imagine something else, something that takes maintenance further away from any contemporary urban demands but that is still tied to considering what this form maintains and how it is built. In continuing a critical project for this type of power, we might imagine it as something without any specific subject or object, something that stands there awaiting a role to play in some nonexistent urban reality: a system of support for a vision of the city desired, but a city that does not yet exist.

NOTES

INTRODUCTION

1. Among the many books on this period, see Robert Stern, Thomas Mellins, and David Fishman, *New York 1960: Architecture and Urbanism between the Second World War and the Bicentennial* (New York: Monacelli, 1997): 94–119; Mathew Gandy, *Concrete and Clay: Reworking Nature in New York City* (Cambridge, Mass.: MIT Press, 2003); Vincent Cannato, *The Ungovernable City: John Lindsay and His Struggle to Save New York* (New York: Basic Books, 2001); Joshua Shannon, *The Disappearance of Objects: New York Art and the Rise of the Postmodern City* (New Haven: Yale University Press, 2009); and Douglas Crimp and L. Cooke, *Mixed Use Manhattan: Photography and Related Practices, 1970s to the Present* (Cambridge, Mass.: MIT Press, 2010).

2. David Harvey, *A Brief History of Neoliberalism* (Oxford: Oxford University Press, 2005); Shannon, *Disappearance of Objects*; Crimp and Cooke, *Mixed Use Manhattan*; Julian Brash, *Bloomberg's New York: Class and Governance in the Luxury City* (Athens: University of Georgia Press, 2011).

3. Among these places and eras are nineteenth- and twentieth-century London, turn-of-the-century Chicago, early-1970s Los Angeles, late-1970s Atlanta, late-1980s Frankfurt, and even twenty-first-century Dubai.

4. See, for example, Fredric Jameson's discussion of the Los Angeles context of the Bonaventure Hotel, or Reinhold Martin on the relationship of mirrored glass to the oil economy in Houston, Texas. Fredric Jameson, *Postmodernism; or, The Cultural Logic of Late Capitalism* (Durham, N.C.: Duke University Press, 1990); Reinhold Martin, *Utopia's Ghost: Architecture and Post-modernism Again* (Minneapolis: University of Minnesota Press, 2010), 94–103.

5. Among the many examples that inspired this approach, see, for example, Walter Benjamin and Rolf Tiedemann, *The Arcades Project* (Cambridge, Mass.: Harvard University Press, 1999); Carl E. Schorske, *Fin-de-Siècle Vienna: Politics and Culture* (Cambridge: Cambridge University Press, 1981); T. J. Clark, *The Painting of Modern Life: Paris in the Art of Manet and His Followers* (Princeton:

Princeton University Press, 1984); and Mike Davis, *City of Quartz: Excavating the Future in Los Angeles* (London: Verso, 1992).

6. John Mollenkopf and Manuel Castells once argued, in their study of New York during this period, "As Chicago was central to Nineteenth Century industrialization, and the founders of modern social science studied it to understand these processes, New York City can be viewed as central to an understanding of the late-20th century post-industrial metropolis." Similarly, the geographers David Harvey and Julian Brash argue that the type of neoliberal economic strategies that spread globally in the early years of the twenty-first century were first staged during the bank crisis of mid-1970s New York. John Mollenkopf and Manuel Castells, *Dual City: Restructuring New York* (New York: Russell Sage Foundation, 1992), 5; Harvey, *Brief History of Neoliberalism*; Brash, *Bloomberg's New York*.

7. On the formation and unraveling of the constituent economic and spatial features of the modern city, see David Harvey, *The Condition of Postmodernity: An Enquiry into the Origins of Cultural Change* (Oxford: Blackwell, 1989); on the disintegration of urban networks, see Gandy, *Concrete and Clay*; and on the autonomy of architecture relative to the city, see Manfredo Tafuri, *The Disenchanted Mountain: The Skyscraper and the City*, ed. Giorgio Cucci (Cambridge, Mass.: MIT Press, 1983). Harvey and Gandy both argue that urban regional planning was economically situated. With the collapse of specific economic instruments, such as bond measures and other forms of municipal leveraging and investment, the physical projects supported by these systems—parks, networks, and water systems—collapsed. Tafuri's argument is similar in that he also understands certain economic superstructures to have a defining role within architecture; but he uses a case study on the development of the skyscraper. Tafuri argues that twentieth-century planners intended to use skyscraper assemblages to direct the form of the city and its environment, but, due to the tower's underlying economic raison d'être, it became a mute object relative to city form and space. Histories of community action and a general questioning of "big" planning also contributed to the downfall of integrated urban and architectural city planning.

8. See Hillary Ballon and K. T. Jackson, *Robert Moses and the Modern City: The Transformation of New York* (New York: Norton, 2007); and Samuel Zipp, *Manhattan Projects: The Rise and Fall of Urban Renewal in Cold War New York* (New York: Oxford University Press, 2010).

9. Similarly, the historian Beatriz Colomina argued that all of modern architecture is haunted by what she called the "tubercular" city. That is, the mantra of light, air, and greenery and their manipulation within a modern architectural language were used to eliminate sickness and disease. Beatriz Colomina, "The Medical Body in Modern Architecture," *Daidalos* 64 (1997): 61.

10. See Gandy, *Concrete and Clay*; and Robert Caro, *The Power Broker: Robert Moses and the Fall of New York* (New York: Vintage, 1975).

11. Nicholas Freudenberg et al., "The Impact of New York City's 1975 Fiscal Crisis on the Tuberculosis, HIV, and Homicide Syndemic," *American Journal of Public Health* 96, no. 3 (2006): 424–34; Harvey, *Brief History of Neoliberalism*, 39–63; Brash, *Bloomberg's New York*, 24.

12. I am drawing a comparison between European urban critiques, such as those by the Situationist International, and American criticisms of urban and architectural planning, such as those by Jane Jacobs. Additionally, I think the early writing within *Oppositions*, the journal of the Institute for Architecture and Urban Studies, is instructive and illustrative of the general shift. The institute was formed in New York City, and its founders were involved in various planning proposals for New York. Many of the early writings in the journal by Peter Eisenman, Kenneth Frampton, and Alan Calquhoun attacked architecture with biophysical pretenses.

13. Jane Jacobs, *The Death and Life of Great American Cities* (New York: Random House, 1961).

14. The residues of architecture's biophysical relation might be found in the large "Eat" sign used to illustrate a new semiological function for architecture, but now it was cast in an entirely communicative language. In addition to the work of Simon Sadler on Archigram's consumerist orientation, see Hal Foster's discussion of Banham, Archigram, and Venturi and Scott Brown and their relationship to postwar consumerism; and Aron Vinegar on Venturi and Scott Brown and his own interpretation of the "Eat" sign: Simon Sadler, *Archigram: Architecture without Architecture* (Cambridge, Mass.: MIT Press, 2005); Hal Foster, *The Art–Architecture Complex* (New York: Verso, 2011); Aron Vinegar, *I Am a Monument: On Learning from Las Vegas* (Cambridge, Mass.: MIT Press, 2008).

15. Theories of architectural autonomy stretch from the rationalist writings on architecture and the city of Aldo Rossi to the more poststructural theories of Peter Eisenman. My proposed narrative extending from "biophysical" to "contextualist" urban engagements contains a few exceptions, including the environmental and experimental work of the late 1960s and early 1970s. Nevertheless, I think the overall criticism of instrumental positivism and its replacement with a visual, aesthetic contextualism define the urbanistically oriented architecture of the 1970s. See, for example, Aldo Rossi, *The Architecture of the City* (Cambridge, Mass.: MIT Press, 1984).

16. Charles Jencks, *The Language of Post-modern Architecture* (New York: Rizzoli, 1977); Harvey, *Brief History of Neoliberalism*, 43.

17. In the 1990s, construction expanded on New York's regional water network, but this expansion lacked any of the liberatory promise of the nineteenth-century Croton system. This is most palpable in the complete lack of visible aesthetic works that celebrated the conveying of water into the city, in the manner of its nineteenth-century analogue. The late twentieth-century expansion of the city's water supply was unhinged from discussions of urban transformation. Maria Kaika and Erik Swyngedouw chronicle the collapse of utopian promise in urban networks in a more general context, and their observations are applicable here. Maria Kaika and Erik Swyngedouw, "Fetishizing the Modern City: The Phantasmagoria of Urban Technological Networks," *International Journal of Urban and Regional Research* 24, no. 1 (2002): 120–38.

18. By the 1990s, New York City's GDP ranked second in the world, behind Tokyo. See the statistics assembled by PricewaterhouseCoopers, UK Media Centre, at http://www.ukmediacentre.pwc.com/imagelibrary/downloadMedia.ashx?MediaDetailsID=1562.

19. This work includes Buckminster Fuller's proposal to dome a portion of midtown Manhattan, excluding it from the industrialized harbors; Archigram's use of the industrialized waterfront as a backdrop for its Walking City of 1964; and the reformed-tenement-block backdrop that forms the scene for SITE's Highrise of Homes project (1981).

20. Harvey, *Brief History of Neoliberalism*; Brash, *Bloomberg's New York*.

21. Tafuri, *Disenchanted Mountain*; Jameson, *Postmodernism*; Stephen Graham and Simon Marvin, *Splintering Urbanism: Networked Infrastructures, Technological Mobilities, and the Urban Condition* (London: Routledge, 2001). For an overview of the environmentalist literature of "urban disconnection," see David Gissen, "Thermopolis: Conceptualizing Environmental Technologies in the Urban Sphere," *Journal of Architectural Education* 60, no. 1 (2006): 43–53. An early example includes Raymond Arsenault, "The End of the Long Hot Summer: The Air Conditioner and Southern Culture," *Journal of Southern History* 50, no. 4 (1984): 597–628; and more recent examples include William McDonough and Michael Braungart, *The Hannover Principles: Design for Sustainability* (Charlottesville, Va.: McDonough Architects, 2003); and Kenneth Frampton, "Technoscience and Environmental Culture: A Provisional Critique," *Journal of Architectural Education* 54, no. 3 (2001): 123–29. On architecture providing a switch from urban "health" to "comfort," see Michelle Murphy, *Sick Building Syndrome and the Problem of Uncertainty: Environmental Politics, Technoscience, and Women Workers* (Durham, N.C.: Duke University Press, 2006).

22. See chapters 1–3 for more on these developments.

23. Roche, Pelli, Anthony Lumsden, and Gunnar Birketts all practiced at Eero

Saarinen's office. Roche took over the office in the early 1960s, Pelli and Lumsden practiced in Los Angeles, and Birketts was based in Detroit. In the mid-1970s, Pelli returned to the East Coast, where he eventually became dean of Yale's School of Architecture and established an office in New Haven, Connecticut. Kenneth Frampton, introduction to *Richard Meier, Architect,* by Richard Meier (New York: Oxford, 1976), 7–17. Also see Cesar Pelli, "Four Days in May: White, Silver, and Gray," *A+U* (September 1974): 15–19.

24. The book engages with these practices as well as with work by an earlier group of architects including Buckminster Fuller, Paul Rudolph, Walter Bird, Brown and Guenther, Edward Larrabee Barnes, and Haines Lundberg Wahler. In focusing on the development of environments within New York City, we gather together a range of "late-modern" architectural practices.

25. See "Late Moderns," issue no. 7 of the online forum of the Los Angeles Forum for Architecture and Urban Design, edited by Tom Marble (2010), http://laforum.org/content/issues-newsletters/forum-issue-7-late-moderns. Architects developing this particular "silver" grammar in New York include Roche, Pelli, Hugh Stubbins, Edward Larrabee Barnes, Brown and Guenther, Horowitz and Chun, and Derr Scott.

26. On miasmatic air and its relation to urban space and interiors in the nineteenth century, see Alain Corbin, *The Foul and the Fragrant: Odor and the French Social Imagination* (Cambridge, Mass.: Harvard University Press, 1988); and William A. Cohen, *Filth: Dirt, Disgust, and Modern Life* (Minneapolis: University of Minnesota Press, 2004). Michelle Murphy also argues that sick-building syndrome revives the miasmatic fears of the nineteenth century: Murphy, *Sick Building Syndrome.*

27. The most representative examples of this literature are Gandy, *Concrete and Clay*; Erik Swyngedouw, *Social Power and the Urbanization of Water: Flows of Power* (Oxford: Oxford University Press, 2004); and Maria Kaika, *City of Flows: Modernity, Nature, and the City* (London: Routledge, 2005).

28. On the idea of influences on the urban production of nature, see Henri Lefebvre, *The Production of Space* (Oxford: Blackwell, 1991); Neil Smith, *Uneven Development: Nature, Capital, and the Production of Space* (London: Blackwell, 1991); Donna Haraway, "A Cyborg Manifesto: Science, Technology, and Socialist-Feminism in the Late Twentieth Century," in *Simians, Cyborgs and Women: The Reinvention of Nature* (New York: Routledge, 1991), 149–81; William Cronon, *Nature's Metropolis: Chicago and the Great West* (New York: Norton, 1992); Bruno Latour, *We Have Never Been Modern* (Cambridge, Mass.: Harvard University Press, 1993); and David Harvey, *Justice, Nature, and the Geography of Difference* (Oxford: Blackwell, 1996). The ideas of Smith and Harvey are particularly criti-

cal for this study. Smith argues for nature as a dialectical form with a capitalist economy between subjects and nature, city and nature, or capitalism and nature. Smith argues for an understanding of nature as a process that emerges from specific tensions that cannot be understood as either externally or internally fixed. That is, nature has no essence but is constantly remade within a modern political, economic, and cultural context. I understand buildings to be sites within which nature is produced. Within the writing of David Harvey, capital appears as the fundamental driver of nature production. The connection to neo-Marxist literature is a critical component within most of the existing literature, but not just for its economic focus. Within literature on the urban production of nature, an otherwise completely flat and "smooth" understanding of urban socioeconomic power (via Latour and urbanists influenced by Deleuze and Guattari) is often discarded in favor of an understanding of power hierarchies that move through urban productions of nature.

29. For Erik Swyngedouw, the appearance of water in the city involves a vast "metabolic network" that links nature and society, nature and city, and, perhaps most significant, nature and capital: "Drinking water from the stand-pipe combines the circulation of productive, merchant and financial capital . . . ; the ecological transformation of hydrological complexes and the bio-chemical process of purification with the libidinous sensation and the physiological necessity of drinking fluids; and the social regulation of access to water with images of clarity, cleanliness, health and virginity. . . . The circulation of water produces a physical geography and a material landscape, but also a symbolic and cultural landscape of power." Erik Swyngedouw, "The City as a Hybrid: On Nature, Society and Cyborg Urbanization," *Capitalism Nature Socialism* 7, no. 2 (1996): 70–71, 76–77.

30. See, for example, Swyngedouw, *Social Power*.

31. See Rosalyn Deutsche, *Evictions: Art and Spatial Politics* (Cambridge, Mass.: MIT Press, 1996); and Neil Smith, *The New Urban Frontier: Gentrification and the Revanchist City* (London: Routledge, 1996). See the more detailed discussion of their ideas in the penultimate section of this Introduction.

32. On Banham's concept, see Reyner Banham, *Architecture of the Well-Tempered Environment* (Chicago: University of Chicago Press, 1984). On historical and contemporary uses of the term "bio-power," see Michel Foucault, *Security, Territory, Population: Lectures at the Collège de France, 1977–78*, ed. Michel Senellart, trans. Graham Burchell (London: Picador, 2009); Michael Hardt and Antonio Negri, *Empire* (Cambridge, Mass.: Harvard University Press, 2001); and Sven Olav Wallenstein, *Biopolitics and the Emergence of Modern Architecture* (New York: Princeton Architectural Press, 2009).

33. Mierle Laderman Ukeles, "Maintenance Art: Proposal for an Exhibition,

CARE" (1969), http://www.feldmangallery.com/media/pdfs/ukeles-MANIFESTO.pdf.

34. Ibid., 4. This last passage also suggests how maintenance contains a more problematic and critical system of acquisition. As maintenance becomes an instrument of care, it becomes further entangled in processes through which material is displaced and fixed within a specific setting—a theme explored in chapters 2 and 3.

35. Patricia Phillips, "Maintenance Activity: Creating a Climate for Change," in *But Is It Art? The Spirit of Art as Activism*, ed. Nina Felshin (Seattle: Bay Press, 1995), 165–93; Miwon Kwon, *One Place after Another: Site-Specific Art and Locational Identity* (Cambridge, Mass.: MIT Press, 2004).

36. Hilary Sample, "Maintenance Architecture," *Praxis*, no. 6 (2004); Jorge Otero-Pailos, "Conservation Cleaning / Cleaning Conservation," *Future Anterior: Journal of Historic Preservation, History, Theory, and Criticism* 4, no. 1 (2007).

37. In my articulating concepts of maintenance and maintenance environments, readers will notice that I often use terms such as "environment" and "socionatural." The architectural "environment" describes the biophysical totality of stuff that appears inside architecture and between the objects and subjects within it. In this sense, "environment" is an assemblage, composed of features that could be positioned in other biophysical relationships in a nonarchitectural context—for example, heat, temperature, humidity, coolth, and light. To paraphrase the French historian of environment George Canghuilhem, the constituent features of environments always point toward the "living" as an ultimate referent. Environment differs from a modern concept of architectural space. Via architectural theory, I understand space as a fundamentally psychoexperiential idea that has a more explicitly representational role in the discipline than environment (the latter almost always being represented mechanically). My continual use of the term "environment" relates to its contemporary and immediate postwar use. But my use of the term is not identical to the manner in which it was employed in the late 1960s and early 1970s (and in some ways is today) to describe the ephemeralization of objects into effects on the human mind and body. In this latter sense, an environment can be created by transforming the role of any representation (such as a painting, object, or photograph) as a source of subjective contemplation into a deobjectified source of sensation to an entranced spectator. My use of the term "nature" is literal in that it describes those forms of matter imagined to be external to human subjects and cities (for example, trees or water). By using the term "socionature," I develop a more satisfying dialectical concept of nature as it is fundamentally experienced in cities.

38. See, for example, Reinhold Martin, "Environment, c. 1973," *Grey Room*

(2004): 78–101; Felicity Scott, *Architecture or Techno-utopia: Politics after Modernism* (Cambridge, Mass.: MIT Press, 2007); Mark Wigley, "Recycling Recycling," in *ECO-TEC: Architecture of the In-Between*, ed. Amerigo Marras (New York: Princeton Architectural Press, 1999), 38–49; and Wallenstein, *Biopolitics*.

39. Keller Easterling, *Enduring Innocence: Global Architecture and Its Political Masquerades* (Cambridge, Mass.: MIT Press, 2005); Sanford Kwinter, *Architectures of Time: Toward a Theory of the Event in Modernist Culture* (Cambridge, Mass.: MIT Press, 2002).

40. See, for example, the journal *New Geographies*, an architecture and geography journal from the Graduate School of Design at Harvard that sees the geographical within urban planning and landscape.

41. Gandy, *Concrete and Clay*; Julie Sze, *Noxious New York: The Racial Politics of Urban Health and Environmental Justice* (Cambridge, Mass.: MIT Press, 2006); Kaika, *City of Flows*; Mike Davis, *Ecology of Fear: Los Angeles and the Imagination of Disaster* (New York: Metropolitan, 1998).

42. Smith, *New Urban Frontier*; Deutsche, *Evictions*; Christine Boyer, *The City of Collective Memory: Its Historical Imagery and Architectural Entertainments* (Cambridge, Mass.: MIT Press, 1996).

43. See, for example, Shannon, *Disappearance of Objects*; Jonathan Mahler, *Ladies and Gentlemen, the Bronx Is Burning: 1977, Baseball, Politics, and the Battle for the Soul of a City* (New York: Farrar, Straus & Giroux, 2006); and Crimp and Cooke, *Mixed Use Manhattan*.

44. From a geographical perspective, we arrive at the end of the "Fordist" era, moving through post-Fordist and into late-capitalist urban economies. From the perspective of architectural periodization, much of the work in this book can be characterized as modern, postmodern, and late modern. I ultimately describe the periodization of the architecture in this book as "late modern." The term relies on Charles Jencks's formulation (described earlier in this Introduction). Although I embrace "late modernity" as the ultimate descriptor of the architecture in this book, I use the term "postmodernism" when appropriate in describing the periodization or aesthetics of certain buildings and spaces, such as the World Financial Center examined in chapter 4, which in fact, from Jencks's perspective, was both late modern and postmodern.

45. See David Gissen, *Big and Green: Toward Sustainable Architecture in the Twenty-First Century* (New York: Princeton Architectural Press, 2003); and Murphy, *Sick Building Syndrome*.

1 PROTECTION

1. Joshua B. Freeman, *Working-Class New York: Life and Labor since World War II* (New York: New Press, 2000), 143.

2. Ibid., 168.

3. The term "gentrification" was coined by Ruth Glass to describe the transformations of Islington, London, in the early 1960s. On the literature of gentrification and its relationship to the demographic transformations in New York City, see Robert Fitch, *The Assassination of New York* (London: Verso, 1993); Neil Smith, *The New Urban Frontier: Gentrification and the Revanchist City* (London: Routledge, 1996); and Rosalyn Deutsche, *Evictions: Art and Spatial Politics* (Cambridge, Mass.: MIT Press, 1996).

4. See Smith, *New Urban Frontier*; and Deutsche, *Evictions*. The "right to the city" is a concept of Henri Lefebvre's: Henri Lefebvre, *Writings on Cities* (Oxford: Blackwell, 1995).

5. In addition to the literature on gentrification cited in note 3, see William Sites, *Remaking New York: Primitive Globalization and the Politics of Urban Community*, Globalization and Community 12 (Minneapolis: University of Minnesota Press, 2003); and Christopher Mele, *Selling the Lower East: Culture, Real Estate, and Resistance in New York City* (Minneapolis: University of Minnesota Press, 2000). An environmentalist examination of gentrification in New York is Miranda Martinez, *Power at the Roots: Gentrification, Community Gardens, and the Puerto Ricans of the Lower East Side* (New York: Lexington, 2010).

6. Deutsche, *Evictions*.

7. Neil Smith, "Toward a Theory of Gentrification: A Back to the City Movement by Capital, Not People," *Journal of the American Planning Association* 45, no. 4 (1979): 538–48; Smith, *New Urban Frontier*.

8. For this latter aspect, see Julie Sze, *Noxious New York: The Racial Politics of Urban Health and Environmental Justice* (Cambridge, Mass.: MIT Press, 2006). Literature on gentrification and environment is scarce but includes Susannah Bunce, "Developing Sustainability: Sustainability Policy and Gentrification on Toronto's Waterfront Local Environment," *International Journal of Justice and Sustainability* 14, no. 7 (2009): 651–67; and Roger Kiel, "Frontiers of Political Ecology," in *Urban Constellations*, ed. Matthew Gandy (London: University College London, 2011), 26–30.

9. Today's "green" building booms are just one example of the ways damaged urban environments and the new architectural environments that have been built in response become settings for engendering particular subjects in the city. This topic is addressed later in this chapter.

10. On Fuller's project, see Buckminster Fuller, "The Case for a Domed City," *St. Louis Post-Dispatch*, September 26, 1965; and on Rudolph's, see Peter Wolf, Ulrich Franzen, and Paul Rudolph, *The Evolving City: Urban Design Proposals* (New York: American Federation of the Arts, 1974).

11. Information on these projects can be found in American Association of State Highway Officials (AASHO), *An Information Guide on Air Rights above and below Interstate Highways* (Washington, D.C., 1961); and Robert Stern, Thomas Mellins, and David Fishman, *New York 1960: Architecture and Urbanism between the Second World War and the Bicentennial* (New York: Monacelli, 1997).

12. State of New Jersey, Department of Transportation, *Air Rights Potentials in Major Highways* (Trenton: State of New Jersey, Department of Transportation, 1969), 15–16.

13. Ibid., 20.

14. AASHO, *Information Guide*.

15. Gail Cooper, *Air-Conditioning America: Engineers and the Controlled Environment, 1900–1960* (Baltimore: Johns Hopkins University Press, 2002), 23.

16. See chapters 3 and 4 on this particular concept.

17. AASHO, *Information Guide*, 13.

18. U.S. Department of Transportation, Federal Highway Administration, Bureau of Public Roads, *A Study of Airspace Utilization*, prepared for the California Division of Highways by Real Estate Research Corporation in cooperation with the Office of Research and Development Bureau of Public Roads (Washington, D.C., 1968), 2.

19. Steven Lowenstein, *Frankfurt on the Hudson: The German-Jewish Community of Washington Heights, 1933–1983, Its Structure and Culture* (Detroit: Wayne State University Press, 1989), 213.

20. Ira Katznelson, *City Trenches: Urban Politics and the Patterning of Class in the United States* (New York: Pantheon, 1981), 97.

21. Ibid., 96–97.

22. Joseph C. Ingraham, "New Bridge Links Planned Uptown," *New York Times*, February 18, 1957.

23. Carl Gerwitz, "Washington Heights Reverses Tide of Urban Decay," *New York Times*, July 1, 1962.

24. Frederick Elias, quoted in ibid.

25. The bus station was used by commuters from surrounding suburban towns and connected to two subway lines in the city.

26. One can contrast the etymological concepts of space with environment via Adrian Forty's analysis of space in State of New Jersey, *Air Rights Potentials*, 15–16.

27. Advertisement, *New York Times*, September 2, 1962.

28. "Bridge Apartments: New York, NY," *Empire State Architect*, September–October, 1963.

29. Donald Canty, "Nervi's Gilded Gateway," *Architectural Forum*, March 1967, 68–73. On the bus station, see "Nervi's First U.S. Work: A New York City Bus Terminal," *Architectural Forum*, May 1960, 7; "Concrete: A Special Report," *Architectural Forum*, September 1962, 78–96; "Nervi Designs Bus Station for New York," *Progressive Architecture*, May 1960, 78; "New York's Uptown Bus Station Dedicated," *Progressive Architecture* 64, no. 2 (1963): 61; "Nervi à New York," *Domus*, October 1963, 1–6; and Paul Goldberger, *The City Observed: A Guide to the Architecture of Manhattan* (New York: Vintage, 1979), 326–27.

30. Fred Bernstein, "Forty-Year Watch: Bridge Apartments by Brown and Guenther," *Oculus* 65, no. 4 (2003): 47.

31. Hazel Henderson, interview by the author, February 2, 2006.

32. Steven Roberts, "Fumes and Noise Plague Tenants," *New York Times*, June 17, 1967.

33. Quoted in ibid.

34. Henderson, interview; ibid.

35. Roberts, "Fumes and Noise Plague Tenants."

36. Bernard Guenther, quoted in Robert E. Tomasson, "Air Rights Building Is 10, and Struggling," *New York Times*, March 24, 1974.

37. David Bird, "Kennedy Warns of Air Pollution Disaster," *New York Times*, June 20, 1967.

38. Robert F. Kennedy, *Statement of Senator Robert F. Kennedy to the Citizens for Clean Air, June 19, 1967* (New York City), Robert F. Kennedy Senate Papers, Speeches and Press Releases, 9/11/66–9/10/67, box 3, John F. Kennedy Presidential Library, Boston, Massachusetts.

39. Office of Research and Monitoring, Environmental Protection Agency, *Indoor-Outdoor Carbon Monoxide Pollution Study* (Washington, D.C., 1972), 1–1.

40. Ibid., 1–3.

41. On cybernetic aspects of planning analysis, see Jennifer S. Light, *From Warfare to Welfare: Defense Intellectuals and Urban Problems in Cold War America* (Baltimore: Johns Hopkins University Press, 2003).

42. Office of Research and Monitoring, *Indoor-Outdoor Carbon Monoxide Pollution Study*, 1–11.

43. See the project by Rudolph and Franzen in Wolf, Franzen, and Rudolph, *Evolving City*.

44. David Shipler, "A Circular Urban Complex Offered for Chinatown," *New York Times*, March 13, 1969. Also see "Project Unites Living and Learning," *New*

York Times, March 2, 1969; "Ground Is Broken for Huge Project Serving Chinatown," *New York Times*, September 12, 1973; David Grant, "Computer Rent Program under Siege," *New York Times*, October 7, 1973; Robert Hanley, "Chinatown to Get 27-Story Towers," *New York Times*, March 28, 1974; Stern, Mellins, and Fishman, *New York 1960*.

45. Although it is referred to in the *New York Times*, very little data are available on causes and outcome of the rent strike. See Tomasson, "Air Rights Building."

46. Reyner Banham, *Megastructure: Urban Futures of the Recent Past* (London: Thames & Hudson, 1976), 128–29. Banham referred to the Washington Bridge Extension Complex as both a megastructure and an "unintentional" megastructure. The latter term positioned it as both within and outside his particular historical trajectory.

47. Ibid., 11.

48. This difference is emphasized within Robert Venturi and Denise Scott Brown's visualization of the desert climate and road in their photo of the "Tanya" sign. The sign represents the climate of Nevada, one sign among many in the Vegas consumerist strip.

49. Banham, *Megastructure*, 44.

50. Peter Sloterdijk, *Terror from the Air* (Los Angeles: Semiotext[e], 2009), 20, 91–92.

51. John Wang, "Developers Readying Three Towers in Chinatown," *New York Times*, September 20, 1981.

52. Compare my analysis here with Reinhold Martin, *The Organizational Complex: Architecture, Media, and Corporate Space* (Cambridge, Mass.: MIT Press, 2005).

2 GROWTH

1. See the discussion of street trees in Max Page, *The Creative Destruction of Manhattan, 1900–1940* (Chicago: University of Chicago Press, 2001).

2. Robert Price, "The Good News about New York City," *New York Times*, September 28, 1986.

3. On suburban office complexes, see Louise Mozingo, *Pastoral Capitalism: A History of Suburban Corporate Landscapes* (Cambridge, Mass.: MIT Press, 2011).

4. Historically, the development of New York City parks involved tensions between green spaces as sources of pastoral pleasures—as in the first efforts at Central Park— and as territories inured with physical, robust activity. The former conceptualization was associated with New York's reformist era, whereas the lat-

ter concept, which reached its zenith in the 1950s, was primarily associated with Moses-era works. See Roy Rosenzweig and Elizabeth Blackmar, *The Park and the People: A History of Central Park* (Ithaca, N.Y.: Cornell University Press, 1992).

5. On the Ford Foundation Building, see Walter McQuade, "The Ford Foundation's Mid-Manhattan Greenhouse," *Fortune*, October 1964, 177–78; "A Great Space Taking Shape in New York," *Progressive Architecture*, November 1964, 192–97; "Kevin Go Bragh," *Progressive Architecture*, May 1965, 190–95; "New York Headquarters Enclosing a Garden," *Architectural Record*, November 1964, 10; "Landscaped Lobby," *Architectural Forum*, June 1967, 52–53; Ada Louise Huxtable, "Architecture: Ford Flies High," *New York Times*, November 26, 1967; Joan Lee Faust, "The Outside-In Building," *New York Times*, March 17, 1968; "Ford's in Its Heaven," *Newsweek*, 1967, 68; H. Sjolund, "Office Building or Greenhouse?," *ASHRAE Journal*, June 1968, 48–51; W. Wagner, "Fresh Forms and New Directions Form a Special Kind of Problem Solving," *Architectural Record*, May 1968, 145, 162; Kathleen Teltsch, "Ford Building Still Drawing Visitors," *New York Times*, August 30, 1970; Francesco Dal Co, *Kevin Roche: Buildings and Projects* (New York: Rizzoli, 1985); and Dan Kiley and Jane Amidon, *Dan Kiley: The Complete Works of America's Master Landscape Architect* (New York: Bulfinch, 1999).

6. Eeva-Lisa Pelkonen, *Kevin Roche: Architecture as Environment* (New Haven: Yale University Press, 2011), 29 and 33; Jeffrey Inaba, "What about Kevin Roche?," *Assemblage* 41, no. 1 (2000): 32; Jeffrey Inaba, "Lost in Space" (lecture at "Thinking Big: Diagrams, Mediascapes, and Megastructures," Yale University School of Architecture, 2010).

7. Pelkonen, *Kevin Roche*, 262–71.

8. Ralph G. Schwartz, quoted in Steven Roberts, "Ford Fund's New Building Has Indoor Woods," *New York Times*, October 26, 1967.

9. Jonathan Barnett, "Innovation and Symbolism on Forty-Second Street," *Architectural Record*, February 1968, 107.

10. Everett Conklin, "Interior Landscaping," *J. Arboriculture* 4 (1978): 73.

11. Robert Stern, Thomas Mellins, and David Fishman, *New York 1960: Architecture and Urbanism between the Second World War and the Bicentennial* (New York: Monacelli, 1997), 99.

12. Kiley and Amidon, *Dan Kiley*, 67.

13. Arthur Galston and T. Sharkey, "Frits Went," *National Academy of Science Biographical Memoirs*, n.d., www.nasonline.org/publications/biographical-memoirs/memoirs-pdf/went-f-w.pdf.

14. Frits Went, *The Experimental Control of Plant Growth: With Special Reference to the Earhart Plant Research Laboratory at the California Institute of Technology* (Waltham, Mass.: Chronica Botanica, 1957), 1–22.

15. Galston and Sharkey, "Frits Went."

16. Georges Canguilhem, "The Living and Its Milieu," *Grey Room*, no. 3 (n.d.): 6–31.

17. Dan Kiley, quoted in Faust, "Outside-In Building."

18. Kiley and Amidon, *Dan Kiley*, 67; Nelson Hammer, *Interior Landscape Design* (New York: McGraw-Hill, 1991), 213–20.

19. Marsha Ackermann, *Cool Comfort: America's Romance with Air-Conditioning* (Washington, D.C.: Smithsonian Institution Press, 2002), 27–42.

20. Faust, "Outside-In Building."

21. Teltsch, "Ford Building Still Drawing Visitors."

22. Hammer, *Interior Landscape Design*, 219.

23. Conklin, "Interior Landscaping," 77.

24. Between 1970 and 1982, midtown Manhattan zoning law allowed developers to build at a floor area ratio (FAR) of 15 to 18, depending on the provision of public spaces. In 1982, the area was downzoned, because of overbuilding, to an FAR of 12 to 13. See Faust, "Outside-In Building."

25. Arthur Drexler, *Transformations in Modern Architecture* (New York: Museum of Modern Art, 1979).

26. New York Botanical Garden, "A Plan for the Buildings and Grounds," New York Botanical Garden, 1974, Edward Larrabee Barnes Collection, Harvard Graduate School of Design; New York Botanical Garden, *Annual Report, 1976–77* (New York: New York Botanical Garden, n.d.).

27. New York Botanical Garden, *Annual Report, 1976–77*, 3.

28. Although the institution was not involved in the planning of the garden, images of the Ford Foundation garden appear on its promotional literature. We might deduce from this that the foundation's garden served as the model for the institute's desire to foster "experimentation with new indoor plants, particularly those for large scale use: malls, atria and indoor parks"—a statement that appears under a picture of the garden in the literature.

29. New York Botanical Garden, "Institute for Urban Horticulture" (promotional pamphlet), New York Botanical Garden, n.d.

30. Stephen Scrivens, *Interior Plantings in Large Buildings* (London: Architectural Press, 1980), 7–13.

31. "More on IBM's Blockbuster," *Interiors* 149, no. 11 (1980): 76–114.

32. Loring and Associates, "Environmental Conditions–Garden" (memorandum), New York Botanical Garden, June 9, 1983, New York Botanical Garden Archives, Institute for Urban Horticulture files.

33. R. S. Hebb, "Report on Bamboo Grove in the IBM Atrium: Present Status and Future Options," New York Botanical Garden, August 2, 1983.

34. On ChemCourt, see Paul Goldberger, "A New Touch of Glass Due on Park Ave," *New York Times*, November 17, 1980; Paul Goldberger, "Aspirations of a Park Avenue Atrium," *New York Times*, April 29, 1982; "A Public Park under Glass on Park Avenue for Chemical Bank," *Architectural Record*, August 1981, 23; "Urban Botanical Park Glassed in at ChemCourt," *Architectural Record*, December 1982; Joan Lee Faust, "Bank's Greenhouse Opens to the Public," *New York Times*, April 29, 1982; Joan Lee Faust, "Buildings with a Heart of Green," *New York Times*, March 9, 1984; ChemCourt correspondence, New York Botanical Garden, May 12, 1982, New York Botanical Garden Archives; John Mini Indoor Landscapes, ChemCourt file, New York Botanical Garden, Institute for Urban Horticulture Files, 1982; John Mini Indoor Landscapes, "Proposed Live Foliage and Flower Installation," New York Botanical Garden, Institute of Urban Horticulture Files, 1982; Chemical Bank, "Chemical Bank to Open 'ChemCourt'" (press release), April 27, 1983, New York Botanical Garden Archives, Institute for Urban Horticulture files; Chemical Bank, "ChemCourt," May 27, 1983, New York Botanical Garden Archives, Institute for Urban Horticulture files.

35. Chemical Bank, "Chemical Bank to Open 'ChemCourt.'"

36. Ibid.

37. Faust, "Bank's Greenhouse."

38. On this aspect, see Dan Graham and Robyn Hurst, "Corporate Arcadias," *Artforum* 26, no. 12 (1987): 68–74.

39. Karnosky's talk was published as the introduction to *Improving the Quality of Urban Life with Plants: Proceedings of the First International Symposium on Urban Horticulture,* ed. David F. Karnosky and Sheryl L. Karnosky (Millbrook, N.Y.: New York Botanical Garden, 1985). The Institute of Urban Horticulture's early 1980s files are filled with articles by horticulturalists on the health impacts of plants in the indoor environment.

40. Faust, "Buildings with a Heart."

41. Dan Graham and Robin Hurst, "Odysseys in Space," *Building Design*, October 1988, 41.

42. Ibid.

43. Michael Sorkin, "The Garden in the Machine," in *Variations on a Theme Park: The New American City and the End of Public Space,* ed. Michael Sorkin (New York: Hill & Wang, 1991), 238–41.

44. On transformations in ornamental horticulture, see Jianjun Chen, Dennis B. McConnell, and Richard J. Henny, "The World Foliage Plant Industry," *Chronica* 45, no. 4 (2005): 9. I am also grateful to Rick Bates at the Pennsylvania State University for clarifying aspects of ornamental-horticulture production; Rick Bates, interview by the author, December 22, 2006.

45. Keller Easterling, *Enduring Innocence: Global Architecture and Its Political Masquerades* (Cambridge, Mass.: MIT Press, 2005), 39–57.

46. Kiley and Amidon, *Dan Kiley*. On the earlier practice, see Scrivens, *Interior Plantings in Large Buildings*, 25; and Chen, McConnell, and Henny, "World Foliage Plant Industry."

47. See "A Tryout for Palm Trees for Battery Park City," *New York Times*, April 22, 1985. All of this activity, of course, has impacted labor practices in the United States and overseas. The plantations in California, Texas, and Florida where indoor plants are grown are a significant employer of Mexican laborers, who come to work in both the ornamental- and the consumable-agricultural markets. Countries such as India and Thailand that also have regions suitably similar to the interior metrics of office buildings are becoming new sites in international ornamental-horticultural production.

48. T. E. Wiley, "Agribusiness Trade in Colombia Offers More Than Just Coffee and Bananas," *Business Week*, September 21, 1992.

49. U.S. Department of Agriculture, *Floriculture Crops, 1984 Summary: Intentions for 1985* (Washington, D.C., 1985).

50. See ibid.; and S. D. Snyder, *Building Interior, Plants, and Automation* (Englewood Cliffs, N.J.: Prentice-Hall, 1990), 7.

51. Mildred Schmertz, "Public Use vs. Private Abuse," *Architecture* 84 (June 1995): 51–57.

52. Lois Weiss, "Fate of ChemCourt Atrium Up in the Air," *Real Estate Weekly*, April 27, 1994.

53. Mathew Gandy, *Concrete and Clay: Reworking Nature in New York City* (Cambridge, Mass.: MIT Press, 2003), 104–7.

3 PRESERVATION

1. One could compare the museum as a contained environment to the efforts of James Stirling or Hans Hollein, where the idea of the museum as an environmental container is downplayed.

2. In 1977, as several of the expansions neared completion, the Metropolitan Museum had 3.5 million annual attendees. In 1978, the British Museum had approximately 4 million. In 2011, the Metropolitan Museum of Art was the second-most-visited museum in the world, immediately behind the Louvre and followed by the British Museum (*Art Newspaper*, April 2012).

3. Sharon Zukin, *The Cultures of Cities* (Oxford: Blackwell, 1995), 113.

4. Faraday and Eastlake wrote, "In considering the position of the National

Gallery, our attention was drawn to the vicinity of several large chimneys, particularly that of the Baths and Wash-houses, and that connected with the steam engine by which the fountains in Trafalgar Square are worked, from which great volumes of smoke are emitted. In the neighborhood also the numerous chimneys of the various club-houses are constantly throwing out a greater body of smoke than those of ordinary private residences." Originally quoted in Charles Lock Eastlake, M. Faraday, and W. Russell, *Report on the Subject of the Protection of the Pictures in the National Gallery by Glass* (London: HMSO, 1850), 140.

5. See the debates regarding the Elgin Marbles and pollution in Athens versus the protected environment of the British Museum in London: Christopher Hitchens, *The Elgin Marbles: Should They Be Returned to Greece?* (London: Verso, 1987).

6. On the relationships of the development of the dam, architectural preservation, and cold-war politics, see Lucia Allais, "Will to War, Will to Art: Cultural Internationalism and the Modernist Aesthetics of Monuments" (PhD diss., MIT, 2008).

7. Quoted in "Egypt Has No Takers for 1 of 3 Free Temples," *Washington Post*, February 16, 1966. The transfer of the objects out of the Nubian Plain and into Western museums entangles deeply with the political webwork of relations that defined the area's regional politics. In 1963, the United States was allied with Ethiopia, a nation that in postcolonial statehood warred with Egypt over control of the Nile. The Ethiopian government protested the construction of the new dam, as it would essentially rob Ethiopian regions of irrigation and the hydrodynamic power of the upper Nile. As Soviet capital virtually secured the dam project, the Kennedy administration did not want to be marginalized in the redevelopment of Egypt. Thus, the stewardship of the monuments was a politically palatable tactic for the United States to be financially involved in the dam project without actually funding its construction and thus completely alienating important regional allies. In 1965, President Lyndon Johnson approved the transfer of funds that would secure the temple for the United States and the movement of Abu Simbel out of the affected area. See Daniel Kendie, "Egypt and the Hydro-politics of the Blue Nile River," *Northeast African Studies* 6, nos. 1–2 (1999): 141–69, for the hydropolitics of the region.

8. Christine Boyer, *The City of Collective Memory: Its Historical Imagery and Architectural Entertainments* (Cambridge, Mass.: MIT Press, 1996), 37.

9. Antonia Lant, "The Curse of the Pharaoh; or, How Cinema Contracted Egyptomania," *October* (1992): 107. See also Brian Curran et al., *Obelisk: a History* (Cambridge, Mass.: MIT Press, 2009); and Peter Tompkins, *The Magic of Obelisks* (New York: Harper & Row, 1981).

10. Sophy Burnham, "A Little Bit of Egypt on Fifth," *New York Magazine,* November 1968, 46.

11. Thomas Hoving, *Making the Mummies Dance: Inside the Metropolitan Museum of Art* (New York: Simon & Schuster, 1993), 58–59.

12. Committee Formed to Make Recommendations to the President of the United States concerning the American Location for the Temple of Dendur, "Guidelines for Application to Committee in Washington, DC, for Dendur Temple," February 20, 1967, Dendur Correspondence File, Metropolitan Museum of Art Archives.

13. Burnham, "Little Bit of Egypt."

14. Committee Formed to Make Recommendations to the President of the United States concerning the American Location for the Temple of Dendur, "Guidelines."

15. "Temple for Washington" (editorial), *Washington Post,* April 16, 1965.

16. Katherine Kuh, "What Home for the Temple?," *Saturday Review,* November 26, 1966.

17. See, for example, Garry Thomson, *The Museum Environment* (London: Butterworths, in association with the International Institute for Conservation of Historic and Artistic Works, 1978).

18. Milton Esterow, "Metropolitan Due to Get Temple of Dendur," *New York Times,* April 25, 1967.

19. For example, the City of New York agreed to pay one-half of the enormous costs of transporting and building the space for the temple; additionally, the influential backing of Senator Robert F. Kennedy helped secure the Metropolitan Museum's bid.

20. Marc Dessauce, *The Inflatable Moment: Pneumatics and Protest in '68* (New York: Princeton Architectural Press, 1999), 1.

21. "660 Dendur Stones Are Given a Temporary Shelter," *New York Times,* November 2, 1968.

22. Burnham, "Little Bit of Egypt," 46.

23. Ibid.

24. On the expansions, see Ada Louise Huxtable, "Metropolitan Museum to Expand in Park and Revamp Collections," *New York Times,* September 29, 1967; C. D. Dillon, "The Second Hundred Years," *Metropolitan Museum of Art Bulletin* 28, no. 9 (1970): 369–76; "The Talk of the Town: Meeting," *New Yorker,* June 20, 1970, 25–26; Jane Schwarz, "A Comprehensive Architectural Plan for the Second Century," *Metropolitan Museum of Art Bulletin* 29, no. 10 (1971): 444–48; and "L'extension du Met," *L'Architecture d'Aujourd'hui,* January 1975, xxi.

25. See Francesco Dal Co et al., *Kevin Roche: Buildings and Projects* (New York: Rizzoli, 1985), 55.

26. Jeffrey Inaba, "What about Kevin Roche?," *Assemblage* 41, no. 1 (2000): 32; Jeffrey Inaba, "Lost in Space" (lecture at "Thinking Big: Diagrams, Mediascapes, and Megastructures," Yale University School of Architecture, 2010).

27. Huxtable, "Metropolitan Museum."

28. "Talk of the Town: Meeting."

29. Burnham, "Little Bit of Egypt," 46.

30. "Dendur-in-New York" (editorial), *New York Times,* November 23, 1967.

31. Bernhard Leitner, "A Master Plan: The Met Plans Its Second Century," *Artforum,* October 1970, 65.

32. Ibid., 66.

33. Leon Golub, "Regarding the Lehman and Rockefeller Gifts to the Metropolitan Museum," *Artforum,* November 1970.

34. Ibid., 40–41 (emphasis in original).

35. Robert Smithson, "Frederick Law Olmsted and the Dialectical Landscape," in *Robert Smithson: The Collected Writings,* ed. Jack Flam (Berkeley: University of California Press, 1996), 67.

36. Ibid.

37. See Gilles Deleuze and Félix Guattari, *Anti-Oedipus: Capitalism and Schizophrenia,* trans. Robert Hurley, Mark Seem, and Helen R. Lane (1977; repr., Minneapolis: University of Minnesota Press, 1983), 257.

38. Grace Glueck, "Drills Sing in Park as Museum Flexes Wings," *New York Times,* March 28, 1974.

39. Grace Glueck, "A Spectacular New Wing," *New York Times,* January 24, 1982.

4 EXCHANGE

1. See the writing of Glenn Collins, "Notes on a Revolutionary Dinosaur," *New York Times*, August 6, 1972; Nadine Post, "Merrill Lynch's High-Wire Act: Data-Hungry Traders Put Technological Twist in New York City Towers," *Engineering News Record* 221, no. 29 (September 1988): 24–27; and Tom Wolfe, *The Bonfire of the Vanities* (New York: Bantam, 1988).

2. See, for example, Rosalyn Deutsche, *Evictions: Art and Spatial Politics* (Cambridge, Mass.: MIT Press, 1996); Christine Boyer, *The City of Collective Memory: Its Historical Imagery and Architectural Entertainments* (Cambridge,

Mass.: MIT Press, 1996); and Stephen Graham and Simon Marvin, *Splintering Urbanism: Networked Infrastructures, Technological Mobilities, and the Urban Condition* (London: Routledge, 2001).

3. Robert Price, "The Good News about New York City," *New York Times*, September 28, 1986.

4. See Charles Brown, "Downtown Enters a New Era," *New York Times*, January 31, 1960.

5. David Ellingson, "Designers Find Bull Market for Human Factors, Electronics," *Industrial Design* 29, no. 2 (1982): 41, 42.

6. Carolyn Iu, interview by the author, March 23, 2012.

7. On the concept of internal and external nature and its relationship to the market, see Neil Smith, *Uneven Development: Nature, Capital, and the Production of Space* (London: Blackwell, 1991).

8. Caitlin Zaloom, *Out of the Pits: Traders and Technology from Chicago to London* (Chicago: University of Chicago Press, 2006), 38.

9. O. A. Abdou and H. G. Lorsch, "The Impact of the Building Indoor Environment on Occupant Productivity–Part 3: Effects of Indoor Air Quality," *ASHRAE Transactions: American Society of Heating, Refrigerating, and Air-Conditioning Engineers* 100, no. 2 (1994): 902–13.

10. W. T. Deacon, "Important Considerations in Computer Room Humidification," *ASHRAE Transactions* 95 (1989): 1273–77.

11. These latter terms appear in writings by William J. Mitchell, *Me++: The Cyborg Self and the Networked City* (Cambridge, Mass.: MIT Press, 2004); and Keller Easterling, *Enduring Innocence: Global Architecture and Its Political Masquerades* (Cambridge, Mass.: MIT Press, 2005).

12. Ogdern Doremus, quoted in Gail Cooper, *Air-Conditioning America: Engineers and the Controlled Environment, 1900–1960* (Baltimore: Johns Hopkins University Press, 2002), 10.

13. Cecil D. Elliott, *Technics and Architecture: The Development of Materials and Systems for Buildings* (Cambridge, Mass.: MIT Press, 1992), 316–17.

14. Ibid.

15. Jeffrey T. Schnapp and Matthew Tiews, eds., *Crowds* (Stanford, Calif.: Stanford University Press, 2006).

16. Elliott, *Technics and Architecture*, 316–17.

17. Iu, interview.

18. This concept of air and gentility is based on an argument regarding ventilation by Dell Upton, *Architecture in the United States* (Oxford: Oxford University Press, 1998).

19. See Cooper, *Air-Conditioning America*; and Anson Rabinbach, *The Human*

Motor: Energy, Fatigue, and the Origins of Modernity (Berkeley: University of California Press, 1992).

20. See Burton Crane, "Funston Notes Need for Space," *New York Times*, January 27, 1960; "Text of Trade Center Report by the Downtown–Lower Manhattan Association," *New York Times*, January 27, 1960; Tim Carrington, "Crowding Plagues Big Board Floor as Machines, Traders Vie for Space," *Wall Street Journal*, October 21, 1981; "Updating Computer Wiring at the NY Stock Exchange," *Electrical Construction and Maintenance* 80 (July 1981): 70–74; and "New York Stock Exchange Main Trading Floor," *Lighting Design and Application* 14 (February 1984): 21–22.

21. Carrington, "Crowding," 29.

22. Quoted in ibid.

23. Ibid., 30.

24. Iu, interview.

25. See Howard Blum, "Shearson Picks Manhattan Site for New Center," *New York Times*, January 16, 1984; Thomas Lueck, "Solomon Will Move to Trade Center," *New York Times*, November 29, 1988; Mark McCain, "The Salomon Solution: A Building within a Building," *New York Times*, March 19, 1989; and Robert A. M. Stern, David Fishman, and Jacob Tilove, *New York 2000: Architecture and Urbanism Between the Bicentennial and the Millennium* (New York: Monacelli, 2006), 253–54.

26. Paul Glickman, quoted in Robert Guenther, "Growth of Computers Causes Some Office-Design Problems," *Wall Street Journal*, November 2, 1983.

27. Carl Hastrom, quoted in ibid., 33.

28. Deacon, "Important Considerations."

29. Post, "Merrill Lynch's High-Wire Act."

30. Adrian Forty, *Objects of Desire: Design and Society since 1750* (London: Thames & Hudson, 1992), 150.

31. Daniel Beunza Ibáñez and David Stark, "Ecologies of Value in a Wall Street Trading Room" (working paper, Pompeu Fabra University, Department of Economics and Business, 2004), 9.

32. Robert Campbell, "Tented City," *Architect's Journal*, November 16, 1988, 25.

33. "Expressing an Image: An Exclusive Serial Story on the Spectacular American Express Tower with Interiors by Swanke Hayden Connell Architects," *Interiors* 145, no. 6 (1986); "Expressing an Image: The Second Installment of the American Express Tower Story Reports Some Unique Fast Track Management Strategies," *Interiors* 146, no. 8 (1986); and "Trading Up: Inside the 4 Million-Square-Foot Merrill Lynch, New York Headquarters, a Spectacular Scene of Financial Glamour and Clamor," *Interiors*, March 1988.

34. "Trading Up," 153.

35. The term is Iu's (interview).

36. Paul Makovsky, "Iconic Workspaces," *Metropolis*, July 2002.

37. Quoted in "Easing the Chaos in Trading Rooms," *Wall Street Journal*, September 21, 1987.

38. Post, "Merrill Lynch's High-Wire Act," 25.

39. "Trading Up," 156.

40. Ibid.

41. Norman Kurtz, cited in Post, "Merrill Lynch's High-Wire Act."

42. Saskia Sassen, *The Global City: New York, London, Tokyo* (Princeton, N.J.: Princeton University Press, 2001).

43. Robert Sobel, *Panic on Wall Street: A History of America's Financial Disasters* (New York: Macmillan, 1969).

44. Quoted in Richard Meislin, "Computers Lose Data Capability in Power Failure," *New York Times*, September 10, 1981.

45. In 1975, U.S. stock markets represented 58 percent of all the stock value traded in the world, but by 1987, that percentage had shrunk to 34 percent, and an understanding of the activity of the other 66 percent of market activity was critical.

46. "Trading Up," 181–82.

47. Travis Longcore and Peter Rees, "Information Technology and Downtown Restructuring: The Case of New York City's Financial District," *Urban Geography* 17, no. 4 (1996): 354–72.

48. Graham and Marvin, *Splintering Urbanism*, 321–27.

49. Robert Fitch, *The Assassination of New York* (London: Verso, 1993).

50. On the Battery Park City development and "the Beach," see Robin Herman, "Nearly 200,000 Rally to Protest Nuclear Energy," *New York Times*, September 24, 1979; Maurice Carroll, "Development Unit Tests Ambitious New Agenda," *New York Times*, January 29, 1981; Grace Glueck, "Engaging Experiments Transform a Sandy Site," *New York Times*, July 31, 1983; Grace Glueck, "Art on the Beach," *New York Times*, July 5, 1985; S. L. Fordham, "World Financial Center: Olympia & York Creates Financial and Leasing Milestones in New York," *Urban Land* 44, no. 9 (1985): 22–26; and Robert Campbell, "Sharkskin and Dreck: The New Urban Landscape, World Financial Center," *Architect's Journal*, November 9, 1989.

51. Michael de Courcy Hinds, "The Shaping of a Landfill," *New York Times*, March 23, 1986.

52. This implied dialogue between the splintered, restructured, and corporate environment inside the World Financial Center and the given historical en-

vironment of the Beach became more explicit during a brief arts exhibition staged within the center in 1988 by the former arts curator of the Beach, Anita Contini. The exhibition, "The New Urban Landscape," staged in celebration of the completion of the Center, displayed the work of artists, many of whom had once displayed their work on the Beach site. Several of the artworks directly commented on the internalization and socionatural artifice of the World Financial Center. The architectural collaborative Hodgetts and Fung and artists Robert Price and Joel Otterson were among a larger group that installed various forms of nature within the recently completed and mostly unleased ground-floor spaces in the financial center. Hodgetts and Fung reworked the atmospheric systems to grow moss on the World Financial Center's columns. Other installations housed trees and animals, and several installations placed these things where they clearly interfered with the intended uses and mechanical equipment of the unleased space. In one installation by Vito Acconci, the artist installed a car in such a way that it suggested smashing through the curtain-wall glass and releasing the financial center's atmosphere across the site. The displayed work implicated the World Financial Center as the facilitator of an emerging nature in the City, one internalized and clearly aligned with financial power. Richard Martin, ed., *The New Urban Landscape* (New York: Rizzoli, 1991).

53. On these interpretations see Campbell, "Sharkskin and Dreck."

54. Cesar Pelli noted that after the World Trade Center's collapse, in 2001, that the Woolworth Building was suddenly visible from the World Financial Center—a building, he said, that partially inspired the architectural form of the World Financial Center. Cesar Pelli, "Connections" (lecture at the National Building Museum, September 2001).

55. Mario Gandelsonas, "Conditions for a Colossal Architecture," in *Cesar Pelli: Buildings and Projects, 1965–1990* (New York: Rizzoli, 1990), 34.

56. Post, "Merrill Lynch's High-Wire Act."

57. Cesar Pelli, "Architectural Form and the Tradition of Building," extra edition, *Architecture + Urbanism*, July 1985, 32.

58. Ibid., 28.

59. Similarly, the Winter Garden can simply be seen as a spatial analogue to the trading rooms surrounding it. Here, public space becomes a container of conditioned air. The twelve palms gathered in this space are as much a tableau of exotic nature as they are indices of the environment that maintains them.

EPILOGUE

1. See Ernst Mandel, *Late Capitalism* (London: Verso, 1972); and the discussion of this phenomenon in the "culture industry" in Rosalind Krauss, "The Cultural Logic of the Late Capitalist Museum," *October* (Autumn 1990): 15. The latter interpretation drives many of my own interpretations of how Mandel's ideas relate to architectural environments.

2. Kenneth Frampton, "Towards a Critical Regionalism: Six Points for an Architecture of Resistance," in *The Anti-aesthetic: Essays on Postmodern Culture*, ed. Hal Foster (Port Townsend, Wash.: Bay Press, 1983), 16–30; Kenneth Frampton, "Technoscience and Environmental Culture: A Provisional Critique," *Journal of Architectural Education* 54, no. 3 (2001): 123–29; Rem Koolhaas, "Junkspace," *October* (Spring 2002): 175–90.

3. Koolhaas, "Junkspace," 176.

4. See David Gissen, ed., *Big and Green: Toward Sustainable Architecture in the 21st Century* (New York: Princeton Architectural Press, 2003). Among the vast literature on the greening of Times Square, see Joseph Giovanni, "Acing to the Deuce," *New York Magazine*, January 2002; "Four Times Square," n.d., Clean Air Counts, http://www.cleanaircounts.org/resource%20package/A%20Book/EStar%20Buildings/Case%20Study%20-%20Four%20Times%20Square.htm.

5. See Gissen, *Big and Green*, particularly the essays by William McDonough and Guy Battle, for this type of critique.

6. Nonetheless, Tschumi's Acropolis Museum certainly comes closest to offering an architectural critique of museological maintenance.

7. See Christopher Hitchens, "Acropolis Now/The Lovely Stones," *Vanity Fair*, July 1, 2009.

8. See William McDonough and Michael Braungart, *The Hannover Principles: Design for Sustainability* (Charlottesville, Va.: McDonough Architects, 2003). This type of argument continues into the present.

9. On the cooling centers in Chicago and New York, see "Cooling Centers," Keep Cool Illinois, http://www2.illinois.gov/keepcool/pages/coolingcenters.aspx, and "Find a Cooling Center," New York City Office of Emergency Management, http://gis.nyc.gov/oem/cc/index.htm;jsessionid=2BCACC3FFD5846ADC624A5BE6BCAC789.

10. S. L. Meyers, "Inspections Mishandled, Cortine Says," *New York Times*, September 17, 1993.

11. See Arup Security Consulting, "The Need for CB Protective Measures in Commercial Property," *Estates Gazette*, October 2003, 1.

12. David Barstow, "Envisioning an Expensive Future in the Brave New World of Fortress New York," *New York Times*, September 16, 2001.

13. James Glanz, "A Nation Challenged: Air Quality," *New York Times*, October 29, 2001. See, for example, the wall-panel text on the Times Building in the Skyscraper Museums 2006 exhibition "Green Towers," which explicitly linked energy-saving cavity windows with "bomb-proofing" and resistance to other violent acts (Carol Willis, curator, 2006).

14. "Urban Dispersion Project," 2005, Center for Visual Computing, Stony Brook University, http://www.cs.sunysb.edu/~vislab/projects/urbansecurity/UrbanSecurity.html.

15. "The Solaire: Live Green" (advertisement), n.d., http://www.thesolaire.com/documents/green_lifestyle.html; and U.S. Green Building Council, http://www.usgbc.org/News/USGBCInTheNewsDetails.aspx?ID=2318.

16. On the health impacts of the collapse of the World Trade Center, see Juan Gonzalez, *Fallout: The Environmental Consequences of the World Trade Center Collapse* (New York: New Press, 2002).

17. Unfortunately, more humanistic and conceptualist distributions of maintenance in architecture and art practices still repeat the contemporary power dynamics of cities (see, for example, the works of Michael Rakowitz and Philippe Rahm).

18. Giorgio Agamben, Homo sacer: *Sovereign Power and Bare Life*, trans. Daniel Heller-Roazen (Stanford, Calif.: Stanford University Press, 1998).

19. By demanding that the environments within this book, and our responses to them, be understood within specific urban episodes, we potentially align future attitudes toward an otherwise vaporous, fleeting, and affective conception of the interior environment with something more monumental and artifactual. See my essay "A More Monumental, Non-naturalistic Environment," in *Tarp: Not Nature* (New York: Pratt Institute Graduate Architecture and Urban Design Program, 2012), 51–53.

20. The classic critique of operative architectural history is Manfredo Tafuri's. See the final chapter of Tafuri's *Theories and History of Architecture*, trans. Giorgia Verrecchia (Cambridge, Mass.: MIT Press, 1980).

INDEX

DAVID GISSEN is associate professor of architecture, visual studies, and visual and critical studies at the California College of the Arts, San Francisco. He is author of *Subnature: Architecture's Other Environments* and editor of the "Territory" issue of *AD: Architectural Design*.